THE EVERYTHING.
GUIDE TO
FORAGING

Dear Reader,

Foraging is a skill that has become almost forgotten. Fears of the outdoors and being poisoned prevent too many people from experiencing the joy of picking and tasting the flavors given to us by nature. Yet, it is a skill that our ancestors knew and used on a daily basis. When I see people hold any one of our native nuts in their hands and not have a clue what it is, or when I hear how others have never eaten a wild blackberry because they didn't want to get poisoned, I realize how disconnected our society has become and how important it is to share the knowledge of foraging.

Then I read survival stories in the newspapers. One in particular was about a young girl who had been lost for five days and had survived by eating raspberries. Or I see on the news the long lines of people waiting for handouts after a natural disaster when there is food all around them. And I realize how important it is that we keep this knowledge alive.

Knowledge that isn't used is lost. It's one thing to know how to identify a particular plant and know it's edible, but you also need to know how to process and prepare it. This book on foraging can be your guide, leading you out into the field and from there to the kitchen, and finally to the table. It provides you with everything you need to know to get you started on your journey of becoming a forager.

Be wild!

Vickie Shufer, BS

Welcome to the EVERYTHING® Series!

These handy, accessible books give you all you need to tackle a difficult project, gain a new hobby, comprehend a fascinating topic, prepare for an exam, or even brush up on something you learned back in school but have since forgotten.

You can choose to read an *Everything*® book from cover to cover or just pick out the information you want from our four useful boxes: e-questions, e-facts, e-alerts, and e-ssentials.

We give you everything you need to know on the subject, but throw in a lot of fun stuff along the way, too.

We now have more than 400 *Everything*® books in print, spanning such wide-ranging categories as weddings, pregnancy, cooking, music instruction, foreign language, crafts, pets, New Age, and so much more. When you're done reading them all, you can finally say you know *Everything*®!

QUESTION

Answers to common questions

FACT

Important snippets of information

ALERT

Urgent warnings

ESSENTIAL

Quick handy tips

PUBLISHER Karen Cooper

DIRECTOR OF ACQUISITIONS AND INNOVATION Paula Munier

MANAGING EDITOR, EVERYTHING® SERIES Lisa Laing

COPY CHIEF Casey Ebert

ASSISTANT PRODUCTION EDITOR Jacob Erickson

ACQUISITIONS EDITOR Ross Weisman

DEVELOPMENT EDITOR Brett Palana-Shanahan

EDITORIAL ASSISTANT Ross Weisman

EVERYTHING® SERIES COVER DESIGNER Erin Alexander

LAYOUT DESIGNERS Colleen Cunningham, Elisabeth Lariviere, Ashley Vierra, Denise Wallace

Visit the entire Everything® series at *www.everything.com*

THE
EVERYTHING®
GUIDE TO
FORAGING

Identifying, harvesting, and cooking
nature's wild fruits and vegetables

Vickie Shufer

Avon, Massachusetts

*Dedicated to the wild plants, that they may be
recognized and appreciated for the gifts they offer.*

An Everything® Series Book.
Everything® and everything.com® are registered trademarks of F+W Media, Inc.

Published by Adams Media, a division of F+W Media, Inc.
57 Littlefield Street, Avon, MA 02322 U.S.A.
www.adamsmedia.com

ISBN 10: 1-4405-1276-0
ISBN 13: 978-1-4405-1276-6
eISBN 10: 1-4405-2511-0
eISBN 13: 978-1-4405-2511-7

Printed in the United States of America.

10 9 8 7 6 5 4 3 2 1

Library of Congress Cataloging-in-Publication Data
Shufer, Vickie.
The everything guide to foraging / Vickie Shufer.
p. cm.
Includes bibliographical references and index.
ISBN 978-1-4405-1276-6 (alk. paper)
1. Cooking (Wild foods) 2. Wild plants, Edible—Identification. I. Title.
TX823.S455 2011
641.6—dc22
2011006239

This publication is designed to provide accurate and authoritative information with regard to the subject matter covered. It is sold with the understanding that the publisher is not engaged in rendering legal, accounting, or other professional advice. If legal advice or other expert assistance is required, the services of a competent professional person should be sought.
—From a *Declaration of Principles* jointly adopted by a Committee of the American Bar Association and a Committee of Publishers and Associations

Many of the designations used by manufacturers and sellers to distinguish their products are claimed as trademarks. Where those designations appear in this book and Adams Media was aware of a trademark claim, the designations have been printed with initial capital letters.

Illustrations by Eric Andrews.
Photo credits on page 291.

*This book is available at quantity discounts for bulk purchases.
For information, please call 1-800-289-0963.*

Contents

Acknowledgments

It is with great pleasure that I can say thank you to all my teachers who have been with me since the beginning, far too many to name individually. I am especially grateful to Dr. James Duke, not only for all his research, but also for sharing his knowledge in classes, workshops, and books. It was he who showed me how to eat cattails out of the marsh, make a soup using burdock and other wild vegetables, and had me testing various wild berries to determine their edibility.

Thanks to all of you who have contributed foraging articles and to the subscribers of *The Wild Foods Forum*, for sharing your knowledge and experience on wild foods. And to all my wild friends, especially Michele Shean and Diane Greiber, who have been testing out my recipes with wild food groups for more years than I can count; and Michele, who helped me recall how we had prepared certain dishes while I was writing this book. Special thanks to Paul, my husband, who has been graciously eating my experiments for more than thirty years. Most of all, I want to thank all of you who have attended my classes, tasted my dishes, and repeatedly asked when I was going to write a book, for the inspiration that you have provided for me to write this.

Top 10 Reasons to Forage

1. Foraging increases awareness of the plant world.

2. The food you find is free for the picking, thereby reducing your food costs.

3. Foraging provides outdoor exercise.

4. It is a source of food in survival situations.

5. Foraging can be a means of weed control in yards and gardens.

6. The food you forage is free of pesticides, herbicides, and genetic modification.

7. A foraged diet provides flavors found nowhere else.

8. Foraged food is highly concentrated in vitamins and minerals.

9. The food you forage promotes health and well-being.

10. Foraging lightens the load of hikers, backpackers, and campers.

Introduction

HAVE YOU EVER THOUGHT about what would happen if you went to the store and there was no food on the shelves, or even worse, you were stranded somewhere away from civilization with nothing to eat? Or maybe you're just curious about those green things that keep popping up in your yard and garden, or growing between the cracks in the sidewalk. If you're one who likes to spend time outdoors, you might be looking for a way to deepen your connection with nature, lighten your load as a backpacker, or reduce your grocery costs by supplementing your diet with wild foods. Maybe you're just interested in plants and want to learn more about how our ancestors used them.

There was a time when every country boy or girl knew where the best blackberry patches were in the summer, or where to go in the fall to gather nuts. Mothers would send their children out in the spring to gather wild greens. Many kids today have never even tasted a wild berry or know what a walnut or hickory nut looks like. Greens are plentiful at the grocery store. Fears of being poisoned are heavily imprinted on young minds. Children are cautioned to never eat anything growing wild.

Many of the plants growing around you have the potential of being transformed into tasty salads, soups, entrées, desserts, and beverages. These are plants that our ancestors knew and used on a daily basis. Some of these are native plants that were growing here when the settlers first arrived. Others are descendants of plants brought over by the settlers, planted in their gardens for food and medicine, and that later escaped their boundaries.

As food became increasingly available on grocery shelves, less interest was given to the wild plants, and for the most part, they became forgotten as a food source. Many became known as nothing more than weeds, in some cases invasive aliens, to be eliminated at all costs. Others were recognized as native plants that needed to be protected. The thought of actually eating wild plants doesn't even occur to most people. Less time is spent outdoors, and as a result, many have become disconnected from the natural world, resulting in what Richard Louv describes as "nature-deficit disorder" in his book, *The Last Child in the Woods*.

Foraging is a means of reconnecting with nature. It gets people outdoors and gives them a whole new perspective on looking at plants. Tasting the plants is a way of using all your senses to explore the natural world. In the event of natural disasters, gathering and eating wild foods would be an alternative to standing in long lines waiting for relief aid. If you find yourself lost in the woods with no food, knowing what to eat or not to eat could be a matter of survival. There are also nutritional benefits. Wild plants are concentrated with vitamins and minerals and have not been subjected to genetic modification. Best of all, they are free for the picking and just good eating, with their own unique flavors.

This book is for anyone who is interested in wild plants and how they can be used for food. It will guide you from your backyard and gardens to the meadows, forests, wetlands, beaches, mountains, and deserts with information on how to identify the plants that you are likely to encounter, harvesting techniques, and recipes for using them. Identifying poisonous look-alikes will help to remove the fears associated with eating wild plants. Using caution and good conservation ethics, this book can help you learn everything you need to know to become a confident forager so you too can enjoy the bounty of nature.

CHAPTER 1

The Way of the Forager

Foraging is a lifestyle. It's a way of connecting with plants and developing an intimate relationship with the plant world by spending time in nature. A forager is attuned to the natural world and to the seasons and follows the cycles of the plants. She sees the plants when they first emerge from the ground, smells their flowers when they burst into bloom, and then tastes their fruits when they have ripened. This is how a forager lives.

Sustainable Foraging

There was a time when people relied on wild foods as a crop to supplement their diet and reduce grocery costs. Wild berries were gathered in the summer to make jelly, jams, and pies; roots and nuts were gathered in the fall to use in baked goods, and greens were gathered in the spring. As wild habitats began declining, concerns were raised about depleting the natural populations and how much can be gathered without harming the environment.

If harvested sustainably, an area will continue to produce year after year. Become familiar with the plants in your area and find out which ones are rare or endangered. Avoid picking from these plants or pick sparingly, depending on the part being gathered. However, you too are a part of the natural world, and by approaching the plants with a conscientious attitude, you can forage in the wild without harming the natural population.

ALERT

When looking for plants to gather, if you only see a single plant here and there, don't pick it. If you see a few here, and a few there, pick only what you need. If the plant is abundant, and especially if it is invasive, pick all you want, but use what you pick.

Gathering Greens

Many wild greens come from plants that are annuals, such as chickweeds or cresses. Others, like evening primrose and thistle, are biennials. They bloom, produce seed, and then die, to be replaced by seedlings that sprout from seeds they have produced. They rely on seed production to reproduce. Others are perennials, like dandelions. Even if you remove all the leaves, they will continue to grow.

If the plant has a rosette of leaves near the ground, you can remove the younger leaves without uprooting or harming the plant. Annuals and biennials often come up thick and can benefit from being thinned by being pulled out and the roots trimmed off. Other greens have branches that can be snipped off at the tips and the plant will continue to grow. Young leaves are generally milder tasting and more tender.

Picking Wildflowers

Flowers are the reproductive part of the plant. Many of them are edible. A number of plants produce both edible flowers and edible fruits or seeds. Gathering the flowers will prevent them from producing fruit and going to seed. Sometimes you have to choose whether to eat the flowers now or wait and pick the fruits later. An ideal situation is when there are enough plants to do both.

Flowers also provide nectar for pollinating insects. Plants in turn depend on the insects to pollinate them so they will produce fruit. Even if it is a wildflower or shrub with no edible parts, the pollinators will still visit their flowers for nectar. Leave these for the pollinators.

Harvesting Fruits

Seeds are contained within the fruits of plants. Fruits may be berries, drupes, hips, nuts, legumes, or capsules that provide food for animals that in turn disperse their seeds. Since many of these fruits are edible, care should be taken to leave some for the wildlife. When appropriate, disperse fruits and seeds to extend their range.

Berries are bird food. Fruit-eating birds rely on wild fruits for survival. Some seeds have to pass through the digestive system of birds before they will germinate. A symbiotic relationship has developed in which the plant provides the fruit for the bird and the bird provides the means for planting its seeds. When gathering berries, remember to leave some for the birds, some to reseed, and some for the next group of foragers.

Nuts provide food for squirrels, turkeys, and other wildlife. Squirrels gather nuts and bury them for storage but don't always remember where they buried them. The forgotten nuts become sprouts the next spring and eventually grow into a tree.

Digging Roots

Digging up roots often means destroying the plants. You don't want to be the cause of a population becoming rare. In some cases roots can be divided and replanted, especially those with tubers. Some roots can have the top part removed and the bottom part containing the root hairs replanted.

Getting Acquainted with Plants

Getting acquainted with plants is a must for anyone interested in eating them. When trying to identify a plant, remember to use your senses. Rub the leaves or crush them to see if they have a scent. Sniff the flowers for their individual fragrance. Look for unusual features that make it distinct. Learning what types of plants there are, leaf shapes and formations, flower structure, and fruit types are all essential to positive identification of an unknown plant. Once you know what to look for, you can use a botanical key to help you identify a particular plant.

Keys vary with different field guides. The time to gather many of the wild greens is before they bloom. Without flowers or fruits, it is sometimes difficult for even the experts to always know the difference. In this case, you can observe the plant's life cycle as it goes through the blooming and fruiting phase. Once you have identified it and determined its edibility, you can harvest it the next year.

Get familiar with those plants that may look similar to each other and whether they are poisonous or not. Identifying a plant is not enough. You may have it identified correctly, but that doesn't mean it's edible. Be sure to check a field guide for positive identification and an edible plant guide for edibility. A medicinal plant guide is also helpful to see if there are medicinal effects. Find out as much information about the plant as you can before eating it.

Flowers

Plants often get lost in the jungle of green. They all blend together, until they bloom. Suddenly they stand out. Some field guides have keys that are based on flower parts. Become familiar with the parts of a flower and how to distinguish between the various types of flowers. Matching a flower to a picture is not always accurate. Look for field guides that show all the parts of a plant, including leaves, flowers and fruits for positive identification.

Fruits

Seeds of plants are contained within different types of fruits. Learn to distinguish between the categories and find out which ones are edible.

Many of the wild fruits have a cultivated counterpart. Usually the cultivated fruit looks larger and juicier, but not necessarily sweeter. Shells of wild nuts are generally thicker and harder to remove than the cultivated variety but the nutmeat has a stronger flavor.

There are numerous inedible berries that are best left for the birds. Often they grow right next to one that is edible. Become familiar with the wild fruits in your area, identify which ones are poisonous, and then find out which ones are safe to eat.

Nuts are probably the easiest to identify of wild foods. With the exception of buckeye and horse chestnut, most nuts are edible. Some are sweeter than others. The nutmeat is contained within the shell that must be removed before eating.

Roots

Roots can be tricky, especially in the winter when the tops of the plants have died back. Gathering roots in the winter often means scouting out an area in the summer when the leaves, flowers, or fruits are present and remembering where you saw it. If appropriate, you can flag it with surveyor's tape to help you find it when the leaves are dormant.

Foraging Grounds

Finding a place to forage can be a challenge in many areas. If you have a yard or garden, this is a good place to start. Otherwise, explore beyond your home. The best spots tend to be the edges of farm fields, forests, and meadows. Permission should be obtained before foraging on any land that is not your own.

Before picking, look for evidence of spraying. An absence of weed diversity is evidence of herbicide spraying. Pesticide spraying is not so obvious. Always wash your plants well before preparing or eating them to remove any pesticide residues that may be on them, especially if you're not certain. If there's a chance the soil might be polluted from dumping or other means, boil the plants for ten minutes before eating.

Old Home Sites

Old home sites or abandoned lots can be found even in urban areas. What was a yard more than likely supports a number of wild greens, especially if no one has been spraying. If there was a garden on the premises, then there's probably going to be more opportunities, since many wild plants like disturbed soils.

A ride out to the country may turn up some interesting foraging opportunities. Abandoned farm fields with grown-up fencerows or barnyards may be worth locating an owner for permission. Look for edges. Many wild fruits grow in the understory of forests but produce more fruit if they get some direct sunlight. These edges may be in empty lots bordering shopping centers, gas stations, or other commercial enterprises. Find out who owns the property and ask permission to forage.

If you're a paddler, you may find that there's more up a creek than just water. Many freshwater creeks and rivers are lined with plants that have edible berries, seeds, and roots. Wild roses bloom in the spring and add a flowery taste to your water bottle. Groundnuts grow along the banks and in the fall the berry bushes have ripe berries. Spicebush and birch often line the banks. In marshes, cattails can usually be found as well as flowering plants, some of which have edible roots. Freshwater marshes have more diversity than saltwater marshes. In some cases, the only way to get to certain plants may be by water. Again, find out in advance who owns the land bordering the waterway where you will be paddling and if it is permissible to forage.

Public Lands

City, county, state, and national parks are all on public lands. Each agency has its own policy for gathering plants in the wild. In some parks, gathering plants for personal use is permitted, depending on how abundant it is. Contact the park manager before picking.

Some state and national forests as well as national recreational areas allow harvesting fruits, nuts, and berries for personal use. In some cases, a permit may be required to harvest plant material. There are also Wildlife Management Areas and Army Corps of Engineers Projects that generally prohibit collecting of plant material. Find out which agency owns the land before collecting.

ALERT

Be aware that the National Wild and Scenic Rivers Act prohibits the removal of plant materials from the area bordering some rivers. The Wilderness Act of 1964 protects the harvest of wild plants in designated federal wilderness areas. Find out what other laws protect plants in your area.

Knowing where not to forage is just as important as where to forage. Roadside foraging is not recommended, unless it is a secondary road with little usage and the part being gathered is not growing right next to the road. Exhaust fumes and leaks from passing vehicles seep into the soil, becoming a part of the plants that are growing there. Also avoid the edges of farm fields or waterways that receive pesticide residues.

The best foraging ground is your own. If you have a piece of property that you can dedicate to wild food, then you can have wild food year round, depending on what you plant or allow to grow. If managed in an ethical manner, it can produce for years to come.

Private Property

Just because a plant is wild does not mean it is free for the picking. If it's on private property, the plant belongs to the landowner, whether it is an individual, a business, or a corporation. Written permission should be obtained from the owner before venturing onto the land.

Homeowners

Many homeowners would welcome the opportunity to have someone pick their dandelions in the spring when they start to bloom or remove the weeds from the garden. Even so, ask permission first and let them know what you're picking. They may be interested in trying them also.

If you are a homeowner, you may want to consider devoting an area of your yard or garden to the wild plants. You can either establish it as a landscaped area or let it go wild and see what comes up. Reducing the amount of grass you have to cut will give you more time to go out and forage.

Farms

Privately owned organic farms and gardens are ideal foraging grounds. Since the soil is free of herbicides, there is a greater diversity of plants. If you don't know any organic growers, contact your local agricultural agent or go online and search for an Organic Growers Association for your area. Many growers are also interested in which weeds you can eat and often include them in their salad mixes.

Bordering most farm fields are hedgerows. They also border woodlands and streams. Hedgerows are made up of shrubs and vines that produce an abundance of wild food. The presence of birds indicates where the fruits can be found.

ALERT

Hunters often use wooded areas and have posted signs along the borders. Find out when the hunting season occurs in your area and avoid going into the woods when hunters might be there. Even if you're not hunting wildlife, it's a good idea to wear a blaze orange hat or vest to make yourself visible.

Some landowners have wooded lots that they are growing for timber or to eventually resell. Often, they have received very little management and are an abundant source of wild plant foods. Get to know the owner and offer to take him out and identify the plants growing there. If it has potential as a foraging area, work out an agreement with the owner.

What Do You Take to the Field?

As a forager, the outdoors is an extension of your life. You may go to the field for different reasons. It may be to release stress and just go for a walk. At other times you may feel the need to be in the outdoors to listen to the nature sounds, take pictures, or sketch plants. Before going on a gathering foray, it helps to scout out the area in advance.

There are certain items that should always be with you, regardless of why you are going to the field. One is a pocketknife that fits comfortably in your pocket and is less than four inches in length. In your other pocket you should have some sealable plastic bags. You never know when you might find yourself in a situation where there's an opportunity to pick something growing wild.

If you're scouting out the area, a sketchpad or camera is handy. A pair of clippers can also be useful. They can be used to snip stems and branches rather than breaking them off or to clip your way through a dense area. A trowel or small shovel is useful for digging up roots. Always carry water. In addition to keeping you hydrated, it can also help to keep the plant material fresh, depending on what you are gathering.

ESSENTIAL

If you find yourself up a creek without a trowel or shovel, and the opportunity to gather roots presents itself, look for a digging stick. The wood must be hard enough not to break when probed into the earth and long enough for leverage. The tip should be tapered to a point.

Containers

For a serious foraging expedition, you're going to need something to put your goods in that you gather. Several sizes of storage plastic bags are recommended. If you're going to your yard or garden, you can use a large basket to put the individual bags in. However, if you're going off to the woods or streams, a cloth bag that drapes over your shoulders or a backpack is handy.

Gloves

Gloves are essential. More than one type of glove with different strengths and durability is necessary. Strong, leather gloves can protect your hands from poison ivy or poison oak, while latex or plastic gloves can protect them from mosquito bites. Cotton gloves with the fingertips cut off are handy for picking blackberries or raspberries. In the winter, gloves should be worn to protect the hands from the cold.

Specialized Tools

More specialized tools are sometimes used for berry picking. A flat, shallow container will prevent berries from getting mashed. If the berries are located in a tree with branches too high to reach, hooked poles or snake sticks with a hook on the end can be used to pull the branches down. Care should be taken not to break the branch and to test its flexibility before pulling it too far. There is also a tool known as a berry picker that is used to comb through the branches of berry bushes to remove the berries. Baskets and containers are used by some people to tie around their waists to free their hands for picking.

Foraging Tips

Wild food doesn't all grow in one spot. You have to have your foraging grounds. It might mean scheduling seasonal foraging expeditions. Being a forager requires being attuned to the plants and their cycles, knowing when the greens emerge, the flowers bloom, the fruits ripen, and the nuts drop from the trees. A forager follows the cycles of plants and knows which plants produce every year, which ones continue to come back, or which ones produce in cycles, with lean years in between prolific years. Very often it's a matter of being in the right place at the right time for a particular harvest. Always be alert and prepared when the opportunity presents itself.

Leaves

Generally, gather leaves when they are tender and showing new growth, either before flower buds appear, or after reseeding, when new fall growth appears. Mid-morning is a good time to gather leaves, after the dew has lifted but before the sun has gotten too hot and wilted the leaves.

Flowers

The time to pick flowers is right before or when they are reaching their peak, while they are still vibrant. After their peak they start fading in color and taste. Flowers are usually best picked in the mid to late morning, after the dew has lifted. Flowers that have just opened don't need to be washed. Avoid washing flowers when possible to retain their pollen.

Fruits

Most areas have a fairly long berry season. Watch the birds and look for seeds in animal droppings. This will let you know what's in season and when it's time to start picking. It is generally best to gather fruits early in the morning. If you wait too long, the birds will get there first and will often pick it clean or leave partially pecked out fruits on the ground. It's also cooler for picking the summer berries. You want to only pick those that are ripe unless it's a fruit that will continue to ripen after it has been picked.

QUESTION

How can you tell if a fruit is ripe?
Some fruits, when ripe, will drop to the ground. Others cling to the plant. If you tug on the fruit and it releases easily into your hand, it's ripe. Color will often reveal the degree of ripeness. Sample taste to find one that is just right and then you know.

Many wild fruits have a short shelf life. If they lie on the ground too long, they start to ferment. If it feels bubbly when you pick it up, the fermentation process has begun. Gathering fruits often means visiting the same area regularly while the fruit is in season.

Roots

In the fall, nutrients are stored in the roots as the top parts die back or go dormant. This is the time to gather roots. The roots continue to grow underground throughout the winter months. They can be gathered up until the plant starts developing new growth above ground. Roots often become tough and woody at this stage.

In areas that experience extreme cold during the winter, roots should be dug before the ground has become too frozen. Otherwise you may have to wait until spring. In warmer climates, early morning or late afternoon is a good time to dig roots.

Sap

Sap begins rising from the roots in late winter and early spring. Tapping trees for sap to make syrup is usually best on a warm, sunny day after a cold spell, before the leaves have developed. This is also when bark peels most easily for harvesting the inner bark of some trees.

Seeds

Seeds should be harvested just before they are ready to drop. It should be done on a clear day, preferably following several days with no rain. Use clippers to snip off the seed head and turn upside down in a brown paper bag. As the seed head continues to mature, the seeds of some plants will release and drop to the bottom.

▲ Wild rice seeds releasing from seed head

Safety Precautions

As with any outdoor activity, there are certain precautions that one should adhere to when venturing out to forage. If you're going out alone, let someone know where you're going, what time you're leaving, and how long you expect to be gone. Make sure you have plenty of water, especially if it's during the summer. A basic first aid kit is always handy. Snakes, spiders, mosquitoes, biting flies, ticks, chiggers, and stinging insects are all a part of the outdoors. Learn to identify poison ivy, poison oak, and poison sumac and avoid them.

Wildlife

Snakes blend in with their environment and often remain unnoticed. Find out which ones are poisonous in your area and learn how to identify them. Be aware of your surroundings and watch where you walk. Most snakes won't bite unless you step on them or try to pick them up.

Spiders are often more visible, especially when you walk into their web stretched across the path. Unless you have an allergic reaction, spider bites react in a similar way as mosquito bites with the exception of the brown recluse and black widow. Use a stick to remove webs from your path.

FACT

Most of the poisonous snakes in this country are pit vipers. They have a heat-sensing pit between the eye and the nostril that they use to pick up the heat from a warm-blooded mammal within eight feet. The head is large and triangular while the pupil of the eye is elliptical.

Mosquitoes, biting flies, ticks, and chiggers can be quite annoying. Avoid using scented soaps or shampoos before going out. Wear plastic or latex gloves to protect your hands. A net worn over a hat can keep them off your face and neck. Long pants and long sleeves can protect the arms and legs from being bitten.

Wasps, bees, and hornets are among some of the insects that can inflict a painful sting. Some caterpillars are also armed with stinging spines. Plantain, the common garden weed, helps to relieve the pain of these stings. Since the herb is edible, you can chew the leaf to form a poultice and place on the sting. Learn to identify it and look for it whenever you go out.

Poisonous Plants

Learn to identify poison ivy, poison oak, and poison sumac. Inspect the area where you will be picking first. Look for plants that look similar to what you're gathering and find out if they are poisonous. If they are poisonous, be careful not to mix them in with what you are picking.

CHAPTER 2

Connecting with Plants

In the process of getting to know plants you will find that you gravitate toward some plants more than to others. You feel a sense of kinship with that plant and want to get to know it better. Make a practice of tasting the individual plants that you know to be edible to see which ones feel good to you. When approaching them, clear your mind of thoughts and focus on the plants. Once you become attuned to them, you will start seeing them everywhere, jumping out at you.

Becoming Aware

Plants are like people. They have individual characteristics that make them different from any other plants. To become aware of plants, all you have to do is step out your back door. Once you've eaten a salad that came from your yard you'll never see it the same way again.

Weeds

What many people think is a weed is actually food. They spend many hours pulling them out of their gardens, weeds that in many cases are more nutritional than the vegetables they are growing. Start noticing which plants are growing around you, even if you can't identify them. Watch for them to bloom. What was once a weed becomes a wildflower when it blooms, and then an herb when you discover how to use it.

Flowers and Fruits

Flowers and fruits are sometimes hidden under leaves and remain concealed to most people while others are more obvious. If a plant is in bloom, look at the color and count the number of petals. Sniff it to see if it is fragrant. If it is a tree, look into the branches for flowers or fruits that may be hidden behind the leaves. Vines climb to the tops of trees reaching for the light. Some trees also have their flowers near the top. To see their flowers requires looking up into the sky. Often it's when they drop to the ground that they are noticed. Some fruits have a green covering that makes them appear to be nothing more than leaves.

Special Gifts

Plants have special gifts for those who are aware enough to receive them. When approaching plants, take a few moments to clear your mind of thoughts and look at them carefully to see how they differ in appearance. Feel the leaves for texture and crush them to see if they have a scent. Look for anything special that makes that particular plant different.

ALERT

Some plants have sharp thorns and can puncture you while others have the ability to sting. Some may cause contact dermatitis and should be avoided. Learn to identify these plants and be aware of them any time you are in the outdoors and avoid them.

Plant Communities

Plants live in communities, sometimes in close association with others. Some like it hot and dry, while others prefer the coolness of shade and water. Explore different types of habitats and start noticing the types of plants found in each one. See if there is a pattern, whether certain plants always grow together or are alone. Some plants form colonies or grow in clusters.

All flowering plants, when in their ideal environment, will bloom. This is when they stand out from other plants and is a good time to get to know them. Browse through field guides with color pictures to get familiar with the different types of flowers. Find out which plants grow in your area by visiting regional nature centers or contacting the Natural Heritage program for your state. Participate in field trips or workshops that focus on the plants in your area. Becoming aware involves spending time in nature.

Plants and People Relationships

The relationship between plants and people dates back to our earliest ancestors. Before there was fire or weapons, there were plants. People and plants have evolved together. Ancient cultures knew and used the plants that grew around them for their sustenance. It was a matter of survival.

Those same plants are available today. All cultivated plants were once wild. As certain plants became more desirable, early people began growing them near their homes. If they saw a particular plant that produced larger or sweeter berries than others, they would select that one and use the seed to propagate more, eventually leading to the development of agriculture.

Plants provide food in exchange for a place to grow. Find out which plants that are growing in your area were used for food by earlier cultures and taste them. If you find some you like, you too can cultivate them and grow them in your garden.

Foraging with Children

Giving children a memorable experience helps them connect with plants. As the leader, you set the example by your attitude toward plants and especially by eating them. Children need to know that some things are poisonous, but certainly not everything. Before allowing them to eat something, help them get to know it and to look around to see what other plants might look like it. Working with children is often not very different from working with adults.

Attuning to Plants

Attuning to plants involves using the senses, beginning with observation and looking for any distinctive features. Start by helping children realize they are not just green things. Each one has a feature that makes them unique, just like each one of them is unique. Scavenger hunts that include finding plants with specific features, such as flower colors, leaf shapes, or types of fruits can help children become familiar with plant characteristics.

Other activities that can help children attune to plants include:

- Seed dispersal—to become familiar with different types of fruits
- Leaf rubbings—to distinguish between leaf shapes and leaf veins
- Sensory activities—using the senses of smell, touch, and taste when appropriate

Cautions

Inform the children that there are a lot of plants that might look like the ones they know, but they may not be edible. Let them know that unless they are with an adult who can positively identify the plant, it's best not to eat anything growing wild. Also, caution them about where to pick and not to pick. They may be able to identify the plant but not realize they can't just pick anywhere.

In the Field

Point out any poisonous look-alikes that grow in the area, if there are any, and show the children how they differ. If it's an area that's okay to pick, have them pick one sample and bring it back to you. After checking what everyone has brought back, take a sample and eat it and have them do the same. Then give the children a collection bag and have them pick enough to make a prepared dish. It's good to already have picked in advance what you need and then supplement with what they pick, making sure it's inspected first.

Food Preparations

Children love to crack nuts. Have several different sizes of rocks and let them practice cracking them. You can also involve them in some of the other preparations such as measuring ingredients, stirring, and mixing that are involved in cooking with wild plants. Taking the plants that have been picked and having the children help prepare a dish that they can then taste provides them with a memorable experience that will carry them into adulthood.

Follow the Cycles

The cycles of plants follow the seasons. They can provide you with what you need when you need it. The gathering period for each plant varies. Being attuned to the plants and knowing when they are in season is important for a forager.

Spring

With spring comes new growth, new beginnings. Buds of woody plants begin swelling as the sap starts rising and patches of green start growing. Young greens emerge to provide vitamins that can boost your immune system and flush out toxins. Flowers burst open, attracting pollinators who will pollinate the flowers so fruits can develop. Some of these flowers can also provide you with food and nutrition.

Summer

The flowers that were blooming in the spring are replaced with fruits that contain the seeds. Among these are the sweet, juicy berries that are available all summer, at a time when you need extra energy and hydration. The early greens of spring are replaced with summer greens that can tolerate the heat. They usually have larger leaves or succulent stems and contain more water than the spring greens.

Fall

Seeds mature in the fall and are dispersed in different ways. The time to gather them is just before they are ready to be dispersed. As fall advances, plants send their starches and nutrients to their roots for storage. This is the best time to start gathering roots. Nuts begin falling in late autumn and provide calories, fats, and oils that can sustain you through the winter.

Winter

Winter is a dormancy period for a lot of plants, at least on the surface. Annuals have died back and the tops of perennials look dead. The growth is happening underground. Roots can be dug throughout the winter, as long as the ground isn't frozen. Cold-weather greens are generally available all winter, unless snow or ice is a factor. The picking season extends into the winter for some berries.

The harvest season may extend over a two- to three-week period that may mean you will have to make repeated trips to the same area. Early morning is a good time to forage. If you wait until later, the birds and mammals will already have been there. Become familiar with the life cycles of the plants and know when they bloom, produce fruit, and go to seed. Following the cycles of plants puts you in touch with the cycles of life.

Plant Features

There are certain features that are shared by all plants. All plants have roots and shoots. Those with similar characteristics are arranged into groups and then into hierarchies, with a Kingdom, Division, Subdivision, Order, and

Class. Among the flowering plants there are two classes: monocots and dicots. Monocots have one seed leaf, veins are parallel in the leaves, and flowers are in threes or multiples of three. Dicots have two seed leaves, netted veins, and four, five, or irregular number of petals.

Knowing what types of plants there are, and having a familiarity with various leaf types, formations, arrangements on the stem, flower structures, and fruit types, is essential to positive identification of an unknown plant. Once you know what to look for, you can use a botanical key to help you identify a particular plant.

ESSENTIAL

Keys vary with different field guides, depending on the type of classification used. Some are based on a few characteristics such as flower color. Others are more evolved and are based on as many anatomical characteristics as possible. Finally there is the phylogenetic classification that is built on evolutionary relationships.

Roots

Roots are the underground part of the plant, whose function is to absorb and conduct food, water, and minerals. They also anchor the plant into the soil. Root division is what some plants rely on for reproduction.

There are different types of roots. Primary roots are those that have developed from the seed root and remain throughout the life of the plant. Tap roots are primary roots and include many of the biennials as well as some trees. Biennials include evening primrose, burdock, and thistle. Dandelions have tap roots even though they are perennials. Adventitious roots are outgrowths from structures other than the primary root such as prop roots or underground stems.

Underground stems are specialized. Rhizomes are underground stems that grow horizontally and are usually fleshy. Tubers are enlarged tips of rhizomes and include groundnuts and arrowheads. Corms are upright, fleshy, and shortened with papery leaf bases. Onions are bulbs and are very short, upright, underground stem tips completely surrounded by fleshy leaf tissue. Stolons run horizontally over the ground and root at the tip, like strawberries.

Shoots

Shoots include the stem with leaves and branches. The stem supports the plant and is where the buds, leaves, and flowers are attached to places called nodes. It also conducts water, minerals, and food from the roots. Stems store and manufacture food by photosynthesis and also sometimes serve as the means for reproduction. They may be either above or below the ground.

FACT

Stems can be either woody or non-woody. Woody stems include trees, which have a single stem and are large. Shrubs are also woody stems but there are two or more stems and they are smaller than trees. Woody vines have weak or trailing stems and usually climb. Non-woody stems include herbaceous dicots and monocots.

Among the herbaceous dicots are annuals, biennials, and perennials. Annuals have a one-year life cycle. They bloom, produce seed, and die all in one season. Biennials live two years. The first year a basal rosette of leaves develops, sometimes in late summer. Over the winter, the tap root develops. The next spring it sends up a flower stalk, blooms, goes to seed, and dies. Perennials come back year after year with an indefinite life cycle. Herbaceous monocots have non-branching stems and are not woody.

Leaves

Leaves store and manufacture food by photosynthesis. They can be either simple or compound and are arranged on the stem in patterns. Some are alternate, growing singly on the stem, while others are in pairs. Whorled leaves have three or more leaves growing from a central point on the stem. The margins on a leaf can be smooth, serrated with saw-toothed edges, or lobed with rounded segments or indentations. Leaves appear in many shapes, sizes, and colors. They may be round, oval, linear, heart-shaped, or triangular. Some may be hairy while others are smooth or have thorns. Look for resinous dots on the surface or underside of the leaf that, when crushed, emit a scent.

QUESTION

How can I tell if it is a simple or compound leaf?
Follow the leaf stem to the main stem. If there is a leaf bud growing in the axil where the two stems meet, it is a simple leaf. Otherwise, there will be multiple leaflets attached to the stem that has a bud in the axil.

Flowers

Flowers come in all shapes, sizes, and colors. If the flower petals all look the same and the flower is symmetrical, it is called a regular flower. Irregular flowers are asymmetrical and the petals may not all be the same size or shape. Some flowers are too small to count and the petals are indistinguishable. An inflorescence, a group or cluster of flowers, attached to a single tip of the stem is a head, and is surrounded by bracts, leaflike structures at the base of the flower. Some flowers have a stalk that is attached to the main stem while others do not. An umbel is a stalk of flowers attached to the stem tip. Flowers that do not have a stalk and are on the same stem form a spike. A raceme is like a spike except that its flowers have a flower stalk. A panicle is a compound raceme. A spadix is a specialized spike of flowers such as the arum family.

Flowers have male and female reproductive parts that are surrounded by the flower petals. The pistil is the female organ and consists of a stigma, style, and ovary. Within the ovary are the ovules that contain the seeds. The style is the stalk of the pistil with a stigma, the part that receives the pollen at the end. The stamen is the male organ that forms the pollen and includes the anther and filament. The filament is the stalk while the anther is the tip where the pollen is born. Some flowers are unisexual, with only male or female parts on one flower, while others contain both sexes. Unisexual flowers rely on the wind, bees, or other insects to bring pollen to them. Some flowers, even though they may have both male and female flower parts, must receive pollen from another plant before the fruit will develop. Special features, such as scent, colors, dotted petals, or stickiness help to lure the pollinating insects to them.

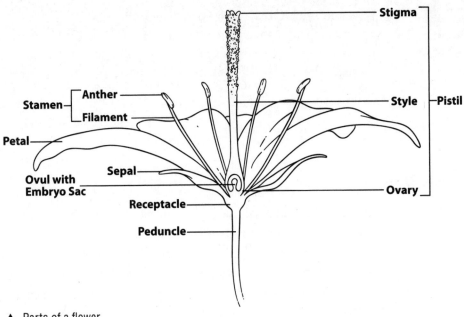

▲ Parts of a flower

Fruits

Once a flower has been pollinated, the fruit begins to develop. There are different types of fruits:

- Berries are sweet and juicy with seeds embedded in the flesh.
- Drupes are fleshy fruits enclosing a pit, which is a hard stone containing a seed.
- Hips are fleshy fruits surrounding several mature ovaries filled with seeds.
- A nut is a fruit with a husk that partially or wholly encloses a shell that contains the nutmeat.
- Legumes are flat pods with sutures that split open when ripe.
- A follicle is a dry fruit that splits open when mature.
- Aggregates are many tiny berries growing clumped together.

Fruits can sometimes be seen hanging from the branches in the leaf axils or clustered at the ends of the stems. They may also grow singly or in pairs.

Fruits contain the seeds of a plant and must be dispersed for the plant to reproduce. Birds and small mammals eat fleshy fruits. Undigested seeds pass through their systems and where they are dropped, if conditions are right, they will germinate and grow. Some seeds are attached to a wing and are propelled through the air when they are mature or carried in a fluff of cotton. Some have burrs and attach themselves to mammals to be transported to another area. Some simply drop to the ground. These may be carried off by squirrels and planted or left to germinate under the parent tree.

Plant Journal

There are many ways to keep a journal. It can be with drawings, photos, or descriptions. In some cases it can be pressed specimens, depending on where the plant is growing. Use a small notebook or tablet that can be carried easily into the field and make a habit of taking it with you. If you forget to take it with you, test your recall by filling it in later. Be consistent and continue through the seasons.

ESSENTIAL

When starting a journal, there is basic information that should always be recorded. This includes the date, location, time, and weather. Also include the type of environment, whether it is a backyard, marsh, woodland, field, or stream. This can be your guide in planning for future foraging expeditions.

Plant Sketching

When learning to identify plants, sketching them will help you to tune in to unique characteristics that later can be used to help identify the plant. This can be extremely useful when in an area where taking a specimen is not appropriate. You don't have to be an artist to sketch plants. The purpose is to record what you are seeing in a way that you can later look it up in a field guide. The sketch can be accompanied with written descriptions as well.

Sometimes it's not convenient to remain in the field to sketch a plant. Insects may be a nuisance, or it may be too hot to sit in the sun for an extended period, or you may not have time, or you may have forgotten your sketchbook. In some cases it may be appropriate to take a cutting of the fresh plant, put the stem in water, and take it inside to sketch.

Sketching plants brings your attention to the special features of the plant. Sketch the plant at different times throughout the year as a part of your journaling. Sketching increases your awareness and is a great tool to help you connect with the plants.

Plant Photography

Photographing plants puts you in direct contact with them. Keeping a photographic journal helps you follow the life cycle of a plant, from the seedling stage to maturity. This along with a written description that also has the location and date included. Photographing a plant can also take the place of sketching the plant if you are in a hurry or if conditions are not appropriate for sketching. Early morning or late afternoon lighting usually produces better results, since the mid-day lighting is usually brighter and harsher. When photographing plants, try to isolate the part being photographed from the background and remove any unnecessary debris or other plant material from around the subject. Zoom in for detail if your camera allows, as well as showing as much of the plant as possible.

CHAPTER 3

Becoming Plant Wise

Becoming plant wise means knowing plants. Wisdom is acquired and is developed by spending time, not just with plants, but also in nature. You know which plants produce every year and which have lean years, as well as those that are rare or abundant. You can know the name of the plant, and even how it's used. But it's not until you actually bite into the fruit, or taste the dish that has been prepared with wild plants, that you can fully appreciate and know the plants.

Rare and Endangered Species

Some plants are hard to find. Populations of certain species have declined over the years and in some cases have even become extinct. Plant populations are determined from field studies and plant surveys conducted by private, local, state, and federal agencies. Sometimes a plant may be considered rare or even endangered. And yet, you may find a large patch of it. At other times, you may see a few specimens here and there spread out over a large area. Then there are those plants that are rarely seen and only occur in a specific area. If there's an abundance of the plant you want to gather, pick sparingly and scatter seed if possible to extend the range.

Most states have a natural resources department. If your state doesn't have one, look for one in a neighboring state. They will most likely have a list of rare and endangered species for your area. Find out which plants are on the list and if a plant that you want to harvest is on the list, look for a substitute elsewhere.

Loss of Habitat

Loss of habitat is one of the biggest contributors to a plant's decline. Increased development is happening all over the country. Farm fields now grow houses and forests are timbered. Shopping centers spring up on every corner and where there is a patch of green, herbicides are used to prevent weeds from growing. Even parks have mowed fields and neatly trimmed edges. When an area is cleared for development, not only are all the trees removed, but also all the shrubs, ferns, and flowering plants that make up the habitat.

Improved farming techniques have all but eliminated hedgerows and natural borders. A manicured look has become the trend. A weedy appearance is considered uncared for. And yet, that's where many of the wild edible plants grow.

Some plants will only grow in certain environments. Along the coast, only those plants that can tolerate salt air and ocean winds will grow there, while in the mountains rocky outcrops support other plants. These specific plants will usually only grow in those areas. Transplanting them to other areas may not be successful and can lead to their decline. Developing the area can also result in those plants becoming rare or endangered.

Overharvesting

Overharvesting occurs when someone picks more than the area can sustain. Whether it is the young shoots, the flower that produces the fruit, or the fruits that contain the seeds. Without seeds to reproduce, the plant will slowly decline.

"Wildcrafting" is the term used when referring to gathering wild plants in their natural habitat for food, medicine, and craft. Herbalists make a living gathering and creating products using wild plants. It provides families with a source of income that otherwise would be lacking. Care should be taken not to gather more than an area can sustain and to make sure seeds are replanted, roots divided, and the populations continue to thrive.

ESSENTIAL

You never want to be the cause of a plant becoming rare or endangered. Plants are renewable resources and if harvested with a conscientious attitude can continue to produce edible parts every year. Use clippers when appropriate to remove only the parts needed. Trim leaves from the plant rather than breaking or denuding the branch.

When gathering annuals, be sure to leave some to reseed. If you are picking berries, leave some for the birds, some to reseed, and some for the next group of foragers. Leaves can be picked from plants without taking the whole plant. Only gather roots when they are plentiful. Roots are the most susceptible to overharvesting. Unless the root is divided and replanted, it means killing the plant.

Before gathering plants, become aware of the plants' life cycles. Observe and notice whether a particular plant comes back every year and produces edible parts. There may be an abundance of acorns one year, but few the next. Notice which annuals or biennials reseed year after year.

Plant Names

Learning plants involves naming them, one plant at a time. Plant names can be very descriptive and add character to the plant. Sometimes they indicate the shape of the flower, the leaf, the color of the fruit, or the way it has been used. For a novice, a field guide alone is usually not enough to positively identify a particular plant. Several plants may have leaves, flowers, or fruits that look similar. Find out the common name used in your area, and when possible, the scientific name as well.

Begin with plants that are already familiar to you. You walk past them every day. Notice how they are different. Many of these are probably on color charts at weed control centers that you may be able to pick up for free. Most of the weeds that herbicides are advertised to destroy are edible plants.

Knowing which plants are indigenous to your area can help. If there is a nature center, botanical garden, or natural area near you, they may have a botanist or checklist of plants in your area. Even better, they may have programs or field trips identifying wild plants. Native plant societies usually have a regional list of native plants. Once you can put a name to the plant, look for the relationship between the name and the plant that will help you remember it.

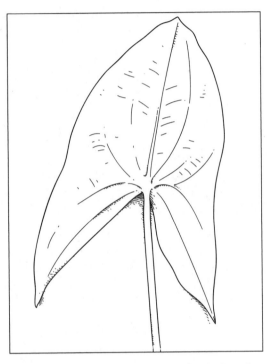

▲ Arrowhead—named for its arrowhead-shaped leaf

Common Names

Plants have both common names and scientific names. Common names can be very regionalized. The same name can be applied to two very different plants, depending on where they are growing. There is a tree that is called hemlock whose needles can be used to make a medicinal tea. There are also herbs that are called hemlock, one is poison hemlock, the other water hemlock. A tea made from the leaves of either one will kill you. Likewise, one plant can have many names.

Common names can also be corrupted. Misspellings, regional accents, or unclear pronunciations can produce some interesting variations of a plant's name. When communicating with people, get to know the regional names they are familiar with. Other people may know the plant you're talking about but by a completely different name.

Scientific Names

Scientific names are in Latin and are used internationally. Identifying and classifying plants is based on anatomical parts that group them in orders and then families. Family names are not a part of the plant's scientific name. Families are divided into the genus and species name, which make up the scientific name.

Sometimes a capital letter will follow the species name. This is referring to the last name of the individual who first published the name with its description and who also has the privilege of naming the new plant. For example, the letter "L" follows a number of Latin names, as in *Daucus carota L.*, the Latin name for wild carrot. The "L" stands for Linnaeus who developed the binomial system of classification, first published in 1735.

QUESTION

What does it mean when you see a genus name followed by the letters spp.?
The letters spp. mean species plural, referring to a particular plant as being one of two or more species of a particular genus. Often this is used when there are many species and distinguishing between them is difficult, as with wild mustards that often hybridize.

The genus name is always a noun whereas the species name is usually a descriptive adjective that relates in some way to the plant. It might be the color of the flowers, the shape of the leaf, or the structure of the fruits. For example, the Latin name for muscadine grape is *Vitis rotundifolia*. *Vitis* is grape in Latin, whereas *rotundifolia* means round leaf, referring to the shape of the leaf. *Angustifolia* means narrow leaves and is frequently used as a species name for plants that have narrow leaves as in *Typha angustifolia*, with *Typha* being the Greek name for cattail, referring to the narrow leaf cattail. *Ilex vomitoria* is a native holly that was used by American Indians to make a strong, concentrated black drink that they would drink in the spring as a ceremonial drink and would literally drink it until they threw up. Sometimes the name is referring to the habitat or location where it was found, as in *Rosa virginiana*, referring to a wild rose that was discovered in Virginia. Names have stories behind them that can help you remember the plant's name.

There is also a trinomial system where the species name is broken down into a subspecies for greater precision. In this case the abbreviation for variety, "var.," is used between the species and the subspecies name.

Food as Medicine

Wild plants that are edible are not just food, they are also good for you. Many of the weeds pulled out of gardens are far superior nutritionally to the vegetable plants that are replacing them. Plants are filled with chemical compounds. Many of the prescription drugs and over-the-counter medications are derived from compounds found in plants. According to Dr. James Duke, more than half of these plant-derived medicinal components come from weeds.

The compounds found in plants are there to protect the plant from being eaten but they can also help protect the human body from disease. If you know which plants are good for certain ailments that you might be experiencing, you can supplement your diet with those plants. The USDA's Phytochemical and Ethnobotanical Database, available online at *www.ars-grin .gov/duke* is a great source for this information.

ESSENTIAL

Many edible plants also have medicinal effects. They may thin the blood, lower blood pressure, or slow the heart rate. They can also be stimulating or relaxing. Before eating wild plants, find out what the medicinal effects, if any, might be. You might be treating yourself for something you don't need to be treated for.

Wild plant foods are an excellent source for many of the vitamins and other nutrients that are sold in health food stores. Many herbal supplements consist of the dried herb in capsule form. Instead of buying the capsules, learn to identify the plant, find out what its habitat requirements are, and either grow it yourself or look for a wild population where it's okay to gather. Eating plants to get your vitamins is far more desirable than taking a capsule in pill form. Plus you get the synergistic benefits, which means that the whole is greater than the sum of its parts.

Spring Tonics

Tonics are those plants that strengthen the body. Flushing toxins out of the body helps to strengthen it and boost the immune system. Some tonics are in the form of teas and are made from the roots, twigs, or leaves of the plant, including sassafras, spicebush, and sweet birch. Others come from wild greens that are often used for detoxification. Dandelions have diuretic properties and are a rich source of iron and vitamin C. Other spring tonics include burdock as a tea or added to soups or vegetables, stinging nettles, chickweed, cresses, and violets. These can be eaten raw in salads, incorporated into meals, or juiced.

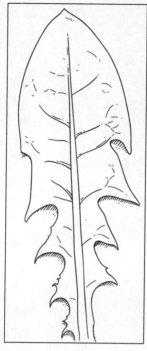

▲ Dandelion leaf

Summer Sweets

In the summer when it is hot and dry, sweet and juicy fruits ripen. These are blood builders, providing sugar for energy and juice for hydration. Among the summer sweets are wild blueberries, wild cherries, elderberries, blackberries, and raspberries.

Fall Foraging

In the fall nutrients descend from the top of the plant to the roots where they are stored over winter. This is the time to gather roots. Burdock, Jerusalem artichoke, and evening primrose are available in your yard or garden, while groundnuts, arrowheads, and water lilies are available in the wetlands.

Fall fruits, such as the pawpaw and persimmon have a higher fat content to prepare the body for cooler temperatures. They are usually not as juicy as the fruits of summer.

Nuts for the Winter

When autumn arrives and leaves begin to fall, this is the time to go to the woods and look for nuts. Typically, nuts are produced by mature hardwood trees and are partially or wholly enclosed in a husk that may be papery, leafy, woody, or spiny in character. Inside the husk is an outer shell and the nutmeat is contained within it. High in protein, rich in unsaturated fats which give them a high caloric value, nuts are just what the body needs to sustain itself through the winter. Nuts were a mainstay in the diet of American Indians and later on, the early settlers. They included hickory, hazelnut, black walnut, chestnut, beech nuts, and acorns from oak trees.

Allergies

Allergies occur when someone experiences an unusually sensitive response to something that is not ordinarily considered harmful. Sensitivity varies with each individual and can vary over a period of time. Almost any plant can cause an allergic reaction in someone.

ALERT

If you're eating a plant for the first time, you don't know that you're not allergic to it. So eat just a little bit. Wait at least twenty minutes to make certain you are not going to have an allergic reaction to it. Then eat a little bit more and wait. After an hour, if no reaction has occurred, you're probably not allergic to it.

Aero-allergens

Allergens are sensitizing substances such as pollen grains or molds that are airborne. Inhaling them can result in sneezing and sniffling, and almost any plant can produce these reactions. In the early spring, some of the more common aero-allergens reach their pollen peak, such as flowering maples, birches, and oaks. Grasses and summer flowering trees reach their peak in mid-summer while the ragweeds and goldenrods bloom from late summer to early fall.

Dermatitis

A few plants can cause a dermatitis rash or inflammation in some people. Dermatitis can result from handling plants or rubbing against them. Poison ivy, poison oak, and poison sumac are the best known of these plants.

If contact has been made with any of these plants, immediately scrub the exposed area with a strong soap. If jewelweed grows nearby, make a wash of the leaves and stems and use it like a washcloth to remove the resin from the skin.

Food Allergy

Food allergies result from sensitivity to certain proteins in plants. Instead of being external, the symptoms are internal. Some may cause itching and swelling in the mouth and throat. Lips may become swollen. Or one can experience nausea, vomiting, and diarrhea. If you are experiencing difficulty in breathing, you may be going into anaphylactic shock and should call rescue immediately. But this is an extreme situation and doesn't happen often.

Pesticide Use

Using pesticides is a common practice in most areas today. It refers to any substance that prevents, destroys, or repels a pest. They include various types of insecticides, herbicides, and fungicides. There are also poisons for rodents and antimicrobials to control bacteria. If it's an abandoned lot, find out what the land was used for before it was abandoned. Chances are pretty good an abandoned area was probably treated with some form of pesticide at some point. Manicured areas, like golf courses, tend to be heavily treated with pesticides.

Insecticides

Insecticides are commonly used by homeowners, gardeners, farmers, and individuals who see an insect and want to kill it. Crop dusters fly over farm fields, and in mosquito-infested areas, mosquito control trucks traverse the residential areas, leaving a cloud of toxic smoke behind them. Ants in the kitchen immediately bring out the sprays in some households, and wasps are prevented from building their nests. Residues from insecticides are on most plant foods. Unless you know they haven't been sprayed, be sure to wash them before eating.

FACT

Federal and state lands, as well as private nature preserves, frequently use herbicides as a management tool to control invasive aliens, both along waterways and on trails. Brown patches are generally evidence of spraying. Check with the manager before picking and to find out if the area has been sprayed.

Before going outdoors, many people spray themselves with toxic insect repellents. If you have applied insect repellent before going out without washing your hands, the plants you gather may be contaminated with pesticide residue. Try switching to an herbal insect repellent.

Many wild fruit trees rely on insects for pollination. Many of these pollinators are being killed by insecticides. If you're getting flowers in the spring but no fruits you may want to try artificial pollination. Using a toothbrush or small paint brush, scoop some pollen off the stamens when they're blooming and brush it on the next flower.

Herbicides

Herbicides are used in the cracks of sidewalks, on golf courses, and at the edges of parking lots. Any landscaped area has most likely been treated with herbicides, especially if you don't see any weeds.

Non-organic gardeners and farmers often use chemical herbicides between the rows and at the edges of gardens and fields. Avoid picking leaves that look spotted and wilted. They have probably been sprayed.

Fungicides

Fungicides are chemical pesticides used to kill fungi that come up in agricultural fields, on plants, or in the soil. Fungi are decomposers of dead, organic matter and include mushrooms, yeasts, and molds. Evidence of their use is harder to detect. If in doubt about whether the plants have been sprayed or not, always make a habit of washing them before eating.

Wild Food Myths

Myths abound concerning wild foods. Often they stem from someone looking for a shortcut to learning the plant. There is no one general rule. Get to know the plants individually and find out which ones are safe to use.

Berry Myths

The color of a berry has been believed to determine whether it is edible or not. You will often hear someone say that red berries are poisonous. There are a number of red berries that are edible. Wild strawberries, cactus fruits, rose hips, and hawthorns are among the edible fruits that are red.

It has also been believed that all blue or blue-black berries are edible. This also is not true. Virginia creeper berries and pokeberries have blue or blue-black berries and are considered poisonous.

Not all white berries are poisonous either. There are white mulberries that taste bland, but are edible nonetheless.

QUESTION

If an animal eats it, does that mean I can eat it?
Some birds love poison ivy berries. There are numerous other berries that are inedible to humans but birds or small mammals are able to eat them without any problems. Squirrels eat mushrooms that would be toxic to humans. However, if you see berries that even the birds don't eat, you may want to find out why.

Bitter Doesn't Mean Bad

Just because a plant is bitter does not mean it's toxic. A lot of wild greens taste bitter. Bitter herbs are actually good for you. They aid in the digestive process plus they are concentrated with vitamins. Many of the bitter herbs are used in the spring as tonics to flush and cleanse the body of toxins.

Milky Sap

One of the myths with wild plants is that if the sap is white and milky, it is toxic. Even cultivated lettuce exudes a white sap when picked, as does wild lettuce and other members of that family. However, the milky sap of dogbane and milkweed is toxic. It's also sticky and forms a hard coating when it dries, making it useful for waterproofing items.

Poison Ivy Myths

Leaves of three, let it be. Many have heard this statement. The fact is, poison ivy does have three leaves, and should be left to be. However, other plants including wild beans and members of the pea family also have leaves with three leaflets and need not be left to be.

It is believed by some people that if you do see poison ivy, look around and you will find jewelweed, used by many as an antidote. In reality, poison ivy grows in lots of different habitats. Jewelweed only grows in damp, partially sunny areas. Poison ivy may be there also, but not always.

CHAPTER 4

Poisonous Plants

Poisonous plants are those that are capable of irritating or causing a harmful reaction in people or animals. Some plants are edible, others poisonous, while some are both edible and poisonous. What makes the difference is the part that is used, how it is prepared, and when it is gathered. With some exceptions, very few plants can really hurt you. Most plants that are poisonous taste so bad you won't eat enough to hurt you.

History of Usage

Poisonous plants have been used since their discovery. They were discovered and used by early cultures before agriculture was known. Knowledge has been gradual, often the result of experimentation. Once a poisonous plant was discovered it was put to use. Among some cultures, knowledge of poisonous plants was kept secret and guarded.

Hunting and Warfare

The earliest usage of poisonous plants dates back to the hunters and gatherers. Arrows were tipped with poisons for hunting and in battle, using both plants and animals. Poisons were added to the drinking water of enemies during war times. Among some indigenous cultures, plant poisons are still used for hunting today.

Using poisonous plants to catch fish was a common practice among American Indians. Certain plants, such as buckeye, were pounded and placed in the water. The poison affected the nervous system without spoiling the meat. As it took effect, the fish would float to the top. The practice of using poisonous plants to kill fish today is illegal.

Murders, Executions

Knowledge of poisonous plants has historically put one in a position of power. Among royalty, taste testers were used to ensure the food had not been poisoned. "Succession powders" were poisons used to guarantee moving up the line of succession. Women would use plant poisons to get rid of undesirable men, while others would use them to get revenge, out of jealousy, or for political reasons.

Poison hemlock is believed to be the source of the poison that was used in the execution drink of Socrates. It contains alkaloids that produce the same results as described by Socrates after he drank his tea. Drinking the tea results in paralysis, eventually paralyzing the heart and breathing muscles.

Magic Potions

Love charms, sleeping potions, or amulets that would protect against harm or injury were all employed by ancient cultures. In some parts of the world, they continue to be used today. Flower baths in some countries are used to bring good luck to an individual. Flowers are steeped overnight in water and massaged into the skin, then left to dry. Other plants are used to bring good luck to hunters.

Plant Medicine

Most plant foods are more than just food. They are also medicine. Either the plants have a high vitamin content or are a good source of minerals or some other desirable substance. These plants are generally recognized as safe (GRAS) by the FDA and are available in most health food stores in either capsule form or tincture. As a medicine, a little bit may be good whereas too much may be harmful.

ALERT

Some plants, even though made into a tea or a soup, are more of a medicine than a food and are used to treat specific ailments. Others are strictly medicine and should only be used by those who are trained. When making tea from herbs gathered in the wild, find out what medicinal effects, if any, there are.

Many of the pharmaceutical drugs in use today were derived from plant materials. *Digitalis,* commonly known as foxglove, is one that contains cardiac glycosides used in heart medicine. Mayapple roots and poke roots, both highly toxic, are used to treat certain types of cancer. False or American white hellebore was used as an analgesic. Many of these plants can be deadly if not used correctly.

Religious Uses

Plants were frequently used among indigenous cultures for religious ceremonies. Often these plants, such as peyote, datura, and morning glory seeds, were hallucinogenic and induced an altered state of consciousness.

Other plants were used to induce vomiting as a cleansing ritual to rid the body of toxins.

Categories of Poisonous Plant Effects

Poisonous plants are those plants that have harmful effects. It may be from touching them, inhaling their vapors, or ingesting them. The effect may be in the form of a rash, upset stomach, heart palpitations, or worse.

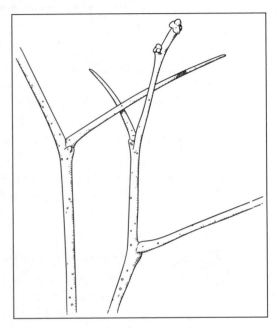

Mechanical Injury

Some plants have thorns and can puncture you, sometimes breaking the tips off under your skin. Blackberries, wild roses, and other brambles have recurved spines that prevent you from moving forward. Yuccas have dagger-like points that can stab you. Climbing vines such as greenbriers can wrap around your legs and scratch you with their sharp thorns.

▲ Hawthorn's dagger-like thorn

ALERT

Cactus pads are armed and dangerous. Each spine on the pad is surrounded by tufts of hairlike spines that attack when you come near the plant. They are so tiny and difficult to see that they often have to work their own way out of your skin. If not cleaned and treated, there's always a possibility of infection.

Other plants, like stinging nettle, have spines that will sting you. Hypodermic-like needles on the stems of the plants inject a compound that produces the stinging effect. Crushing up the leaves of yellow dock and rubbing them on the affected area can relieve the sting.

Allergic Reaction

An allergic reaction is an unusually sensitive response to something ordinarily not considered harmful, as with nut or wheat allergies. Since all plants can possibly cause an allergic reaction in someone, the plant that produced the allergen is not necessarily poisonous. However, there is a greater sensitivity to some plants, such as poison ivy, poison sumac, and poison oak that cause a contact dermatitis reaction in some people and are what most people think of when you mention poisonous plants.

Internal Poisoning

Internal poisoning is the most serious poisoning as a result of effects from toxic substances. Certain alkaloids affect the central nervous system while others affect the liver.

Alkaloids

Alkaloids are toxic substances that affect the central nervous system and are found in a number of wild plants. Some affect nerve function without visible effects while others act through the nervous system, including false hellebore and death camas, both in the lily family. Other alkaloids affect the liver. Crotalaria and groundsel can cause severe liver damage.

The nightshade family is well known and includes many garden plants that have both edible and poisonous parts, for example tomatoes and peppers, whose leaves are poisonous. Some nightshades, such as the ground cherry, grow wild. The fruits of the ground cherry are edible when ripe, whereas the unripe fruits are poisonous. Nightshades also include datura, which contains alkaloids that can have dramatic hallucinogenic effects and can result in convulsions and coma, even death.

Another type of alkaloid that is widely distributed in the plant kingdom is found in ergot, a fungus that grows in grain, rye, and other grasses. It produces effects similar to LSD, which was derived from it. Alkaloids derived from ergot are used as uterine-contracting drugs.

Glycosides

Glycosides are compounds that can be broken down into simple sugars plus other substances and are found in a number of plants, most of them nontoxic. The cardiac glycosides in digitalis can strengthen the heart in small amounts but can be fatal in larger quantities. Dogbane and oleander also contain cardiac glycosides and should be handled with care.

QUESTION

What causes the soapy froth that I sometimes see at the edge of streams or bays?
Saponins are non-cardial steroid glycosides that have a soapy-like reaction when agitated. These are the substances that are found in yucca, bouncing bet, and other plants that have been used for soap. When taken internally they can irritate the digestive system.

Cyanogenic glycosides are the most dangerous. Cyanide poisoning is the result of the breakdown of the cyanide-producing glycoside molecule found in certain members of the rose family, including wild cherries and wild plums. Scratching the bark and sniffing it for the bitter almond scent reveals the presence of the compound that breaks down into cyanide. Wilted cherry leaves have resulted in deaths of livestock and horses that grazed on trimmed branches bordering their pastures. Seeds and pits also contain this molecule.

Goitrogenic glycosides are found in members of the mustard family and can cause goiter. Persons who have hypothyroidism should only eat members of the mustard family cooked.

Oxalates

Oxalic acid is the substance that adds a lemon-like flavor to a number of wild greens, including sheep sorrel, wood sorrel, and yellow dock. Too much, however, is not good. Calcium oxalate crystals in large quantities can damage the kidneys.

Members of the Arum family, including Jack-in-the-pulpit and arrow arum, contain calcium oxalate crystals that when bitten into produce an intense burning sensation. It can cause swelling at the back of the throat and tongue, and in extreme cases, block breathing.

Resinoids and Resins

Resinoids are chemical substances left over after plant materials have been extracted and are sometimes toxic. Mountain laurel, azaleas, and other members of the heath family contain a toxic resinoid, as do members of the milkweed family, water hemlock, and mayapple. Urushiol is the resin in poison ivy that causes contact dermatitis in some people.

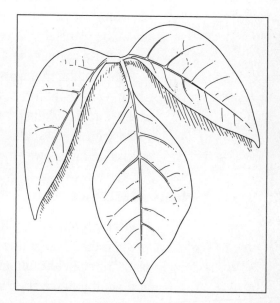

▲ Water hemlock

Photosensitization

Photosensitization looks like sunburn and occurs when sunlight reacts with certain pigments that are hypersensitive to sunlight. Buckwheat and St. Johnswort are among the plants that have photosensitizing pigments and can cause one to become sensitive to the sunlight. Taking St. Johnswort or eating products that include buckwheat may cause one to burn more easily when exposed to the sun than they normally would.

▲ Poison ivy—leaves of three

Ways to Avoid Plant Poisoning

Prevention is the best way to avoid poisoning. Only eat those plants that you know without a doubt are edible. Practice moderation. Just because something tastes good and you know it's good for you does not mean it's okay to gorge yourself. Avoid experimenting with unfamiliar plants for food or medicine. In the spring, numerous green leaves emerge at the time wild greens are being harvested. Be mindful of what you are picking and don't add anything you can't identify.

Child Poisoning

Most plant poisonings involve children, who are naturally curious and want to explore the world by taste. Many plants that are used in landscaping are poisonous. If you have children, find out which plants in your yard and neighborhood are poisonous and show them to your children with cautions not to eat them. Make sure they can identify poison ivy, poison oak, or poison sumac if they are in your area.

Children sometimes use plants as playthings. Know which ones they are using and whether or not they are poisonous. If you're not sure of the identity of the plants they are playing with, make sure they know not to eat them or put them in their mouths.

Many children have sucked the nectar from honeysuckle flowers. There are other fragrant flowers, such as yellow jessamine, that also grow on vines and are toxic. Identify any flowering vines in your area that may be confused with honeysuckle and point these out to your children. Keep plant seeds and bulbs away from infants when working with them.

Plant Identification

Before eating any plant, make sure you can identify it first. The best time is when the plant is in bloom or has fruit. Use a field guide to identify the plant. You can also photograph the plant and send it to the botany professor at a nearby university, field botanist with your state's natural heritage program, or other knowledgeable botanist in your area.

ESSENTIAL

Only eat those plants that you can positively identify as an edible plant. Never assume a plant is edible just because it bears a resemblance to an edible plant or because an animal eats it. When eating a plant for the first time, eat just a little bit and then wait to make sure it agrees with you.

You can use the taste buds to confirm a plant's identity after using the key in a field guide. Take a small bite of the plant and roll it around in your mouth. If it tastes bad, spit it out and wash your mouth out.

Plant Medicine

If using plants as medicine, find out as much information about the plants as you can and what to expect as side effects. Many plants have medicinal properties, and very often those properties can be toxic. Listen to your body, and if you feel nausea, dizziness, or other discomfort, discontinue the use of the plant.

Smoke Exposure

Avoid smoke from burning plants unless you know what's burning. Resins from poison ivy, poison oak, and poison sumac can be carried by the wind and may result in a dermatitis reaction in those who are exposed to the smoke.

Emergency Action

If poisoning is suspected or has happened call your physician. If the physician is not available, call the poison control center. Gather as much information as you can before making the call. If you are in an out-of-the-way place, you may want to induce vomiting, depending on what the poison is.

Plant Information

If possible, provide the common and scientific name of the plant. If you don't know the name of the plant, provide a detailed description, including any flowers or fruits that might be present. Crushing the leaves or scratching the bark to sniff it for any scents can also be helpful in identifying the plant.

Plant Remains

Save as much of the plant as possible. Be able to tell them the part that was eaten and how much. Also let them know how long ago it was. Whether the plant was ripe or unripe, rotten, or moldy is also important.

Personal Information

Providing the age, weight, and physical condition of the person sus-pected of being poisoned is important. Also describe any physical symp-toms that the person might be experiencing.

Poisonous Plants to Know

For those interested in foraging, finding out which wild plants are poisonous and which ones might be confused with an edible plant is important. It is recommended that you learn the poisonous ones first and then feel free to experiment with the ones that you know are edible.

Green Leaves

In the spring when gathering wild greens, there are a few plants to be aware of. Buttercups hide among the leaves of chickweed and dandelion and are sometimes picked with them. Members of this family contain glyco-sides that have caused irritations among livestock. Spurges are also common in gardens and lawns. They produce a milky sap that can also be irritating. Pokeweed leaves, when eaten raw, will make you throw up, even though they are edible when cooked. Milkweed is another plant that is edible when cooked but toxic raw.

Flower Nectar

Just because a flower is beautiful and smells good, doesn't mean you can eat it. Yellow jessamine flowers are an example. Honeybees have been poisoned from foraging on the nectar of these flowers. The showy, fragrant flowers of the jimsonweed are also toxic and have poisoned children suck-ing their nectar.

Azaleas are in the heath family, with flowers that are also tubular and fra-grant, and like the yellow jessamine, are toxic. The swamp azalea is some-times called swamp honeysuckle, making it even more confusing.

Poisonous Fruits

Eating a poisonous fruit by mistake has probably happened many times to many people. Suffering from the effects of a poisonous berry is more rare. Most fruits that are poisonous are so bitter that you won't eat enough to be poisoned. This includes members of the holly family that have berries that may be red or black and are considered toxic. If you eat enough of them, they can cause vomiting, diarrhea, and even death.

Pokeberries contain poisonous seeds. While the fruit may not taste bitter, poisoning can result if the seeds are ingested. Mayapple fruits are edible, but the seeds are poisonous.

Poisonous Grape Look-Alikes

Moonseed is a vine with heart-shaped leaves that looks like a grape vine and has fruits that look like grapes. Grapes have many seeds imbedded in the flesh, whereas moonseed fruits have a single seed that is in the shape of a crescent moon, which is where it got its name. Grape vines also have tendrils that are usually forked at the tip.

Virginia creeper berries are also grape-looking in appearance. The vines, however lack tendrils and leaves are made up of five leaflets. Berries of both moonseed and Virginia creeper are poisonous and should be avoided.

Poisonous Legumes

Legumes are bean-like pods that are characteristic of members of the pea family. Even though some of these species are edible, others contain toxic alkaloids that can result in nervous disorders.

Lupines are common herbs that grow in the western United States and Canada. Even though some may be edible when cooked, others contain toxic alkaloids and positive identification is difficult. It is best to avoid the lupines.

Locoweeds in the western part of the U.S. have reportedly been the cause of poisoning of horses, cattle, and sheep. The word *loco* refers to the crazy behavior shown by the horses and cattle who ate the weed.

Precatory beans, also known as rosary peas, grow in pods similar to peas with seeds that have a glossy red coating tipped with black. Seeds contain abrin, a deadly toxin.

Poisonous Nightshades

The nightshade family has many members, some are edible and some are poisonous. It is the family that tomatoes and peppers belong to. Ground cherries, also known as husk tomatoes, are also in this family and are edible. They can be identified by their papery husks. Although edible when ripe, unripe fruits and leaves contain solanine and other alkaloids that could be toxic.

Members of the nightshade family that have poisonous berries include:

- **Horse nettle** has yellow-orange fruits that look like ground cherry but lack the papery husk.
- **Black nightshade** has black berries that contain solanine, an alkaloidal glucoside.
- **Bittersweet nightshade** has bright red berries that also contain solanine.

Datura is in the nightshade family and has seeds that, when ingested, can cause hallucinations, seizures, coma, and even death. The fruit of the jimsonweed, also called thornapple, is a prickly, egg-shaped capsule containing numerous black seeds. Leaves, roots, and seeds contain the toxic alkaloid hyoscyamine.

Roots

Some of the deadliest poisons are contained in the roots of plants. This includes the water hemlock and the poison hemlock, both members of the carrot family. Young leaves of wild carrot and poison hemlock look very similar, and they both grow in meadows and fields. Mistaking the two can be fatal.

Water hemlock and water parsnip both grow in wet areas and look very similar. Water parsnip is edible whereas water hemlock can kill you. Also growing in wet areas are members of the arum family, arrow arum and skunk cabbage, that have calcium oxalate crystals. In the woodlands, Jack-in-the-pulpit can be found. This is another member of the arum family that has calcium oxalate crystals in the roots.

In a garden or meadow, burdock and pokeweed may grow side by side. Burdock is frequently used in wild food cooking. There have been occasions when poke was used instead of burdock and resulted in violent vomiting for several days.

Members of the lily family can be toxic. This is the family that wild onions and garlic belong to. If it looks like an onion or garlic, but is lacking the smell, don't eat it. It could be death camas, which can cause vomiting and, as its name implies, can be deadly. Daylilies are also in this family and even though many people have eaten them, occasionally they have caused vomiting.

Poisonous Mushrooms

Mushrooms can be deadly. There's not much room for error. Even though the mushroom tastes okay and you feel okay after eating it, by the time you realize you've eaten the wrong thing it's too late. Symptoms may not show up for several hours or even a few days. Anytime mushroom poisoning is suspected, get medical help immediately.

Mushrooms are also difficult to identify. Positive identification often involves getting spore prints or using a microscope for closer examination. Unless you're an expert, or go out with one who is, it's best to leave the wild mushrooms in the field.

Amanitas

Amanitas are the most deadly and account for most of the mushroom poisonings. Just beneath the cap is a ring that encircles the stem that can help to distinguish them. The poison damages the liver and treatment is not always successful. Symptoms include intense abdominal pain and vomiting.

False Morels

True morels are a popular mushroom among foragers. But there is a false morel that one should be aware of that can be deadly. True morels have deep pits and hollow fruiting bodies whereas the false morels have a wrinkled but not pitted cap. They also have a smooth stalk. Symptoms may not occur until several hours after ingesting and may include severe abdominal pains, vomiting, and diarrhea.

CHAPTER 5

Plant Families

Plants have families that are named and classified in groups based on anatomical parts, generally the characteristics of the flowers or fruits. In the plant world, this is called *taxonomy*. Even though members of one family may have similar characteristics, they don't all share the same edibility properties. Members of one family may be very toxic while others are considered safe to eat. In some families, all members are edible. When learning plants, it's important to get to know the individual plants within a family.

Wild Greens

Green plants alone are able to capture the sun's energy and convert it into food that can be consumed by other life. This food is called chlorophyll and contains carbon, hydrogen, oxygen, and nitrogen. Most of the wild edible greens can be found in backyards and gardens in the form of weeds. These greens are packed with vitamins and nutrients that can boost the immune system and treat common ailments.

Buckwheat Family

Buckwheat family members have knots where the leaves are attached to the stem, giving some members of this family the nickname of knotweed. Small flowers with petal-like sepals are clustered in a spike at the top of a flower stalk. Sheep sorrel and yellow dock are examples of this family with edible leaves.

Mustard Family

The mustard family, also known as the crucifers, is quite large and includes many members that are cultivated in gardens. The leaves are often basal, sometimes divided or deeply lobed. The flowers have four petals that form a cross, giving it the name of crucifer. The colors vary from white and yellow to pink and purple. Seed capsules can be either flat like peppergrass or long and slender like wild mustard. All mustards have a spicy odor and taste, some more so than others and almost all of them are palatable.

Nettle Family

Nettles consist of mostly herbs, sometimes with stinging hairs on the stems. Flowers are small and greenish, often in clusters in the leaf axils. The leaves are edible, including stinging nettles and wood nettles once they have been cooked or the stinging hairs crushed. Plants that look like nettles but lack the stinging hairs are called false nettles and are included in the nettle family. These are also edible but don't have the same nutritional value as the stinging nettle.

Pokeweed Family

The pokeweed family includes herbs, trees, and shrubs, mostly in the tropics and subtropics. Pokeweed that grows in this country is a tall, branching herb with reddish stems in the fall and purple berries. Young leaves and shoots are edible after cooking in two changes of water.

Other Edible Families

Other plant families that produce edible greens, flowers, or vegetables include the following:

- **Amaranths** are edible herbs with bristly flowers that can be green or red and form tight clusters at the tops of the stalks.
- **Bedstraw** is an edible herb that has whorled leaves and white flowers with four petals.
- **Chickweed** is an edible herb in the pink family that is distinguished by five divided petals.
- **Corn salad** is a member of the Valerian family with edible basal leaves that are round at the tip.
- **Heal-all** is in the mint family and has clusters of short-stalked purplish flowers at the tops of the stems.
- **Lambsquarters** is in the goosefoot family and has triangular, edible leaves with a white powdery substance beneath them.
- **Plantain** forms a basal rosette of edible leaves with parallel veins and small flowers in a spike.
- **Purslane, miner's lettuce,** and **spring beauties** are in the purslane family and have edible leaves.

Edible Flowers, Roots, and Vegetables

Some of the edible greens are annuals, others are biennials, and still others are perennials. The flower buds and flowers of some of these greens are also edible. When certain biennials send up their flower stalks the second year, it can be used as a vegetable, like celery.

Evening Primrose Family

Mostly herbs, this family includes the evening primroses, whose flowers open in the evening and close up the next morning. The flowers have four petals followed by capsules with numerous little black seeds.

The common evening primrose is the species most frequently used for food. It is a biennial that germinates in late summer or early fall after the seeds from the previous year have dropped. Leaves have a reddish midrib and form a rosette in the fall. They remain on the plant through the winter. The next spring it sends up a flower stalk with alternating leaves that get smaller as they near the top. Their roots are starchy and can be eaten. Young leaves, flowers, and seeds of the evening primroses are also edible.

Laurel Family

The laurel family consists of mostly trees, sometimes shrubs, with aromatic bark and leaves. Many small flowers grow in clusters followed by fruits that are either a berry or a drupe. The flowers and buds of some species are edible. Leaves of most members of this family can be used as a spicy seasoning. In some species, the twigs or the roots are used to make a tea.

Mallow Family

Although mallows are mostly herbs, there are a few that are shrubs or even trees. They are fairly easy to recognize, with five petals that are often quite showy and a center that looks like a bottlebrush from the way the male stamens are attached to the sides of the female pistil. Numerous male stamens form a column that unites and surrounds the female pistil.

Most members of this family have edible parts, including the roots, leaves, flowers, or fruits. They also contain mucilaginous properties that make them slimy. While okra is the species

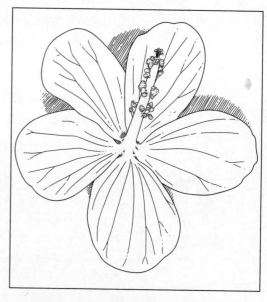

▲ Mallow flower showing male stamens surrounding female pistil

that most people associate with as edible, none are poisonous and most have been used as food by early cultures.

Milkweed Family

Milkweeds grow throughout the country in open fields or roadsides and can easily be recognized by their flowers that have five down-curved petals. Leaves are oval-shaped and in pairs or whorls. Milkweed fruits are distinct, with pod-like follicles filled with many seeds attached to fluffy hairs.

The common milkweed has pinkish-purple flowers and is the one most commonly eaten by foragers. Young shoots, flower buds, and young pods are eaten after being boiled through two changes of water. Milkweeds contain cardiac glycosides and can be dangerous if not prepared properly. Not all species can be recommended as food, since the toxic properties may remain in some species even after cooking.

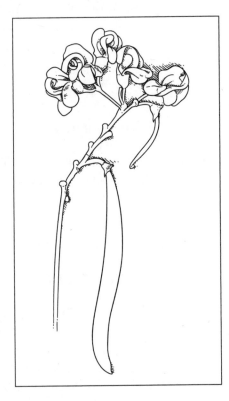

▲ Groundnut flowers and pods

Pea Family

The pea family is a large family that includes trees, shrubs, vines, and herbs throughout the world. They have characteristic pea-like flowers with irregularly shaped petals. A common trait among all members of the pea family is the fruit that is a legume similar to beans grown in gardens, with one or more bean-like seeds inside.

ALERT

There are both edible and poisonous members of the pea family. For some species, the pod is the part eaten, at other times it's the seed, and in some cases the flowers or the roots can be used. Some pods are tough, thick, and inedible. Others have tiny seeds that are poisonous. Wild beans should never be eaten raw.

Members of the pea family that have edible parts include black locust, honey locust, redbud, wild beans, groundnuts, and mesquite.

Sunflower Family

As its name implies, members of this family have disks of central flowers surrounded by ray-like petals of assorted colors. Most members of this family are herbs, including the typical sunflower. The fruit is a one-seeded nutlet with a hard shell that is edible.

Some members of this family also have edible roots, including dandelion, burdock, chicory, and thistle, as well as edible leaves. Flowers of some species such as dandelion, thistle, and oxeye daisy are used as food or in a beverage by foragers.

Other Edible Families

Other plant families that produce edible flowers, roots, or vegetables include the following:

- **Agave** family members have basal leaves that are long and dagger-like surrounding a central flower stalk that is edible when young and edible flowers among some species.
- **Lilies** generally have showy flowers borne on stalks that arise from bulbs or corms, some of which are edible.
- **Mustards** have edible flower buds and flowers that resemble broccoli and other cultivated members of that family.
- **Violets** have irregular flowers with two upper petals and three lower, most of which are edible.
- **Wood sorrel** is recognized by its clover-like appearance and has edible flowers with five petals.

Spring and Summer Fruits

In most areas fruits begin ripening in late spring and continue through the summer and into the fall. Summer fruits are generally juicy and sweet.

Gooseberry Family

The gooseberry family includes gooseberries and currants. The gooseberries have spines at the leaf nodes, while the currants do not. Both have palmately lobed leaves that resemble a maple leaf, with lobes extending from a central "palm." Flowers are tubular with five petals and five stamens. Gooseberry and currant fruits are berries that are edible.

Heath Family

The heath family is a large family of plants that consists of mostly shrubs, some evergreen. The flowers are often bell-shaped with four or five petals. The fruit is either a berry or a capsule.

This family includes the edible blueberries and huckleberries and also the toxic rhododendrons and azaleas. Throughout the west are a number of species of manzanitas, all sharing the same common name except for kinnikinnick and bearberry, which are also in this family.

Mulberry Family

Mulberries are mostly trees or shrubs that are found throughout the United States. Only the red mulberry and the Texas mulberry are native. Several species have become naturalized and can be found growing wild. The fruit is similar to a blackberry, made up of many one-seeded fruits. Leaves are sometimes lobed with three distinct veins arising from the base.

Muskroot Family

The muskroot family now contains the elders, which formerly had been included in the honeysuckle family. Elder is a native shrub with representatives throughout the United States. Large, flat-topped clusters of small, white flowers make their appearance in late spring. Fruits soon follow and are small berries that may or may not be edible. Blue and black-berried elder fruits are generally safe to eat, whereas those with red berries are not.

Other Edible Families

Other edible spring and summer fruits:

- **Serviceberries, strawberries, cherries, plums, hawthorns, and wild roses** are members of the rose family with fruits that are berries, drupes, hips, or pomes.
- **Mayapples** are low-growing herbs in the barberry family that have large umbrella-like leaves and yellow, lemon-scented edible fruits.
- **Ground cherries** are in the nightshade family and have edible berries when ripe that are enclosed in a papery husk.

Fall Fruits

Fruits that ripen in the fall and linger through the winter are generally not as juicy as those in the summer. For some of them, sweetness is enhanced by the frost. The time to start looking for the fall fruits is when the leaves begin changing colors.

Black Gum Family

Several species of trees make up the black gum family. Leaves are alternate and turn scarlet red in the fall on the black gum trees. The fruits are drupes that hang on long stalks, often in pairs, from the branches.

Cactus Family

The cactus family consists of mostly herbs with succulent stems and tufts of sharp spines. They are found mostly in dry, sunny areas like deserts. Flowers are usually large and colorful and appear near the top of the stem. Stems are either segmented or ribbed and the spines are actually modified leaves.

Cacti are edible, mostly the fruits. In some species the flattened stems can also be eaten.

Custard Apple Family

Members of the custard apple family are usually tropical. Pawpaw is an exception and has large, banana-like leaves that emit a pungent odor when crushed. Flowers are maroon-colored with three triangular petals.

Pawpaw fruits are berries with large seeds and thick skins that turn yellow as the fruit ripens. The edible pulp that surrounds the seeds is smooth and yellowish, like custard.

Ebony Family

The common persimmon is the only member of the ebony family in the eastern United States and has brownish, almost black bark, somewhat like ebony. The trees are small to medium-sized and have alternate, oval-shaped leaves. The fruits develop through the summer, first green before turning into a round, orange to purplish berry when ripe.

ESSENTIAL

You must have two persimmon trees, one male and one female, to get fruits. Only the females produce the fruits. Male and female flowers are on different trees and bloom in late spring. Female flowers are greenish-yellow and larger than the male flowers that are white and bell-shaped. Fruits begin to develop soon after the petals drop.

Persimmon trees can be found in the eastern part of the United States from southern Connecticut to Florida and west to central Texas in abandoned fields or clearings. The Texas persimmon grows in southeastern and central Texas and also has edible fruits that are black in color.

Vining Fruits

There are lots of vines that produce fruits in the fall. Some are edible while others are best to leave for the birds.

Grape Family

Grapes are deciduous, woody vines with tendrils that are sometimes forked on the end. Leaves are usually toothed and heart-shaped. The fruits are berries with several crunchy seeds inside.

Passionflowers

Passionflowers are more of a southern species, with most members growing in the tropics. It is a climbing herbaceous vine with leaves that are alternate and often deeply lobed. The flowers are quite distinct, with three to five petal-like sepals plus three to five petals overlaid with a starburst pattern of thread-like filaments.

Winter Fruits

There are a number of wild fruits that ripen in late fall and remain on the plant throughout the winter. These are generally dry, often without much flavor, but are a good survival food.

Barberry Family

Members of the barberry family include both herbs and shrubs. Among the shrubs are several species of barberry that grow in the eastern part of the country. Members of this family have flowers that grow in clusters or racemes and leaves that are sometimes spiny. Oregon grape is also a member of the barberry family and grows throughout the western United States. It is an evergreen shrub with thick and prickly leaves. Small, yellow flowers appear in the spring followed by bluish-purple fruits that ripen in the fall and are edible.

Madder Family

The trailing woody groundcover that is common in many eastern forests is the partridgeberry and a member of the madder family. The fruit is a two-eyed berry that is actually two blossom scars that result from two flowers that join to produce a fruit. Fruits are edible but lack flavor.

Muskroot Family

A family that formerly only consisted of small herbs, it now contains the elders and the viburnums. Both have paired leaves, with the elder's leaves also being compound. Flowers are small with five petals that grow in flat-topped clusters. Fruits are either berries or drupes and may or may not be edible. The fruits of viburnum species ripen in the fall.

Rose Family

In addition to having fruits that ripen in the spring and summer, some members of the rose family also have fruits that ripen in the fall and remain throughout the winter. Crabapples drop to the ground and get covered up and protected by fallen leaves. Rose hips, hawthorn, and chokeberries also begin ripening in the fall and may remain on the plant through the winter.

Seasonings

Many of the fragrant scented leaves can be used as a seasoning in soups or stews. Some of them can be made into a tea. In some cases, twigs or even roots are used to brew into a tea. Some plants have a high salt content and can be used as a salt substitute for seasoning.

Goosefoot Family

Orache has triangular-shaped leaves and resembles lamsquarters, a close relative. Flowers are small and grow in the leaf axils. Orache grows in or near saltmarshes. It has adapted to this environment by storing salt in its leaves and can be used as a salty seasoning with other vegetables.

Salicornia is also a member of the goosefoot family and, like its cousin orache, is tolerant of salt and grows in salt marshes. Salt is stored in the succulent stems, giving it a salty taste.

Laurel Family

The laurel family consists of mostly trees, sometimes shrubs, with aromatic bark and leaves. Leaves of most members of this family can be used as a spicy seasoning. In some species, the twigs or the roots are used to make a tea.

Waxmyrtle Family

The waxmyrtle family consists of shrubs or small trees with alternate leaves that are aromatic when crushed. The flowers are small, green or yellow, and in short clusters. The fruit is a drupe. Leaves of this family are sometimes used as seasoning or to make a tea.

Tea Families

Teas are beverages made from flowers, leaves, roots, bark, and fruits of many types of plants. You can always find something to make tea from. However, there are some plants that are used primarily for making tea, whether it be as a tonic in the spring, a stimulating beverage in the summer, or a relaxing tea in the evening.

Birch Family

The birch family is made up of trees or shrubs with alternate leaves that have straight veins. Male flowers hang in long catkins while the female flower is in short, cone-like clusters that produce small nuts or nutlets. Sweet birch twigs are used for tea.

Holly Family

The holly family contains several species whose leaves are used to make tea, the most popular being the yaupon holly. Not only does it have caffeine in its leaves, but it also tastes good. However, the berries on all hollies could be toxic if consumed in large doses, so only use the leaves for tea-making.

Mint Family

Mints are mostly aromatic herbs or shrubs with square stems and opposite leaves. Flowers have irregular petals with upper and lower lips. Many members of this family can be used as a seasoning or to make a tea. Some species, such as heal-all, also have edible leaves but are lacking in menthol and are not aromatic like other members of the mint family.

Sumac Family

The sumac family consists of trees, shrubs, and vines, the most notable being poison ivy. Leaves are usually compound with three or more leaflets. Sumac flowers are in dense clusters and are followed by tight clusters of one-seeded drupes.

QUESTION

Aren't sumac berries poisonous?
There is a poison sumac and a non-poisonous sumac. The poison sumac has white berries that hang in loose clusters while the non-poison sumac has red, tightly clustered berries. Red berries can be used to make a tea, whereas the white ones are poisonous and can cause a contact dermatitis reaction, similar to poison ivy.

There are about fifteen species of sumac scattered throughout the United States. In the east there are at least three species that are fairly common, all ripening at different times. Staghorn sumac is the largest of the three with hairy twigs and leafstalks that resemble the velvet on a deer's antlers. They begin blooming in mid-summer, with clusters of small, pinkish flowers. The flowers quickly develop into one-seeded fruits. About the time the fruits start ripening in late summer, the winged sumac starts blooming. Their flowers are more of a yellowish-green color. The smooth sumac is similar to the staghorn but has smooth twigs and leafstalks.

On the west coast there are also at least three species that include lemonade berry, sugar bush, and basket bush. They grow in the coastal sage scrub, chaparral, and oak woodland. Any of the sumacs that have red berries can be used to make a tea by steeping the berries in hot or cold water. Cold water results in a fruitier flavor but has to steep for a longer period of time than hot water. Poison sumac has white berries and should be avoided.

Other Tea Families

Other tea plant families include the following:

- **The laurel family** includes sassafras with aromatic roots for tea and spicebush with twigs used to make a tea.
- **The ephedra family** includes several species commonly known as mormon tea, with stout, leafless-looking stems and cone-like flowers used to make a tea.

Nuts

Nuts are partially or wholly enclosed in a husk that may be papery, leafy, woody, or spiny. A shell that may be hard and bony or thick and leathery surrounds the nut itself. The time to look for nuts is after the leaves have started falling. Except for buckeye and horse chestnut, most nuts are edible. Some are more bitter than others, especially with hickory nuts and acorns. Soaking them first can help remove some of the bitterness.

Beech Family

The beech family is mostly trees or shrubs with alternate leaves that are toothed or lobed with straight veins. The male flowers hang in catkins. Fruits are nuts enclosed in a cup-like outer hull. The beech family includes the American beech, oaks, and chestnuts.

Birch

The birch family is made up of trees or shrubs with alternate leaves that have straight veins. The fruits are one-seeded nuts that grow in a cluster, sometimes with a leaf-looking outer hull. The birch family includes the birches and hazelnuts.

Walnut

Walnuts are trees with long, compound leaves. The male flowers hang in long, drooping catkins, while the female flowers are in short clusters. The fruit is a nut enclosed in a thick outer hull, which sometimes splits open at maturity.

Seeds

Seeds are small and often require a lot of work to gather and prepare. However, a little bit goes a long way. Some seeds can be collected by cutting the seed stalk and turning it upside down in a paper bag, allowing the seeds to drop to the bottom. The seeds can then be winnowed or strained to remove the chaff or other plant material.

Grasses

Grasses have long leaf blades and jointed flowering stems. Small flowers without petals form a spike, head, tassel, or branched panicle. Young leaf blades are edible as a juice or dried and powdered. Seeds of all grasses are edible. However, the seed must be separated from the chaff. The seeds of some grasses drop easily as they dry while others cling to the chaff.

FACT

Johnson grass is an introduced grass that grows in fields and thickets and has a corn-like appearance. Wilted or frost-damaged leaves develop cyanide and have poisoned animals that have ingested it. Healthy, living plants have low levels of cyanide and can be consumed safely.

Pine Family

Pines are cone-bearing trees with needle-like leaves that grow throughout most of the United States and are characteristic of acid soils, often sprouting after a fire. They are sometimes referred to as the "pioneers of the forest" as they are one of the first of the woody plants to move into an area that has been cleared or allowed to be reclaimed by nature. Pines are part of a large family that also includes larches, hemlocks, firs, spruces, and Douglas firs.

Pines are mostly evergreen and provide some part for food year round. In the fall, pine seeds are collected from some species, while in the spring the pollen can be collected and added to flour. The inner bark is most easily harvested in the spring and can be used as a survival food. The tips of pine sprouts can be eaten raw or in salads while the needles from older trees can be used to make tea year round.

Water Plants

Some plants require standing water to grow while others only need wet soil. Some can tolerate a short drying period. There are some plants that float, some that are submersed and grow beneath the water while still others are immersed and grow out of the water. Some of these plants have edible roots or seeds. Others have shoots that can be harvested as a vegetable in the spring.

ALERT

One of the benefits of wetland plants is their ability to filter pollutants from the water. It is important to know the quality of the water before gathering and eating wetland plants. If in doubt, boil the parts being used for at least ten minutes before using in a recipe.

Aquatic Roots

There are a number of wetland plants that have edible roots. Roots are best gathered in the fall or winter, usually after the leaves have dropped and the water is cold. They are generally embedded in the muck, which makes removal difficult.

Arrowhead Family

Arrowheads are emergent wetland plants with long-stalked basal leaves. The flower stalk is leafless and bears small flowers with three petals in whorls of three.

The roots of some members of this family have been called duck potatoes because they look like small potatoes and ducks eat them. Roots extend outward from the plant with edible tubers on the ends.

Arum Family

A family of herbs, usually in or near the water, but occasionally on land, that are characterized by a spadix that consists of numerous small, stalkless flowers crowded together on a thick stem. It is often surrounded by a large, showy bract that is referred to as a spathe. The leaves have long stems.

Several members of this family contain calcium oxalate crystals that can cause an intense, burning sensation when eaten if not prepared correctly.

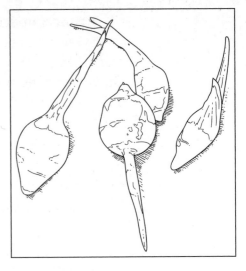

▲ Arrowhead tubers, also known as duck potatoes

Cattail Family

Cattails are marsh plants that can be found throughout North America. They are what some people think of as a "hot dog on a stick." They have long, sword-like leaves that are flat. Tiny yellowish-brown male flowers form a spike above the female spike of flowers that develop into the brown seed spike characteristic of cattails. They form colonies with their horizontal rhizomes that spread underground.

Aquatic Seeds

Many of the aquatic plants, including grasses, contain edible seeds. Usually these are seeds that are best left for the birds. However, there are a few that are worth harvesting.

Lotus Lily Family

Sometimes referred to as water lilies, the large leaves usually emerge above the water rather than float on top. Flowers are large and showy followed by the edible seeds that are contained within a circular receptacle. Roots are also edible but difficult to remove.

Pickerelweed Family

Pickerelweed has large, heart-shaped leaves that emerge from the water on long stalks. The leaf veins closely parallel the margins of the leaf that emerges from an underground rhizome. It produces spikes of blue flowers during the summer months that are followed by edible seeds.

Water Lily Family

Water lilies are aquatic plants, usually with floating, heart-shaped leaves. Flowers are large and showy. Seeds and roots are edible. However, the roots are usually deeply embedded in the muck and sometimes taste like muck.

CHAPTER 6

Where the Wild Things Grow

Wild plants spring up wherever they are given space to grow naturally without sprays or mowing, some forming their own communities. Foraging requires knowing where these communities are and the time of year to visit them. It may be an abandoned lot, a hedgerow that has grown up at the edge of a field or forest, a meadow, swamp, desert, or your own backyard where weeds, fruits, and nuts often abound. The altitude, humidity, rainfall, temperature, and soil are some of the factors that determine which plants will grow in a particular area.

Your Big Backyard

Your backyard or garden is a great place to begin looking for wild foods. If the area is free of herbicides, the wild plants are already there. Gardens and disturbed soils make excellent foraging grounds for wild greens and other wild vegetables. Many of the so-called weeds that people work hard to eradicate are edible plants, often providing more nutrition than what they typically grow in gardens. Some of these are native plants while others have become naturalized.

QUESTION

What is the difference between native plants and naturalized plants?
Native plants are those plants that were already growing here when the settlers first arrived in the "New World." These settlers brought herbs with them to grow for their food and medicine. Many escaped cultivation and now grow naturally. In many cases, these naturalized plants out-compete native plants because of their lack of predators. Barberry is a common fruit-bearing shrub that is naturalized in the United States, while the blueberries are popular native plants among foragers.

If you pull weeds from your gardens, you may already be familiar with a lot of the plants. All they need is a name to go with them. If left in the ground long enough, and the conditions are right, all plants will bloom. If you don't know what it is, leave it until it blooms. Be observant of the plant while it is developing. It often goes through several stages before blooming. After it has bloomed, watch to see what kind of fruit it produces. Or, if it blooms and becomes a wildflower, you can look it up in a wildflower guide.

Patches of Green

Many of the wild greens grow in patches, either from roots that spread underground or because conditions are favorable for that particular plant. A good time to look for these patches is in the winter, when the grass has died back. If allowed to bloom and produce seed, the patches of green will grow. Some of the most common edible green weeds are also considered to be pests by many people who are unaware of their nutritional value. Some of these include:

- Chickweed
- Corn Salad
- Mustards
- Dandelion
- Sheep Sorrel
- Violets

Many of these green patches are annuals, such as the chickweed, cresses, henbit, and dead nettle. If they've never had a chance to get established, they may not be growing in your garden. Others, like the dandelions and violets, are perennials. These plants are generally difficult to get rid of and are excellent additions to your recipes and meals.

Wildflowers in Your Yard

If you wait until a little later in the spring to mow your lawn, all those herbs forming green patches will send up a flower stalk and bloom. This includes edible dandelions, violets, chickweed, and cresses, which will add vibrant yellow, white, and blue colors to your yard. The blooming flowers also act as signposts, making it easy to identify the opportunities for foraging that are growing right outside your house.

ALERT

People who use a lawn service that controls weeds are missing out, not only on having wild greens to eat, but also the wildflowers that follow. Many of the weeds that herbicides are advertised to kill are edible herbs. If you have a lawn service, find out what chemicals are being applied to the soil before you consider doing any foraging in your yard.

Gardens often have more diversity of plants than yards. Disturbed soil is a good environment for many seeds to germinate in. Learn to identify plants before removing them. They may have more nutritional value than what you are planning to grow.

Poke Habitat

Poke is easy to spot and identify in late summer, when the stalks are red and the berries are turning purple-black. Birds flock to the berries to feast, dropping their seeds behind them. While you shouldn't eat the berries, you *should* leave the stalks through the winter, or mark the spot and come back in the spring to harvest the young, tender shoots around the old stalks as well as new sprouts just emerging. If overgrowth is a concern, you can pull up the entire plant, but be sure to remove and discard the root that is the most toxic part of the plant. Prepare the young sprouts the same as the shoots by covering with cold water and bringing just to the point of boiling. Pour the water off and then repeat the process once, to make sure any traces of bitterness and the mildly toxic compounds are removed.

▲ Lambsquarters just emerging in the spring

Shade Trees

Trees are often planted in yards to provide shade. Shade trees can provide edible fruits. Acorn-bearing oaks are often planted in yards and around schools and other public buildings, and dump lots of nuts on the lawn and sidewalk in the fall. Understory trees such as redbud, serviceberry, mulberry, and black cherry are also frequently planted for their ornamental and wildlife value. The beautiful, fuchsia-colored flowers of the redbud tree are mildly sweet and can be gathered in the spring to add to salads and desserts. As the young pods develop they can be used in stir-fries like snow peas. Serviceberries begin ripening about the same time, followed by the mulberries, both of which are edible. You have to get out early to beat the birds however. Black cherries ripen in the summer and can be made into a refreshing juice drink.

Sun Lovers

Some plants require a lot of sunlight to grow. They are usually fast growers and often produce showy flowers during the summer months. Cow pastures, abandoned farm fields, or forests that have been logged provide an opportunity for the sun lovers. Occasionally an old tree will come down in a mature forest, bringing with it vines and smaller trees. This opens up a light gap in the forest and allows plants to grow that otherwise would not be there.

Fields and Meadows

Abandoned fields that are only cut periodically become a meadow habitat that is dominated by grasses. Biennials such as burdock, wild carrot, evening primrose, chicory, and thistle come up in late summer, remain green all winter, send up a flower stalk in the spring, bloom, and go to seed. The young leaves and first-year roots of some biennials are edible and should be gathered in late winter or early spring, so make sure to plan your meadow foraging accordingly if you are looking for these plants.

ESSENTIAL

Learn to recognize and identify poison hemlock when venturing to the field. It is in the same family as wild carrot and has similar characteristics. Poison hemlock can be distinguished from wild carrot by the smooth leaf stalk and the trademark purple streaks on the stem. The stalks of the wild carrot are covered with hairs.

Perennial wildflowers are also found in sunny areas, including milkweed and pokeweed. Brambles form colonies when the opportunity arises and seedlings of trees and shrubs emerge. If allowed to grow they will eventually produce fruits.

Hedgerows

Hedgerows are thickets with a thick tangle of small trees, shrubs, and climbing vines that are dense and almost impenetrable. They develop at the edges of woods, between farm fields, or at the edges of ditches, canals, or waterways. Many of these are berry plants, as is indicated by the number of birds visiting them. Wild cherries, elderberries, and mulberries are among the edible varieties of trees and shrubs that grow here. Once you positively identify a plant, you can pick the berries from it. However, do not assume that because birds are eating the berries, you will be able to as well. Several types of berries, like the poke berries mentioned before, are delicious for birds but dangerous for humans. Foraging for berries is discussed in detail in Chapter 10.

Woodlands

Woodlands contain layers of plants. Shade-loving herbs grow on the forest floor. In the east, partridgeberries, wintergreen, and wild ginger are among the herbs to look for. In a deciduous forest, they generally bloom early before the leaves have emerged. Many of these herbs have food or medicinal value.

Woody shrubs make up the next layer. They are also early bloomers, usually after the herbs. Many of these are berry bushes, including blueberries and huckleberries, and may produce berries, especially in the late summer, which is when many foragers look for them. But the most abundant producers are those on the edge that receive more light.

QUESTION

What is the understory?
The understory of the forest is the layer of trees and shrubs that grow beneath the canopy. These plants are shade tolerant and include small trees that even when mature, are towered over by the canopy. If it is a young forest, the understory includes those trees that will eventually replace the trees in the canopy.

Small trees make up the understory. Their flowers are often unnoticed until their petals drop to the ground. Serviceberries, hawthorns, and crabapples are some of the understory trees that are most easily approached in the autumn, when their fruits have had a chance to ripen and their leaves have begun to drop.

The canopy is made up of tall trees that tower over the forest. In a mature forest these tall trees are generally deciduous hardwoods. A number of nut-bearing trees, including tall oaks, hickories, and beeches, live in the canopy. Thankfully, these canopy trees generally drop their nuts in the fall and winter, making these otherwise inaccessible treats easy to find and eat.

Coniferous Forests

Conifers are cone-bearing trees that are mostly evergreen. In more northern areas of the country, they can be the most common plant species in boreal forests, but they can also be found at high elevations in more southern areas. Pines are the most common and recognizable of these types of trees, and are widely distributed. Also included among the conifers are cypress, cedar, hemlock, and fir, the traditional American Christmas tree. Most of these trees have easy-to-spot needle-like leaves, while some are more scale-like.

FACT

Pine seeds are attached to thin, membrane-like wings that are carried by the wind when they are released from the cone. Numerous seeds are produced and can be carried great distances. When conditions are right, they germinate and send up new sprouts. Most of these sprouts will die since they need a lot of sunlight to grow. Pine sprouts are a good source of vitamin C. At this stage you can pick the sprouts and eat the tips.

Older conifers have needles that are too tough to eat. Instead, you can use them to make a tea that is rich in vitamin C by steeping them in boiling water for a few minutes at a time. In the spring male catkins, which are long, drooping clusters of small flowers and pollen, are produced by pines and can be nibbled on. When the pollen develops it can be collected and added to flour. The inner bark of some pine species, including white pine, can be dried, powdered, and used as an emergency flour substitute.

Pine Barrens

Pine barrens are unique habitats in the eastern United States that have deep, sandy soil and oak pine forests. Contrary to their name, they are not barren. At one time the pine barrens extended from New Jersey and southeastern Virginia, along the coastal plain to Texas. In New Jersey the pines are mostly pitch pine, while in Virginia longleaf pine is the dominant tree. The dry surface soil and resinous pines are highly flammable and result in frequent fires that help shape the ecology of the area. Both regions have an open canopy with fire-resistant pines.

Sandy soil and plenty of sunlight are favorable for the growth of members of the heath family, including blueberries and huckleberries, which form a thick shrub layer in the understory. Wintergreen is abundant in both areas, forming a thick, evergreen carpet on the forest floor. In New Jersey there are Atlantic white cedar swamps interspersed with the oak-pine forests. In the bogs is a lush layer of sphagnum moss with cranberries and other herbaceous plants.

Cedar Glades

Eastern red cedar is characteristic of cedar glades. The bark is thin and peels easily from the tree. They are woody, evergreen trees and shrubs with needle-like to scale-like leaves. The thick canopy prevents a lot of growth in the understory. What appears to be a berry is actually a cone. When looked at under a magnifying glass, you can see tiny cones with scales pressed so tightly that they appear to be round. The fruits are aromatic and turn blue when mature.

Juniper berries have traditionally been used for flavoring in a variety of dishes. The flavoring in gin comes from juniper berries. Berries should be gathered when they have turned dark blue and are juicy. They can be used fresh or dried and stored for future use. Even though juniper berries are used as a seasoning, their medicinal uses outnumber their food uses. For this reason, they should be used sparingly and only for short periods of time as a seasoning or a tea.

Mixed Deciduous Forests

A mixed deciduous forest is a combination of hardwoods and conifers, all competing for sunlight. They form a dense understory with a diversity of young trees, shrubs, vines, and herbs. These forests can be found east of the Mississippi River, across the Ohio valley to the Potomac, the mountains of Tennessee, Kentucky, West Virginia, and Virginia and in the southern Appalachian mountains of North Carolina and Georgia.

Deciduous Forests

Deciduous forests have mostly hardwood trees that drop their leaves in the fall. Elevation, soil type, temperature, and rainfall determine the types of trees that grow in a particular region. An older forest has a denser canopy and therefore a more open understory for early wildflowers to grow, including wild ginger, Indian cucumber root, and wintergreen.

Some soils are more acidic than others. In forests where there are oaks, pines, beeches, or other members of those families, the leaf litter builds up, keeping the soil layer thin and acidic. Other trees, such as maple and basswood, have leaves that are quickly broken down and recycled, forming a thick layer of topsoil that supports a greater diversity of plant life.

Mountain Forests

Altitude, humidity, amount of rainfall, and rock deposits are some of the factors that influence the types of forests found in the mountains. Higher elevations support plant life not found on lower sites and vice versa. The Appalachian mountain system of eastern North America is much older than the Rocky Mountains in the west, with peaks that rise not even half as high as those in the rockies. While the scenery may be spectacular in the west, the vegetation is greener with a lot more diversity in the east.

Aspen-Birch Forest

The aspen-birch forest is a pioneer forest in northern regions that springs up in disturbed soils and grows rapidly, thriving in full sunlight. Quaking aspen, big-toothed aspen, and paper birch are among the dominant trees that grow here. In the understory are hazelnuts, brambles, and chokecherries. As these trees age and eventually die they will be replaced by the spruce-fir forest that is more shade tolerant than the aspens and birches. This forest also includes sugar maple, basswood, beech, and hemlock. These trees have been growing slowly in the shade of the aspens and birches, waiting for the opportunity to fill in the gap when they are gone.

Spruce-Fir Forests

There are high elevation and low elevation spruce-fir forests and low elevation spruce-fir forests that develop in northern regions. A wide-spreading root system anchors them to the thin layer of soil that has built up on bedrock. Hobblebush and blueberry are common shrubs in this habitat with bunchberry and trillium on the forest floor.

Oak-Hickory Forest

Oaks and hickories form mature forests that can be found in the eastern part of the country. A thick canopy in the summer blocks the sunlight from the forest floor. This prevents a lot of understory vines and shrubs from being able to grow there, giving it an open appearance. Shrubs that do grow in the understory include blueberries and their relatives, viburnums, sourwood, spicebush, and sassafras.

In the spring, before the trees have leafed out, wildflowers make their appearance. Some of these wildflowers are edible and include violets, partridgeberry, and wintergreen. While trilliums and orchids are also edible, the populations have declined so much that these are best left in the wild. Many of the wildflowers are either medicinal or poisonous and should also be left undisturbed.

Wetlands

Wetlands, as their name implies, are wet and develop along the edges of rivers, streams, lakes, or other aquatic areas. They either have standing water or the soil is saturated with water during some part of the growing season. Wetlands vary, depending on the type of soil, whether it's flat or moving water, climate, and the types of vegetation that grow there. Near the coast there are tidal marshes and swamps that may be either fresh or salt, depending on how far they are from the sea. Plants that grow in these marshes have to adapt to fluctuating water levels that range from completely drying out to being totally submerged. Not a lot of plants can grow in salt marshes. Those that grow there have special adaptations that enable them to survive. There are also nontidal wetlands that can be found in low areas anywhere from the coast to the mountains. These wetlands generally have a greater diversity of plant life.

Forested Swamps

Swamps are wetland areas that border creeks, bays, and waterways and are found throughout the United States. They are characterized by trees that have adapted to wet conditions. Bald cypress and water tupelo trees are able to grow in standing water and are common in the southeast. Wide buttresses add support and stability to the trees. Cypress knees emerge above the water surrounding cypress trees, also helping to stabilize them.

As plants accumulate in the knees and break down into soil, a microhabitat is formed as seedlings emerge from seeds that have germinated in the soil.

In the spring and summer, a number of flowering plants add color to the swamps. This includes sundrops, irises, wild roses, and several species of lobelias. These plants provide nectar for pollinating insects. Other plants produce fruits that are edible, including the fruits of wild roses, known as "hips," that are especially versatile, and can be used both as a food and to make a mild-flavored tea. Blueberries, serviceberries, viburnums, and chokeberries also produce edible fruits.

Bogs

Layers of peat, which is partially decomposed organic material, mainly dead leaves and other plant material, characterize bogs. Long, cold winters, short cool summers, sufficient moisture, and trees with acidic litter are vital for peat formation. Once they are established, the acidity of the bog slows down the decomposition of added plant material and they continue to grow, providing a unique wetland habitat.

Cranberries grow in bogs and are in the heath family, along with blueberries and huckleberries. There are three species native to the United States. The large cranberry is the same species that is cultivated and sold in grocery stores around Thanksgiving time, but it also grows wild in boggy areas.

Riparian Habitats

Riparian habitats develop along the banks of freshwater creeks, streams, and rivers that are prone to flooding. Land is moved as new streams are dug out by moving water. Plants that grow here have adapted to these changing conditions. Spicebush, sweet birch, river birch, and black willow are sometimes seen growing on these banks. In addition to stabilizing the banks, they also filter pollutants from the water and provide habitat for wildlife.

Marsh Margins

Marshes are wetland areas that develop along the edges of bays, rivers, or canals. They are characterized by grasses and grasslike plants, including sedges, rushes, and cattails. There are both freshwater marshes and saltwater marshes. In some areas there are freshwater tidal marshes, where the waterway is beyond the reach of salt but is still influenced by the tide. There are also saltwater marshes whose water level is influenced by the wind rather than the moon.

Marshes have historically been referred to as wastelands and not good for anything but to breed mosquitoes. However, marshes are a very productive ecosystem. Not only do they provide food for wildlife, but they also offer an abundance of food for humans, as long as they know where to look.

There are some wildflowers in the marsh that are edible. The large showy flowers of several species of mallow, the most easily recognized marsh flower, as well as the purplish spike of flowers of the pickerelweed are both edible, as are the fruits. Bacopa forms a mat on some marshes and has succulent, edible leaves. It blooms all summer with small, white flowers.

Freshwater Marshes

The water level of freshwater marshes is generally influenced by the amount of rainfall and is a more stable environment than the fluctuating water levels of salt marshes. As a result, there is a greater diversity of plants in freshwater marshes. Cattails, arrowheads, groundnuts, and pickerelweed all grow in freshwater marshes.

Along the banks of streams, creeks, and rivers is a low-growing herb known as pennywort. There are a number of different species scattered across most of the country. It is in the carrot family and has small, white-topped clusters of flowers that appear during the summer. The most distinctive feature is the leaf, which is round and has the leaf stalk coming out of the center for some species. Pennywort is related to gotu kola that is sold in health food stores. The leaves are edible, but bitter.

There are a number of roots that can be harvested from freshwater marshes. These are generally deeply embedded in the mucky soil, making removal a difficult and somewhat messy procedure! A digging fork or any similar instrument works best to pry them loose from the mud. Some of the roots that can be harvested in a marsh include those from the easily recognizable cattails, arrowheads (discussed in detail later in the book), and water lilies. Groundnuts also grow along the banks in somewhat sunny areas. Their roots grow just beneath the surface of the soil in long strings, making them easy to harvest.

ALERT

Mucky soil, which is partially decomposed plant material, characterizes marshes. The muck is like a giant sponge that slowly absorbs and releases water. When you step on a sponge it compresses and then expands when you lift your foot off. If you find yourself stuck in the muck, drop to your knees or all fours to center your weight and free yourself.

Salt Marsh

Salt marshes develop around bays or estuaries that have an opening to the sea. The plants that grow here have to adapt to the salt water as well as the fluctuating water level. Some plants, like the black needlerush, store the salt in their tips. Saltmarsh cordgrass excretes the salt onto the surface of their leaves. Salicornia and orache dilute the salt in their stems.

Seaside Foraging

Salt air and ocean winds influence the types of plants that grow near the ocean. Plants have developed special adaptations to be able to live there. The roots of sea rocket, which grows in the upper beach zone at the base of the dunes, extend deep into the sand to get water. A waxy coating on the leaves protects them from drying out. The leaves of live oak trees are thick and succulent to store excess water. Dusty miller and false heather have a coat of down to protect them from the sun. Seaside evening primrose and dune beans grow close to the ground in the shade of other plants, where they are protected from the harsh conditions.

Dunes

Sand that is carried by the wind from the beach builds up into hills of sand wherever there is an object to block it. As the sand builds up around the object, a hill is formed that eventually becomes a dune. As grasses take root and grow, they stabilize the dunes, allowing other plants to grow there as well.

Sea rocket is a member of the mustard family and one of the first plants to establish itself at the base of the dunes as you come up from the beach. It has adapted to the sandy soil and intense heat by storing excess water in its leaves and seeds. The seeds look like miniature rockets and when you bite into them the juice shoots out, giving them the name sea rocket.

On the dunes, you'll mostly find sea oats and beach grasses with horizontal rhizomes that help hold the dunes together. Horizontal rhizomes are underground root stems. Ground cherries, wild beans, and seaside evening primrose are among the low-growing herbaceous plants found in the shade of the grasses.

As you move away from the ocean the diversity of plant life increases and woody plants establish themselves. Bayberries, beach plums, wild black cherry, and persimmons are included among those plants that often can be found within a few hundred meters of a beach environment.

Maritime Forest

Maritime forests develop on the back side of dunes where they are protected from the ocean winds and salt air. The trees in the maritime forest are often stunted, usually growing no higher than the highest dune, often giving the appearance of being pruned, as the tips are killed by the salt air. Live oak trees spread their branches out horizontally instead of vertically as an adaptation to these harsh conditions. They can be completely covered up with sand and will continue to send out new growth.

Deserts

Deserts are dry, usually sandy areas with sparse vegetation and less diversity than other regions. Plants have to adapt to long periods without rain as well as tolerate torrential downpours. Some plants adapt to drought by sending roots deep into the soil. Others, like ocotillo, drop their leaves until after a rain and then when the soil dries out, they drop them again. Chaparral is a well-adapted plant that has a greasy coating on its leaves to prevent water loss through transpiration. Some plants produce seeds that are drought resistant and then germinate after a heavy rain. Some of these are annuals that grow very quickly, bloom, and produce seed before dying back.

Chaparral Community

The chaparral community is characterized by dry summers and wet winters. It also experience wildfires as a natural occurrence. Chaparral, also known as creosote bush, is a scrubby plant that can be found in communities that include mesquite, ocotillo, yucca, and several species of cactus.

Buckwheat is a common plant in southern California's chaparral community. It forms low mounds with round flower heads rising above it in the spring, with white to pink flowers that turn brownish as they mature. The old flowers are ground and sifted in with other flour to make buckwheat pancakes and breads.

Coffeeberry, in the buckthorn family, is also found in the chaparral. It is a spreading, evergreen shrub from three to seven feet high with bright green leaves. It has edible berries that turn red in the fall.

High Desert

High desert communities consist of open flatlands as well as steep mountains with streams running through them. Canyons, gorges, and mesas have been carved out of sedimentary rock deposits and provide a variety of habitats for plants. Along the streams look for the characteristic wetland plants that include cattails, sedges, watercress, and willow trees. On the higher elevations, pinyon pines, sagebrush, mormon's tea, and miner's lettuce are some of the plants found growing on the northern slopes. Yucca, agave, and various cactus species like the southern slopes.

The high desert community is characterized by hot summers and cold winters. Storms can pop up suddenly resulting in extreme temperature changes. Dress in layers when planning a trip to the high desert and take plenty of water. Stay on designated trails to avoid getting lost and always be on the lookout for rattlesnakes.

CHAPTER 7

Invasive Aliens

Invasive aliens include plants that are not native and were either brought to this country for a purpose or, in some cases, came here by accident. They are also referred to as exotic or non-indigenous. Alien plants have played an important role in agriculture, landscaping, and soil stabilization. While most aliens do not persist in the wild, those that do sometimes become aggressive and spread rapidly, crowding out desirable native species. One way to control or prevent plants from spreading is to find a use for them.

Autumn and Russian Olive

Deciduous shrubs or small trees, autumn olive and Russian olive are in the oleaster family and are very similar. There are several other related species across the country, most of which are not native. Silverberry grows in the western part of the country along the banks of streams or on hillsides. They all share the characteristic of having silvery scales on the underside of the leaves and dots on the fruits.

QUESTION

How can you tell the difference between Russian olive and autumn olive?
Autumn and Russian olive both produce yellow, fragrant flowers in the spring that are small and have four petals. The fruit of autumn olive is red, sweet, and juicy, while the fruits of Russian olive are dry and mealy and may be yellow or silvery.

The area in which you live can help you to determine which species grows there. Russian olive covers much of the central and western part of the United States as well as some areas in the east. It does best in low, moist, sandy areas and can be found along streams and edges of fields. Autumn olive was planted in the eastern and central United States from Maine south to Virginia. It is drought tolerant and has nitrogen-fixing root nodules that enable it to thrive in poor soils including roadsides, pastures, and fields whose soil has been depleted of nutrients from farming. It does not do well in wet or densely forested areas.

Origins

Russian olive is native to southern Europe and Asia. It was introduced in the late 1800s as a windbreak and for its ornamental value. Autumn olive was introduced from eastern Asia in 1830, first as an ornamental and then to restore vegetation in disturbed areas. Its ability to fix nitrogen in the soil made it useful to also improve the soil. Forests that had been cleared in national and state forests and along the highway were replanted with autumn olive. Some conservation groups were promoting using it to create a wildlife habitat in backyards, parks, and other natural areas. Birds are attracted to the fruits and disperse the seeds across fields and forests. The plant grows rapidly and in a short time forms a colony.

Food Value

The fruits of both species, autumn olive and Russian olive, are edible. Autumn olive fruits are sweeter and more desirable than those of the Russian olive. The fruits begin ripening in late summer and continue into November.

Taste can vary from shrub to shrub, so it's a good idea to sample a few before picking, especially if there's more than one tree in the area. Branches are generally loaded with fruits, making it easy to pick a lot of fruits in a short time. Some people believe they become sweeter after a frost. Fruits can be nibbled right off the tree or made into a juice. The fruits are a rich source of lycopene, which is good for the prostate.

Garlic Mustard, the Gourmet Green

As its name implies, garlic mustard has properties of garlic as well as properties of mustard, giving the crushed leaves a scent that is a combination of both plants. Even though it is a member of the mustard family, it is lacking the deeply lobed or divided leaves that are characteristic of many of the mustards. Leaves are more rounded, somewhat heart-shaped at the base, with toothed margins. Basal leaves grow through the winter, sending up the flower stalk in the spring. Flowers are typical of the mustards with four petals, followed by capsules containing small black seeds.

Origins

Garlic mustard is native to Europe and Asia. It arrived in this country in the 1800s presumably by settlers who used it for food and medicine. It can now be found from Canada south to Virginia and west to Kansas and Nebraska.

Garlic mustard grows best in moist, shady conditions found in many woodlands, often growing through the winter when many plants are dormant. In the spring it produces thousands of seeds that are dispersed throughout the woodlands, probably carried by animals. Eventually it becomes the dominant plant on the forest floor.

Food Value

All above-ground parts of the garlic mustard are edible. Younger leaves are less bitter than older leaves, although both can be used to spice up a meal. As a member of the mustard family, the flower buds resemble miniature broccoli florets and are edible, as are the flowers. Even the tiny seeds, when crushed, release a garlic-mustard flavor.

Garlic mustard grows in many natural areas and nature preserves and is considered highly invasive. You can volunteer to pull it out in the spring before it has a chance to produce seeds.

Japanese Honeysuckle

Japanese honeysuckle is a vine that is known to most people, if for no other reason than they're constantly pulling it out in areas where they are trying to grow other plants. The older stems have a brownish bark that may peel off in sections.

Honeysuckle vines are flexible, making them useful as a weaving material or for basketmaking. It is a climbing vine and twists around young saplings of trees and shrubs, often growing with the tree, giving it a spiral-shaped tree trunk. It also spreads out across the ground, rooting at the leaf nodes and creating new plants.

Leaves of honeysuckles are in pairs, sometimes with lobes. The part that is most familiar and stands out is the fragrance of the flower. It stands out above all other scents in the area. Follow the scent to its source and you will find the white flowers of the honeysuckle which turn yellow as they age. Flowers are tubular, with five fused petals that contain nectar at the base. The fruits are inedible blue-black berries.

Origins

Japanese honeysuckle is native to Asia and was originally introduced in 1806 as an ornamental. In 1862 a more vigorous variety was introduced and was planted for erosion control and as a food for wildlife. It has spread across most of the eastern and southern parts of the country by underground rhizomes or runners. Where the leaf nodes touch the soil, roots develop and new plants are formed. The berries are a source of food for birds and other wildlife that disperse the seeds to new areas.

Food Value

The nectar from the base of the flowers is very sweet and can be sucked straight from the flower. You can also make flower tea by steeping the flowers in hot or cold water. Tea made from hot water is more bitter than tea made from cold water.

QUESTION

Can nectar be sucked from any honeysuckle flower?
There are other species of honeysuckle, all characterized by tubular flowers. However, only the Japanese honeysuckle is endowed with the perfumed fragrance. Some species may possibly be poisonous in large quantities. For safety purposes, it's best to avoid those that don't have any flavor. Yellow Jessamine is a vine that has yellow, tubular flowers that are mildly fragrant, but they are poisonous and have been mistaken for honeysuckle.

Honeysuckle leaves can also be used to make a tea. Dr. James Duke has used honeysuckle leaves and forsythia buds to make a tea to drink upon feeling the first symptoms of the flu, and has been successful in preventing the onset.

Japanese Knotweed

Japanese knotweed, sometimes referred to as Mexican bamboo, looks more like a bamboo than it does a knotweed. It even has a hollow stalk like bamboo. A member of the buckwheat family, it has the characteristic knots at the nodes. It may grow ten feet in one season and then die back in the fall. It spreads with horizontal rhizomes and very quickly colonizes an area.

In the spring, when the young shoots of Japanese knotweed emerge from the ground, they resemble asparagus. The leaves are broad and triangular, with a long, pointed tip. Small greenish-white flowers grow on long flower stalks that emerge from the leaf axils. Summer is the time to look for the colonies. That's when it's easiest to recognize. Remember where you find it, and come back in the spring to harvest the shoots.

Origins

Originally introduced from Asia in the late 1800s as an ornamental and for erosion control, Japanese knotweed now occurs throughout much of the United States. It prefers roadsides and railroad tracks but also forms dense colonies along stream banks and in damp, low-lying areas. Once it has established itself it's hard to get rid of.

Food Value

Like other members of the buckwheat family, Japanese knotweed has a tart flavor. Young shoots emerge in the spring and resemble asparagus. The time to gather them is before the leaves have emerged, when they are about six to eight inches tall.

ESSENTIAL

If you want to have a healthy heart, eat more Japanese knotweed. According to Dr. James Duke, former economic botanist for the USDA, Japanese knotweed is a rich source of resveratrol, the same compound found in grapes that is good for the heart and is sold as an herbal supplement in health food stores.

Young shoots of Japanese knotweed can be eaten raw or cooked like asparagus. The stalk gets tough and hollow as it ages. If you cut it off at the ground, in a few days it will be back again, allowing for another harvest.

Kudzu—The Weed That Ate the South

Kudzu is a trailing vine that looks like a giant bean. It has three leaflets that are sometimes as much as four inches wide. The purplish pea-like flowers grow in clusters and are very fragrant. They can be sniffed in late summer while driving down the road in areas where it grows. Brown, hairy pods soon follow, each containing three to ten seeds.

Origins

Kudzu originated in China and was brought to this country from Japan in the late 1800s. It was originally introduced as an ornamental and forage crop for animals. Farmers were encouraged to plant it to prevent erosion and as a soil stabilizer. It was also widely planted for erosion control by the Civilian Conservation Corps under President Franklin Roosevelt.

Today, kudzu covers much of the southeast, reaching as far north as Pennsylvania and Maryland and west to Texas. It branches out from a single taproot, extending in all directions, growing up to a foot a day. Roots develop at the nodes where the leaves are attached to the stem and new plants are formed. It grows best in well-drained soils but will grow in any disturbed area where it gets an opportunity, such as abandoned fields or lots. Repeated cuttings have proven to eliminate it in some areas.

FACT

According to research by several Harvard scientists, kudzu has more value than just food. After kudzu extracts were given to alcoholic hamsters, they voluntarily chose not to drink the alcohol. It was concluded that a compound known as daidzin that was found in kudzu had enabled alcoholic hamsters to withdraw from alcohol. Another study by a psychiatric professor associated with Harvard Medical School conducted a study on humans and found that those who took kudzu drank alcohol more slowly and consumed about half as much alcohol as those who did not take kudzu.

Food Value

Not only has kudzu invaded fields, but in some cases, it has also invaded kitchens. Grown as a shade vine in the south, it would grow up lattices and entice southern cooks with its fragrant flowers. Kudzu flower jelly, fried leaf chips, and other dishes were created and displayed at kudzu festivals.

Kudzu leaves, roots, and flowers are edible. Starch from the large taproots, which can grow to depths of six feet, can be used as a substitute for cornstarch. Young leaves are edible as a green vegetable and can be used as a spinach substitute. Flowers are used to make jelly.

Multiflora Rose

Multiflora rose is most common in the eastern part of the United States. It grows along the roadsides, in fields and pastures, and at the edges of forests and streams. Arching stems have curved, sharp thorns. In the spring it is covered with clusters of white, fragrant flowers with five petals. The fruit of the rose is a small hip containing many seeds. The fruit develops through the summer, ripening and turning red in the fall, and sometimes remaining on the plant through the winter. Birds feed on the fruits and in the process disperse the seeds.

Origins

Multiflora rose was brought to the United States in the 1880s by horticulturists from Asia. It was later planted as food and cover for wildlife habitats and on highway medians to prevent erosion. It forms dense thickets throughout most of the United States.

ALERT

Rose hips are a natural source of vitamin C. Even though the multiflora rose hips are small, they are very sweet and highly concentrated in vitamin C. A little bit goes a long way. Drinking an excess of rose hip tea can result in diarrhea. Always practice moderation when eating anything wild for the first time.

Food Value

The fragrant flower petals of the wild roses can be added to water to give it flavor. They can also be nibbled on, added to salads, or even used to make jelly. The fruits of the multiflora rose can be used to make tea, jelly, or wine.

Phragmites, Reed Gone Wild

Also known as common reed, phragmites towers over all other grasses in the marsh, reaching heights up to thirteen feet. In addition to its height, you can also pick it out by the gray-green patches of color. In late summer, feathery plumes develop at the tops of the stalks.

Origins

Phragmites is believed by invasive plant working groups to have arrived in this country by accident in the early 1800s at a port along the Atlantic coast. It was grown commercially in Europe as fodder for animals and for thatching material.

Phragmites likes it wet and grows in sunny, marshy areas along the edges of bays, rivers, canals, and estuaries. It has underground rhizomes that spread in all directions. Fragments can break off and are easily transported to new sites where they quickly form new colonies. It is often found in some of the most polluted waters and possibly helps filter pollutants from the water.

▲ Phragmites seed head

Food Value

Phragmites is edible. The roots and young shoots can be prepared in the same way as cattails. The stalk of young shoots can be peeled and the inner stalk eaten, while the roots can be pounded to release the starch used as a flour substitute. Avoid using plants that are growing in polluted waters, since they absorb and filter out the pollutants. If unsure of the water quality, boil the parts being used for at least ten minutes.

Garden Weeds

Many of the weeds that come up in your gardens every year are not native. Some of them were once cultivated and have continued to reseed. A number of them are considered invasive in some areas. They sometimes grow along the edges of woodlands or streams in natural areas.

Common Chickweed

Chickweed is a European native that now grows throughout the United States. It tends to sprawl on the ground, forming a mat as it matures. Leaves are small and in pairs with long stalks. Small, white flowers with five deeply cut petals grow in small clusters at the tips of the stems.

Chickweed is an annual that germinates in the fall and grows through the winter. In extremely cold conditions it may die off and then re-emerge in the spring when the soil becomes warm enough for the seeds to sprout. It grows quickly and when the temperature starts climbing, it blooms and soon goes to seed.

This is also about the time when gardeners are preparing the soil for the spring planting. If you want to prevent chickweed from spreading, pull up the entire plant before it produces seed. Leaves, stems, and flowers are edible and can be eaten raw in salads, made into herb spreads, or added to vegetable dishes. A side benefit from eating chickweed is its cancer preventive properties, which according to Dr. James Duke, include genistein and saponins.

Asiatic Dayflower

A native of China, the Asiatic dayflower is in the spiderwort family. The narrow leaves give it a grass-like appearance as it sprawls across the garden. Roots develop where the stem nodes touch the ground, forming new plants. The flowers are the most distinctive part. A pair of rounded blue petals sits on top of a small petal beneath. The flowers only last for one day, followed by the seeds found at the base of the flower.

Young leaves are mild tasting and can be eaten raw in salads. Flowers and seeds are also edible as a nibble or sprinkled in salads.

Sheep Sorrel

Sheep sorrel is a native of Europe that now grows throughout the United States in yards, gardens, roadsides, and other disturbed areas, spreading by runners on the ground. It is a perennial in the buckwheat family and is a miniature version of the cultivated garden sorrel that is grown for its tart flavor. The leaves are flared at the base, giving it a heart-shape appearance. Flower stalks develop in the spring with clusters of tiny greenish or reddish flowers that grow in a spike.

The tart flavor can be attributed to the oxalic acid in the leaves. Boiling the leaves for two to three minutes and pouring the water off can help reduce the amount of oxalic acid. They can be eaten raw in moderation.

Sheep sorrel is one of the herbs included in the Essiac anticancer formula that has become popular in recent years. Sheep sorrel is rich in cancer-preventative vitamins and was historically used as a cancer folk remedy. It is also high in oxalic acid and, in large doses, may cause poisoning.

Yellow Dock

Yellow dock originated in Europe, Asia, and Africa and now grows in disturbed areas throughout the United States including gardens, fields, and edges of forests. It can be identified by the long taproot that is yellowish when cut open, giving it the name yellow dock. Emerging leaves are long and narrow with wavy or curly margins that have reddish veins. Yellow dock seeds usually germinate in late summer. Leaves grow through the winter and the next spring the plant sends up a flower stalk with small, greenish flowers in whorls at the top of the stem. These flowers are followed by numerous brown nutlets that are prolific reseeders.

Like its relative the sheep sorrel, leaves of yellow dock also contain oxalic acid, giving it a tart flavor. Leaves are edible raw or cooked. Older leaves tend to get tough and more bitter. Cooking helps to remove the bitterness.

Young roots can also be eaten, although they fit more in the category of medicine than food. Roots should be harvested before the flower stalk develops. Even when young, they have a bitter taste.

The brown nutlets that develop at the tops of the stalks are also edible. Once they have been stripped from the plant, the seeds can be winnowed and ground into a flour.

CHAPTER 8

Spring Emergents

As daytime temperatures begin climbing, as early as March or April in some areas, the drab colors of winter give way to the bright colors of spring. Tree buds swell as sap begins moving up from the roots of trees and shrubs, lawns turn green, not from grass but from the weeds mixed in, and wildflowers burst open. Many of these emerging plants are edible. Teas can be made from roots and leaves and wild salads from leaves and flowers. Additionally some of these plants can be cooked as potherbs.

Backyard Greens

Herbaceous plants that have survived through the winter start growing as spring approaches. Seeds of annuals and biennials sprout and new leaves emerge from the ground. The greens provide vitamins, minerals, and other nutrients. Some may have a higher content of one property than another but they all contain beta carotene; vitamins A, E, and C; iron; calcium; and other nutrients.

Wild Salad Greens

Many of the wild greens in the spring can be eaten raw and make tasty salads. Usually younger leaves are more tender and milder tasting than older leaves that can be used as cooked greens.

Heal-all

Although heal-all is not native to this country, it has become naturalized and volunteers in lawns and moist, shady spots. It is often seen growing along damp, woodland trails year round. Small, almost triangular leaves develop through the winter. The surfaces of the leaves have small bumps that can be felt when you rub your fingers across them. Leaves are edible, raw or cooked, and have a mild spinach-like flavor.

In the spring a flower stalk develops. The stem leaves are paired, oval-shaped, and are larger than the basal leaves. The purple, snapdragon-like flowers are about one-half inch long and form a dense spike at the top of the stem. After the plant has bloomed, the seed stalk will dry on the plant, making it easy to identify in the fall and winter. Even though the top dies back, at the base is a rosette of leaves that remains green all winter and starts growing as soon as it starts warming up in the spring.

Chickweed

By the time spring has arrived, chickweed is starting to bloom and has formed a thick mat. The flowers are small, white, and on long stalks at the tips of slender stems with leaves that are also small and in pairs. Even though the flowers only have five petals, it appears they have ten because of the deep notch in the center of each one. Leaves and flowers are edible raw.

Violets

Violets are perennial herbs that emerge in the early spring. The blue violet is the one that is the most common and grows in backyards in somewhat shady areas. They have heart-shaped leaves on long stalks with toothed margins. The flowers have five irregular, bluish-purple petals at the top of a long flower stalk. Other violet species have white, pale blue, or purple flowers. The leaves have a mild flavor and can be added, along with the flowers, raw to salads.

ALERT

Violets with yellow flowers have been reported to cause nausea and vomiting. These should be avoided, and if you're not sure what color the flower is, wait until it blooms before you eat it. There is also a member of the buttercup family that is poisonous and has heart-shaped leaves when it is young that look similar to violet leaves.

Mustards

If you like to have a little bite added to your salad, look for members of the mustard family. They generally have deeply lobed or divided leaves. These are generally cool-weather plants and will sprout as soon as the soil is warm enough. Some members have smooth leaves and flower buds while others have leaves that are hairy. Rub them between your fingers for texture to determine if you want to eat them raw or not. Some have a strong flavor that can be tempered with heat. Many come up in your garden if it hasn't been treated with herbicides, including bittercress, winter cress, peppergrass, wild mustard, and wild radish.

Some mustards are picky about where they grow. Watercress will only grow along shallow streams or wet areas. Garlic mustard likes the shady forest floor while sea rocket only grows near the shoreline.

Mustard seeds sprout prolifically and can be thinned by pulling them out and adding them to a salad mix. Leaves are also edible and are usually best when picked while they are young. Older leaves get tough and more bitter.

Leaf texture varies among different species. It may be smooth on some and rough and hairy on others. The hairy ones are best if they are cooked before eating.

Dandelions and Their Look-Alikes

There are several species in the sunflower family that have leaves that look very similar. Dandelions are familiar to most people as a common weed in their yards, open fields, roadsides, and other sunny areas. Basal rosettes of deeply lobed leaves emerge early in the spring before the yellow flowers appear. The best time to gather the leaves is before they have bloomed. Young dandelion leaves can be eaten raw, even though they are somewhat bitter. Cooking them removes the bitter taste.

In the same habitat is a false dandelion with thicker, tougher leaves. They are very bitter. Wild lettuce also grows in the same habitat and has leaves that look similar to dandelion but are paler underneath and have fine hairs on the underside of the midrib. The young leaves are edible but gain in bitterness as they mature. The plant sends up a flower stalk that may reach ten feet in height topped with yellow flowers that look similar to dandelion but are smaller. At this stage the leaves are bitter and have sedative-like properties in them. Sow thistle has sharp spines on the leaf margins. Young leaves can be eaten.

Nettles

Stinging nettle is a perennial that spreads by runners or underground rhizomes. The square stems are covered with stinging hairs. Leaves are opposite and have toothed margins, coming to a point at the tip. They also have spines. The spines are like miniature hypodermic needles that inject several chemicals, including histamine, that cause the stinging sensation.

Nettles grow close to the ground in the winter. As soon as the days start warming up, new leaves emerge. The plant grows rapidly and within several weeks it may be two to four feet tall. This is the time to pick nettles for their greens. When gathering nettles, always remember to wear rubber gloves.

Nettles can be safely eaten after boiling them in water for two minutes. They can also be placed in a blender or food processor and chopped to release the chemicals that cause the stinging sensation.

FACT

"Nettle puts the sting in, dock takes the sting out," is a country saying. If you do find yourself in a patch of nettles and you need relief from the stings, look for yellow dock. It is a common weed that can be found in most disturbed areas. Look for the basal rosette of long, narrow leaves with wavy margins, usually with reddish veins, growing in open, disturbed areas. In the summer it sends up a flower stalk with greenish flowers growing in a terminal cluster followed by brown, seedlike fruits. Crush the leaf until it's moist and rub on the sting.

Tree Leaves

Most tree leaves are too tough or bitter to eat as food. There are a few exceptions. In a forest with beech trees, beech nuts that were left on the ground from the previous fall, sprout and produce a pair of distinctive, almost rectangular-shaped seed leaves that are edible raw or cooked. Young beech leaves can be cooked as a potherb.

Sassafras has distinctive mitten-shaped leaves. At least three, sometimes four, different leaves can grow on one plant, including a mitten for the left hand, one for the right hand, some with two lobes, and some with no lobes. Sassafras leaves have a completely different smell than the roots. They are spicier and lack the root beer smell. Leaves are edible raw or cooked.

Sourwood is an understory tree of oaks and pines and a member of the heath family with blueberries and huckleberries. White, bell-shaped flowers hang in drooping clusters in the summer. Elliptical-shaped leaves turn a distinctive peachy-red in the fall. This is the time to mark the location and return in the spring to harvest the young leaves as they emerge. At this time they are a yellowish green and have a lemony flavor when eaten.

Roots and Shoots

Many of the roots that are gathered in the spring are those of the biennials and sometimes perennials that have wintered over. While the plants above the ground have gone dormant or have ceased to grow, the roots below the ground have been growing. The time to harvest them is before they develop a flower stalk that emerges from the center of the rosette of leaves or before the leaves have started to grow.

The stalks of some biennials, once they have emerged, are also edible and can be used as a vegetable. Some of these can be eaten raw while others must be cooked first.

Spring Lilies

Lilies have bulbs or corms, often forming clumps, and send up new shoots in the early spring. The bulbs or corms of some species are edible while others are deadly.

Familiar members of the lily family include several species of wild onions and garlic, sometimes collectively referred to as onion grass because of their grass-like leaves and strong onion scent. The emerging young leaves are edible raw or added to cooked vegetables or soups. The bulbs can be used as a substitute for onions and garlic.

Ramps, also known as wild leeks, grow from Canada to Georgia in rich, moist soil in deciduous hardwoods. The leaves are wider than those of garlic and onions, and the bulb is larger and stronger in smell. When harvesting ramps, cut off the top part and replant the part with the root hairs to prevent the population from declining.

ALERT

The young shoots of milkweed and dogbane, side by side, look very similar. Dogbane contains cardiac glycosides and is highly toxic. Both species have leaves that are in pairs and are oval-shaped and both exude a white, milky substance when a leaf is broken off. Milkweed leaves are somewhat wider and more robust. Positively identify milkweed before eating.

Milkweed

The common milkweed is a perennial and in the spring sends up new shoots that are edible. The time to gather the shoots is before the leaves have unfolded. All parts of the milkweed are poisonous when raw. To prepare for eating, cover with boiling water and boil for one minute. Strain, cover with boiling water a second time, and boil for one minute. Strain and use as a cooked vegetable.

Pokeweed

Pokeweed is a tall, perennial herb that comes up every year in gardens, edges of fields, and other disturbed areas. It has oval-shaped leaves and a thick stem that turns red as summer progresses. Fruits develop in late summer or early fall and turn purplish-black. The plant may grow up to six or seven feet in one season before dying back for the winter. New growth emerges from the same roots the next spring.

It is among the dead stalks that you look to find the new growth in the spring. Look for plants that are less than a foot tall. Young leaf tips may also be picked. Poke must be cooked before eating. Peel the stems by pulling the leaf stalks downward. Prepare the stems by boiling through two changes of water and then use as a substitute for asparagus. Young poke seedlings also emerge in the spring and can be picked, boiled through two changes of water, and eaten.

Thistle

Thistles are biennials in the sunflower family. Fleshy roots of some species are edible, although somewhat bitter. Early in the spring of the second year, a flower stalk develops. The best time to harvest it is just before the flower bud opens. It can be eaten raw as a celery substitute or cooked as a vegetable.

ESSENTIAL

Skinning a thistle is an essential skill if you are going to eat thistle stalks. Strong leather gloves and a sharp knife are also recommended. Begin by removing the stalk leaves and then cut it off at its base. Chop the head off next, and then use your knife to peel and remove the outer skin.

Cattail Shoots

Cattails form colonies in wetland areas with an interconnecting root system made up of horizontal rhizomes that are edible. In the early spring young shoots emerge from the mucky water. The best time to harvest them is when they are less than a foot tall. Cut the shoots off at the base and strip the outer leaves to the inner core that is whitish or yellowish-green. These cattail hearts can be eaten raw in the field or chopped and added to salads. As the plant continues to grow, the core becomes tough and fibrous.

Edible Buds and Flowers

Buds swelling on trees and shrubs are one of the first signs of spring. Some of these early blooming trees have buds and flowers that are edible. Some of these have a fragrant scent that lead you to them while others come up in your backyard.

Flowers have a variety of tastes. Many flowers have a taste similar to their scent and range from spicy to sweet to almost no taste at all. How they are used is equally variable. Get familiar with the different tastes by nibbling on them before adding to a dish.

Dandelions

Dandelions start blooming early, with flower heads appearing randomly in lawns. This is the time to start looking for the buds located in the center of the rosette. Flower buds and flowers are edible. But the best flowers are when you see a profusion of yellow flower heads covering the lawns, growing out of the sidewalks, or popping up in landscaped gardens. These are the sweetest. As the season progresses, the flowers tend to get bitter as do the leaves.

Mustards

Members of the mustard family have flower buds that look like miniature versions of cultivated broccoli. When the flower buds open, the four petals form a cross, giving them the generic name of crucifers. The colors vary from white and yellow to pink and purple. All mustards are edible and have a spicy odor and taste, some more so than others. Almost all of them are palatable in some form. Flower buds and flowers are edible, either raw or cooked.

Mustard Fruits

The fruit of members of the mustard family is a pod-looking capsule containing seeds inside. Some are long and narrow while others are short and round. Some split open easily while others are tough and hard. The seeds, even though small, are quite spicy and can be ground up and used as a spice or seasoning.

Violets

Violets are familiar weeds for most people. They come up in lawns, in the forest, along stream banks, and just about every place where people go. Some have blue flowers, others have white, and one has yellow—this is the one you don't eat.

Violet flowers taste mildly sweet. They can be eaten raw, infused in water for a flower tea or candied and made into jams, jellies, and syrups.

Elder

Elder is a native shrub with representatives throughout the United States. The most common one in the eastern states is common elder. There is also another elder, the red-berried elder, which is considered poisonous. Common elder grows along ditches, stream banks, hedgerows, and edges of swamps and blooms in the later part of spring with an abundance of large, white, flat-topped clusters of flowers.

ALERT

Elder often grows in areas where you don't want to gather, such as the roadside, edges of fields that have been sprayed with pesticides, or near polluted waterways. Inspect the surroundings before gathering flowers. Also, learn to distinguish it from water hemlock that also has white, flat-topped clusters of flowers.

Finding elder is easy. The large, white flowers can be spotted from the car while driving down the road. Once the flower heads have filled out, use pruning scissors to snip off the tops. Elder flowers are edible, either dipped in batter and fried or infused in water for a tea. They can also be dried and used later to make tea.

Herbalist and botanist Christopher Hobbs, at an herb conference, referred to elder flowers as a blood mover. If you are holding heat in one part of your body, as with eczema or other skin conditions, elder flowers will help clear the blood of heat and toxins.

Legume Flowers

Legumes are in the pea family and have the characteristic pea-like flowers. Redbuds and black locusts are both members of this family that have edible flowers.

Redbuds are easy to recognize in the spring with their fuchsia-colored flowers that appear before the leaves have unfolded in the early spring. They grow along the branches and sometimes the trunk of the tree. The flowers have a sweet-tart flavor and can be added to salads or desserts.

Two different species of redbuds grow in the east and the west. In the east it can be found from New Jersey south to central Florida and west to Texas and Nebraska. In the western part of the country it grows on dry slopes and in canyons and foothills.

There are eastern and western species of black locust trees. Both species have thorns and pinnately divided leaves, which means there are multiple leaves arranged on each side of a common axis. The word "pinnate" comes from a Latin word meaning "feather." The flowers of the eastern species are white, while those of the western species are pinkish-purple. Both are edible.

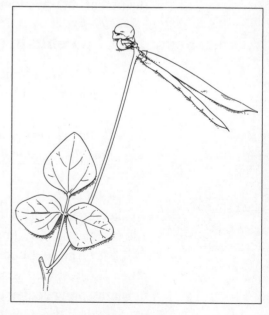

▲ Wild bean with pod and flower

Sassafras

In the spring before the sassafras leaves have emerged, small yellowish-green flowers appear at the end of the stems. Male and female flowers are usually on separate trees. Flowers are mildly spicy and can be nibbled raw or added to salads or cooked dishes.

Spring Teas and Beverages

Teas made in the spring are cleansing and stimulating. Getting to the roots before the leaves and flowers burst out is important for those whose roots are used, as is watching the plants for the first leaves and the peak flowers.

Mormon Tea

Mormon tea is in the ephedra family and is native to deserts and grasslands throughout the arid west and southwest of the United States and the drier regions of Mexico. It is a low, shrubby plant with branching stems and small scales for leaves, giving it a leafless look. The stems and leaves can be steeped in hot water for tea.

Sassafras, Spicebush, and Sweet Birch

Sassafras, spicebush, and sweet birch are woody plants in the eastern United States that can be made into individual teas or brewed together to make what was once referred to in Appalachia as the SSS Tonic. The SSS Tonic is still available today as an iron and vitamin booster but with no mention of the herbs originally used.

Sassafras

Sassafras is a plant that most people have heard about, especially if you add root beer to the name. This is the plant that was originally used to flavor root beer. The root beer smell of the root distinguishes this root from any other. The best time to dig up the roots is before the leaves have unfolded in the early spring or after they have dropped in the fall.

Sassafras has a wide range and can be found from southern Maine to Florida, and west to Texas and eastern Kansas. It grows as a tree or shrub in the understory of the forest and has horizontal rhizomes that spread out in all directions, sending up new shoots as it goes. The time to locate it is in the summer when it has leaves. It has at least three different leaf shapes on one plant and has been called the mitten tree because of the shapes of the leaves. Deep lobes on the left or right side give it the appearance of a mitten. Some leaves have deep lobes on both sides while others have no lobes at all.

Sassafras never grows alone. Look for the parent plant first and then look for the young shoots around it to dig up to make tea. A dozen or so pencil-sized roots are enough to make a good pot of tea.

Spicebush

Spicebush is a shrub that grows in shady areas, sometimes bordering streams, where the soil is moist. The leaves are oval and simple, so simple they are often overlooked. In the early spring it produces small, yellow flowers on the branches. The twigs are distinctive with a spicy aroma when scratched and sniffed. This is the part used to make tea.

Sweet Birch

Sweet birch grows in cool, moist upland forests with smooth, dark brown bark. Leaves are doubly toothed and come to a sharp point at the tip. The cone-like fruit is small and brown and contains two-winged nutlets. The twigs and branches of sweet birch, when scratched or broken, smell like wintergreen and can be made into a tea.

Yaupon Holly

Yaupon, or "cassine" as it is known in some parts, is a native shrub or small tree, often forming thickets along the Atlantic coast from Virginia south to central Florida and along the Gulf coast to southern Texas. It can grow in dry,

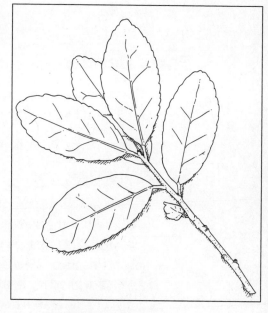

▲ Yaupon leaves for making tea

sandy soil near the ocean and can withstand strong winds and salty air. It is evergreen, with small, oval-shaped leaves up to one inch long, with rounded teeth. It blooms in the spring with numerous tiny, white fragrant flowers followed by shiny, red berries that mature in autumn and often remain attached throughout the winter.

Yaupon is the only holly in North America with caffeine in the leaves. Other holly leaves can also be used for tea but lack the flavor and caffeine that the yaupon has. Until the 1970s it was sold in restaurants on the outer banks of North Carolina where it grows in abundance. With coffee and imported tea becoming readily available, yaupon was eventually forgotten.

FACT

Yaupon holly was used by American Indians to make a ceremonial drink in the spring. They would travel to the east coast and gather branches of yaupon to brew into a strong, concentrated black tea. They would then drink it until they threw up, giving it the species name of *vomitoria*.

Early Berries

The berry season begins in the spring, about mid-May in some areas. Trees, shrubs, and herbs whose flowers were among the early bloomers produce the berries.

Serviceberries

Serviceberries are one of the first trees to bloom in the understory of the forest in the spring before the leaves have come out. They are easily spotted at that time of the year when the tree is covered with white flowers. Members of the rose family, the flowers have five petals and are about an inch wide. This is the time to look for the trees. Once the flowers are gone and the leaves have developed, the trees blend in with the forest and disappear.

About a month after the tree has bloomed, the fruits begin to ripen. They are best when they turn a deep red or purplish color. You have to get out early to pick them before the birds get to them. They will eat them until they're gone. The fruits are mildly juicy and have a slight, almond-like flavor.

Mulberries

Mulberries are medium-sized trees with fruits that look like blackberries. All are edible but some have more flavor than others. White mulberries are mostly bland tasting, while red or black berries are sweet.

Wild Strawberries

Wild strawberries look like strawberries, except they are much smaller. What they lack in size they make up for in taste. They are usually found in light areas within the forest or along its edges. A member of the rose family, they have flowers with five white petals in the early spring.

QUESTION

How can you tell the difference between a wild strawberry and a mock strawberry?
True strawberries have white flowers, whereas mock strawberries have yellow flowers. Also, the fruit of the mock strawberry has seeds on the surface and the inside is a whitish pulp with no flavor. The true strawberry looks and tastes like a strawberry.

Wild strawberries are the ancestors of the cultivated strawberries that have been bred to produce larger berries but less flavor. Wild strawberries also have more nutritional value than their cultivated counterparts, which are mostly water.

CHAPTER 9

Summer's Harvest

Summer is a lazy time, when the days are long and the heat can sometimes be stifling. Many of the cool-weather greens have gone to seed and have been replaced by those that like the heat. Spring fruits give way to summer fruits that are usually sweeter and juicier. Early morning or late afternoon is the best time for gathering and sometimes necessary to beat the birds to the berries and also to avoid the midday heat.

Summer Sweets

At the peak of summer, when the sun's rays are the most intense, and temperatures climb to record highs, the sweet and juicy berries ripen. They provide extra sugars for energy and fluids for hydration at a time when they're most needed.

Heath Berries

Blueberries, huckleberries, and manzanita are all woody shrubs in the heath family. Blueberries and huckleberries both have blue berries while those of the manzanita plants are red when ripe. There are also dangleberries, farkleberries, deerberries, and sparkleberries. All have blue berries and are edible.

Blueberries and huckleberries look very similar. True blueberries bear terminal clusters of fruits that turn blue or sometimes black when ripe, with many seeds in the center. True huckleberries have flowers in the leaf axils and fruits with ten large seeds and resinous glands on the underside of the leaves.

▲ Star shape pattern on tip of blueberry

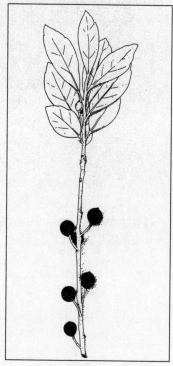

▲ Poisonous Inkberries with no star

Blueberries can be grouped into two kinds, the highbush and the low-bush. Both are shrubs and are common in the eastern United States. The highbush blueberry is the tallest of the blueberries and can get up to fifteen feet tall. This is the ancestor of the cultivated blueberry and is a common understory shrub in the eastern half of the country. Leaves are oval shaped with green, sometimes red stems that are somewhat zig-zagged, making them easy to identify in winter. The lowbush blueberries are much smaller, usually no more than three feet high. The fruits ripen a little later than the highbush but they are equally sweet.

QUESTION

When is a blue berry not a blueberry?
Look for the star at the top of the berry. Where the five sepals join together, a star-shaped pattern is formed. The star generally, but not always, indicates it is one of the edible blueberries. If the star is missing, it may be one of the poisonous look-alikes. Some members of the holly family have inedible, blue-black berries growing next to blueberries but no star.

Manzanita species can be found along the western coast from southern California to Alaska and along the northern part of the United States to Maine. These are woody, evergreen plants that sometimes sprawl on the ground. They bloom in the spring with small white or pink flowers that are followed by green berries that look like little apples. The berries turn red when they are ripe. Manzanita berries are edible and can be used for jellies, jams, or cobblers.

Cherries and Plums

Cherries and plums are closely related, both sharing the same genus Prunus. There are about thirty species scattered across most of the United States. Birds eat the fruits and widely distribute their seeds. They both belong to the rose family and have clusters of white flowers in the spring that are followed by fruits that ripen from late spring to early fall.

Wild cherries are small with a large stone in the center. They can be eaten raw but are best when made into juice or jelly. Plums are in the same genus as cherries, and like cherries, have fruits that are drupes with a large stone in the center. There are a number of species of native plums scattered across most of the country with colors that range from deep red to yellow or orange when ripe. When ripe, cherries and plums will drop easily into your hand. Unripe fruits cling to the branches. However, both are a good source of pectin when unripe, and if making jelly, a few should be included in your harvest.

Ground Cherries—Native Tomatillos

They look like miniature lanterns, hanging from the stems of a low-growing herbaceous plant. Ground cherries are really not cherries at all. They are in the nightshade family and are related to tomatoes, with tomato-like fruits enclosed in a papery husk. When the husk starts turning brown, the fruits begin to ripen. The ripe fruit is similar to a ripe tomato and can be used in the same way. Unripe fruits are poisonous.

Mayapples—Fruits of the Forest

Mayapple is a member of the barberry family and is found in the eastern part of North America in damp woods or shaded clearings and often grows in large colonies, spreading underground by thick, creeping rhizomes. The best time to look for mayapples is in the early spring when the miniature, umbrella-like leaves emerge from the forest floor. Standing from one to one-and-a-half feet tall, the leaves partially hide the large solitary flower appearing in the fork where the stem branches into two leaves. Some plants have only a single stem, in which case there is no flower.

The name "mayapple" is referring to the flower, which was thought to resemble an apple blossom and opens in May in some areas. There are usually six to nine white, waxy petals, unlike apple blossoms that have only five petals. It has also been called mandrake due to the similarity of the root to the unrelated European plant.

You know the mayapple fruits are ripening when you step into the woods and catch a scent of lemon in the air. While the plant is easy to locate in the spring, by the time the fruits are ready to harvest, most of the leaves have died back and other plants have grown up around them. Finding the fruits is most easily done by using the sense of smell. When they ripen they turn yellow and look and smell like lemons. The fruit is a large berry with many seeds and is edible when ripe. The pulp surrounding the seeds can be eaten raw or can be made into a juice or jelly.

ALERT

The roots, leaves, seeds, and green fruit are all toxic and are strongly cathartic. The most poisonous part of the plant is the root, which contains podophyllum, a bitter resinous compound that is a gastro-intestinal irritant and, in large doses, is fatal. Etopiside and teniposide are two synthetic derivatives that are used to treat certain types of cancer.

Ramblin' Brambles

Blackberries, raspberries, dewberries, and wild roses are all considered brambles, and they do ramble. They grow in a tangle of thorny stems and spread in all directions, reaching out and grabbing innocent passersby. To go forward when in their grip is inviting trouble, due to their backward-directed bristles. The only way out is to back out.

Even though the fruits ripen in the summer, it's best to scout out the areas when they're blooming in the spring. Dewberry is usually the earliest bloomer and is similar to blackberry but grows closer to the ground, being more of a creeper than growing upright. They like moist woods and clearings.

Blackberries, raspberries, and wild roses all bloom about the same time in mid-spring. They generally like open, sunny areas. All the brambles have flowers with five petals, which may be either white or pink, and compound leaves with three or more toothed leaflets. The fruits of dewberries, blackberries, and raspberries consist of many small, juicy drupelets, each containing a hard seed. Blackberries and dewberries look very similar, turning black when ripe. Raspberry fruits may be red or black when ripe, depending on the species, and differ from dewberries and blackberries in that they separate from the fleshy stalks when picked, forming hollow shells. The fruit of the rose is a hip and ripens in the fall.

Elder

Even while the elder is still blooming, the tiny green fruits at the base of where the flower petals meet are developing. The color goes quickly from green to red, then deepens to a purple and finally turns almost black before they are finally ripe. The berries can be removed by rubbing the stems gently between your fingers.

ESSENTIAL

According to Dr. James Duke in *The Green Pharmacy,* black elderberry has two compounds that are flu preventive. Elderberry extract is available on pharmacy shelves and health food stores as a flu preventive. Common elderberry is similar and may have the same flu prevention properties.

Elderberries can be used to make jelly, syrup, pies, or wine. Fresh berries have a strong flavor that can be mellowed somewhat with drying.

Summer Wildflowers

Plants that bloom in the summer are often sun lovers and can be found in fields, at the edges of forests, and in open, marshy areas.

Cattails

Cattails are common in most wetlands, and in late spring the flower buds begin to develop. You will notice first a slight swelling at the top of a central stalk. Feel with your fingers to determine if it is mature enough to harvest. If so, pull the top leaves back to reveal the greenish flower spikes, two of them, male and female. The male is at the top and the female, which later becomes the part we refer to as the "hot dog," is on the bottom. The immature flower spikes are edible, although the male is more tender.

As the flower buds mature, the male flower begins to turn yellow. When you tap the spike and see the pollen being dispersed, you know it is ready to collect. Put a plastic bag around the spike and strip the pollen from the stalk. The pollen can then be added to cornmeal or flower for bread. Once it has turned brown, it's past its peak. Eventually the male flowers dry up and drop off, leaving only the female spike.

Mallow Flowers and Fruits

Mallows are found worldwide. The habitat varies from coastal marshes to fields, gardens, and meadows. They are members of the same family that includes okra, hibiscus, hollyhock, and cotton, plus about 1,500 other species that grow throughout the world.

Some mallows begin blooming at the peak of summer, producing shades of white, pink, and lavender flowers. The hibiscus flowers used in commercial herb teas are in the mallow family. There are several species of hibiscus that grow wild. Wild mallow flowers can be eaten raw in salads or added to tea blends.

Immediately following the flowers are the fruits. Mallow fruits are capsules with chambers that contain the seeds. The size varies with the different species. Rose mallows grow in wetland areas and have fruits that are larger than those of the weedy common mallow that grows in lawns and gardens and are referred to as cheeses because of the flat, wheel-like shape of the fruit. Rose mallow fruits measure up to two inches in length. Like okra, they get tough quickly and should be picked while young and tender.

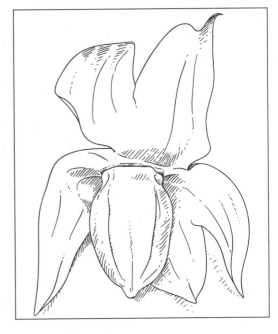

▲ Rose mallow fruit

Milkweeds

While there are a number of milkweeds, the common milkweed is the one most frequently used for food. In ideal conditions, it may get up to six feet tall. Flower buds begin developing in mid-summer and soon open into fragrant, pinkish-colored flowers. A pod-like fruit with a rough surface soon follows. Flower buds, flowers, and young pods are all edible after preparing by boiling for one minute, pouring the water off, and boiling a second time, after which you can strain and use as a cooked vegetable.

Yucca

Yucca is in the agave family and is easily recognized by its sharp-pointed, dagger-like leaves that form a rosette. Curly, fibrous threads line the edges of the long leaves. In the late spring and early summer, a flower stalk arises from the center and produces large, white, bell-shaped flowers at the top. The flowers require cross-pollination for the greenish, oblong fruit to develop, and the only pollinator is the yucca moth, which can usually be found inside the flowers.

QUESTION

Are the yucca roots they sell at the grocery store from the same plant?
The yucca root sold at the grocery store is not related to the native yucca at all. It actually belongs to the genus Manihot and is imported from the tropics. The native yucca roots contain saponins, a group of glycosides that form a soapy foam when dissolved in water. The roots taste very bitter and are not easily digested.

The young flower stalks of yucca are edible when they're about a foot tall. They resemble asparagus at this stage. Some taste better than others, even when growing side by side. Do the taste test before including them in a recipe. Yucca flowers are also edible. The reproductive parts in the center are bitter and should be removed. Flowers can be eaten raw or cooked with other vegetables.

Luscious Legumes

Legumes are plants that have bean-like pods and are easily recognized in the wild because of their close resemblance to the many cultivated variet-ies that occur. Not all beans are edible. Some contain toxic alkaloids and should be avoided. Seeds of wild beans contain varying amounts of cyanide and should be cooked before eating.

Groundnuts

Groundnuts are members of the pea family that have bean-like vines with compound leaves. Look for them along the sunny edges of waterways, climbing up trees and shrubs along the banks. In mid-summer they develop clusters of maroon-colored blossoms that are followed by pods containing edible beans that look and taste like garden peas.

Mesquite

In the southwest is the mesquite, a small tree in the pea family that grows along streams and in areas where the water table is relatively high, from southern Kansas to southeastern California. Look for the spikes of greenish-yellow flowers in the early spring, followed by pods that become brittle and brown when fully ripe, usually in the fall. Gather the pods when they are mature and make a flour by grinding the pods to make into cakes or mush. The seeds are hard and should be discarded.

Redbud—the Bean Tree

Soon after the redbud tree has finished blooming, pods begin developing. It is while the pods are developing that the distinctive heart-shaped leaves begin unfolding, partially hiding the flat pods. In the beginning the pods are greenish-pink in color, becoming pink and finally turning dark brown by the end of the summer. They are best when picked while still in the greenish-pink phase, when they are between one to two inches in length. This is when they are the most tender. As they mature they become tough and not palatable. Redbud pods have a somewhat tart flavor and can be used as a cooked vegetable.

Wild Beans

Wild beans are climbing vines, often with three leaflets, looking similar to poison ivy until they bloom. The flower is a characteristic pea-like flower that may be white or varying shades of pink and lavender. The fruit is a bean-like pod that is very similar to our garden vegetables.

Native beans include the genus Strophostyles that grows in the eastern part of the United States and has flowers and fruits that grow in small clusters. In the southwest is the tepary bean in the genus Phaseolus, which has many cultivated species. In the same genus is another wild bean that grows along the Mississippi and Ohio Rivers and the Gulf and Atlantic coastal plains. The pods, when very young, can be cooked like green beans. After the seeds have developed, they can be shelled and used as a cooked bean.

Summer Greens

Many of the summer greens are annuals and come up in backyards and gardens. They like sunny, disturbed areas and grow rapidly, with some species such as lambsquarters and amaranth reaching as much as eight to ten feet tall. These are best picked in the early morning before they droop from the heat of the sun.

Goosefoots

Lambsquarters is the best known member of the goosefoot family and can be found throughout the world. It is a European native and readily becomes naturalized in areas where it is introduced. The leaves are mild tasting and can be eaten raw or cooked as a spinach substitute.

Other goosefoot members include:

- Epazote has become naturalized in southern states and has leaves that are used as a bean seasoning.
- Orache grows near salt marshes and has leaves that add a salty seasoning to foods.

Grass Grazing

Chewing on the ends of grass blades is a common practice for some people. The milky juice is refreshing and thirst quenching. Young leaf blades can also be juiced like wheat grass. Avoid actually eating the leaves since the cellulose in the leaves is indigestible. A tea can be made by steeping the leaves in hot water or they can be dried and powdered. Barnyard grass, crabgrass, foxtail grass, and orchard grass are some of the grasses whose leaf blades can be used.

Some plants look like grasses but instead are sedges, rushes, or cattails, especially in wetlands. Chewing on the stems of these plants should be done with caution, especially if uncertain of the water quality. Sedges can often be identified by their triangular stem, while the rushes have round stems without jointed leaves. Cattail leaves are flat.

Mallow Greens

Mallow leaves, especially when they are young and tender, can be eaten raw in salads or cooked as a potherb. The mucilaginous leaves give a thickening quality to vegetable dishes or casseroles. They are rich in nutrients, including vitamins A, B_1, B_2, and C; iron; calcium; and essential fatty acids.

Purslane

Purslane is a low-growing, succulent herb that waits until after the last frost to emerge, which is usually late spring. Leaves are rounded at the top and may be either alternate or opposite. These can be trimmed and the plant will continue to grow and sprawl out in different directions. The trimmings can be added raw to salads and soups or eaten as a cooked green.

ESSENTIAL

According to Dr. James Duke, purslane contains several antioxidants that fight against cancer. It is rich in vitamin C, beta-carotene, glutathione, and vitamin E and is one of the best sources of omega-3 fatty acids in the plant world, which have been linked with lowering cholesterol levels.

Small, yellow flowers appear in mid-summer followed by black seeds. Leaves, stems, flowers, and seeds are all edible.

Summer Teas

In the summer when it's hot and you want something more than just water, there are a number of plants that can be used to make refreshing herbal teas. Adding ice to the drink can make it even more cooling. Herbs add flavor to the water, plus additional minerals and nutrients. Some herbs can have a calming effect while others may be stimulating. For maximum benefits, pour boiling water over the herbs, cover with a tight lid, and let steep for twenty to thirty minutes.

Daisy or Aster-like Flowers

The sun-lovers make their appearance all summer. Daisies and asters are in the sunflower family, which has lots of members. The flowers of most species are bitter; however, some of these make a dainty-tasting tea that is refreshing to drink when it's hot.

Oxeye Daisy

Oxeye daisy flowers look like large chamomile flowers and taste very similar in a tea. The dark green leaves with deep lobes form a rosette of basal leaves and continue up the flower stalk, getting smaller as they near the top where the large, white flower, up to two inches wide, is located. The petals are white with a yellow center that has a depression in the middle. They can be found in fields, pastures, and roadsides.

Sweet Goldenrod

This is a goldenrod that can be distinguished from all other goldenrods by its taste, which is a sweet, anise-like flavor. The leaves are from one to four inches long and narrow, with smooth edges. About mid-summer the yellow clusters of flowers appear along one side of arching branches. Look for it in dry fields and open woods in the eastern United States.

Life Everlasting

Life everlasting blooms later in the summer and looks like a lot of other plants blooming at that time. The scent is the trademark. It's unlike any other. The leaves are several inches long and feel wooly to the touch with whitish hairs underneath. The flowers are white and cotton-like and fragrant, as are the leaves. It grows in dry clearings, fields, and edges of woods throughout the eastern United States.

Mints

All mints have a square stem, but not all plants with a square stem are mints. There are a number of mints that have been planted in yards and gardens and have escaped into the wild, often mixing with other mints. They can be recognized by their square stems, opposite leaves, and flowers with five petals that form an upper and lower lip. Most members are aromatic.

Horse Balm and Bee Balm

Horse balm and bee balm are members of the mint family that bloom in late summer with a smell that resembles thyme. Horse balm has yellowish, purple-dotted flowers that grow in whorls in the upper leaf axils with white or pale purple bracts at their base. It grows in dry, sandy soil along the coastal plain and in prairies of the Midwest. Bee balm has bright red, tubular flowers and grows in moist soil along streams.

FACT

According to Dr. James Duke's phytochemical database, *www.ars-grin .gov/duke*, horse balm is the best source of carvacrol. Research studies have shown carvacrol helps prevent the breakdown of a compound that seems to be lacking in people with Alzheimer's. It seems probable that drinking a cup of horse balm tea might be an effective medicine against Alzheimer's disease.

Horse balm is in the genus Monarda along with several other species that occur over most of the United States and southern Canada. The fresh or dried leaves can be used to make a tea.

Skullcap

There are several types of skullcap, but the one that is most frequently used for making tea is mad-dog skullcap. It grows in moist woodlands near swamps and blooms in late summer with small, bluish-purple flowers that grow in one-sided racemes from the leaf axils. Its name comes from its folk use for treating rabies. As a tea, it helps relieve nervous conditions including insomnia and anxiety.

Red Clover

Red clover is in the pea family with alternate leaves divided into three leaflets with a V-shaped pattern near the end of each leaflet. Tiny, pinkish-purple flowers develop into a head at the top of the stem. They should be gathered when the flower heads are fully open, before they start turning brown. Red clover grows in fields, meadows, and disturbed areas through-out the United States and is often planted for its nitrogen-fixing abilities. Flowers can be used fresh or dried in tea blends.

Wintergreen

Wintergreen is in the heath family, along with blueberries and cranber-ries. It is a low-lying, evergreen herb that grows in acid woodlands from Newfoundland to Manitoba and south to Georgia and Alabama. It spreads on the forest floor with horizontal rhizomes just beneath the surface. The leaves contain compounds that add a wintergreen flavor to tea. Look for the little black, resinous dots under the leaves for positive identification.

CHAPTER 10

Fall Foraging

When the edges and tops of the forests start turning yellow and red, and the fields and grassy areas turn golden, you know that fall is approaching. It is often marked with warm, sunny days that are ideal for being outdoors harvesting what has been developing all summer. Fruits are ripening, seeds are maturing, and nuts are falling. When squirrels and chipmunks can be seen scurrying around trees gathering nuts and storing or burying them, it is a sure sign that another harvest season has arrived with yet another crop ready to be picked.

Hips, Haws, and Mini Apples

The rose family contains a number of species with edible fruits that ripen in the fall, some beginning to ripen in late summer. These fruits tend to be less sweet than the serviceberries and cherries that ripen in the spring and summer. These fruits are high in vitamin C and E and help boost the immune system against the cooler temperatures.

Hips—The Fruit of the Rose

One of the easiest to recognize and also one of the most common bushes found throughout the United States are the wild roses. They grow in the mountains, at the edge of the forest, in fields and cow pastures, and in swamps and marshes. The fruit of the rose is a hip that contains several mature ovaries filled with seeds. Calyx lobes are prominent at the tip of the fruit. The fruits are edible and can be nibbled raw or steeped in hot water to make rose hip tea.

Nature's Mini Apples

Hawthorns and crabapples are shrubs or small trees in the rose family that produce fruit that look like miniature apples. They grow in the understory of the forest or along the edges of fencerows or abandoned fields where they sometimes form thickets with stout thorns that arm branches and trunks. In the spring, clusters of flowers with five fragrant petals are borne on the branches.

ESSENTIAL

Hawthorns are considered by many herbalists to be a heart tonic and have been used for heart problems including high blood pressure and angina. According to Michael Murray in *The Healing Power of Herbs*, hawthorns are rich in flavonoids and have been studied for their antioxidant effects.

There are a number of species of hawthorns, most being small trees or dense shrubs. Fruits are generally red and somewhat resemble the fruit of their close relative, the wild rose. One way to distinguish them from roses is by their long, stout thorns. A tea can be made by steeping the fruits in hot water, or they can blended be with other fruits to make a juice drink.

Crabapples

Crabapples are ancestors of apples and have also been domesticated. Several species that are native to the United States include:

- Sweet crabapples extend from New York west to northeast Arkansas and south to northern Georgia.
- The southern crabapple is found from Virginia south to northern Florida and west to Louisiana.
- Prairie crabapples grow from northern Indiana south to Arkansas and from Oklahoma north to southeastern South Dakota.
- Oregon crabapples occur on the west coast from west-central California northward to Alaska.

Native crabapples can be distinguished from cultivated crabapples by their taste. Most are extremely tart, with no sweetness at all.

Berries and Berry-like Fruits

There are lots of berries that ripen in the fall. A lot of them are best left for the birds. But mixed in among them are hidden treasures—flavors found nowhere else. Once you have identified which ones to leave for the birds, start experimenting by taste to see what the individual fruits taste like.

Black Gum—the Lemon Tree

Black gums are one of the first trees to start changing colors in the fall. The leaves are oval-shaped and turn scarlet red while most other trees still have green leaves. This is also about the time the fruits start ripening, turning blue-black in color. Biting into this fruit is like sucking on a lemon.

There are several species in this family with edible fruits. Swamp black gum is similar to the black gum, but the fruits are more bitter and leave an aftertaste. Taste is often the best way to distinguish between these two species. The Ogeechee gum grows in wooded swamps from Florida to South Carolina, with sour-tasting fruits that turn red when ripe.

Pawpaw Patches

Pawpaws grow in patches, usually as an understory tree in the forest. The fruits develop through the summer and look like short, green bananas. They grow in clumps of three to four on the branches of the trees and begin to ripen in late August, reaching their peak in late September, about the time the leaves start to turn yellow. Pawpaws drop to the ground when ripe and should be gathered right away before they turn black. If they are not fully ripe, you can place them on a table at room temperature and they will continue to ripen.

Persimmons

Persimmons look like miniature pumpkins and, coincidentally, ripen about the same time. It is believed by many people that you have to wait until after the frost to eat a persimmon but this is not always true. While there may still be persimmons on a tree when the frost occurs, they actually start ripening before the frost.

ALERT

Persimmon fruits must be ripe before eating and at that time are very sweet, like dates. Unripe fruits contain astringent tannic acid and leave a drying, chalky sensation in the mouth. Ripe persimmon pulp can be used in the same way as pumpkin but with a superior flavor.

Ripe persimmons sometimes develop dark, mottled coloring and feel soft to the touch. When ripe, they drop to the ground. Strong winds will sometimes blow unripe persimmons to the ground as well. If they still feel firm, they are not ripe. If they lie on the ground too long and feel bubbly, they have started to ferment.

Passionfruits

Passionfruits, also called maypops, are berries about the size of an egg that look like miniature watermelons. Juicy pulp is contained within a thick skin that turns yellow and wrinkly when the fruits are ripe. The juice can be extracted and made into a drink that has somewhat of a citrus flavor.

Spicebush

Spicebush is a shrub that is found in the eastern United States from Maine south to Florida and west to Texas in the south and Missouri and Iowa to the north. It grows in the understory along streams and in damp woods and blends in with the greenery for most of the year. In the spring it makes its appearance with yellow flowers that appear before the leaves. After the leaves come out, it remains invisible again until the fruits ripen and turn bright red. This is the time to pick them. They can be dried and used later as a spicy seasoning in desserts.

Sumacs

Sumacs are distinguished by their large, compound leaves and dense clusters of fruits that develop on the branches. Poison sumac has white berries. All species that bear red fruits can be used to make a tart, lemonade-like beverage. The fruits are covered with bright red hairs that are tart with malic acid. They also contain ascorbic acid and tannic acid.

The fruits of sumac remain on the plants well into the winter, offering a source of food for wildlife when other foods are scarce. Several game birds rely on sumac as a winter food source, as do some of the songbirds that winter in the north.

Colorful Cacti

Cacti are succulent, spiny herbs with rounded, cylindrical, or flattened stems that are an adaptation to the hot, dry conditions where they grow. Even though cacti are normally associated with the southwest, several species of prickly pear grow throughout the United States and as far north as Canada in dry, sandy and open, rocky areas. Most cactus species have edible fruits.

Some taste better than others. Depending on the location, some species start ripening in late summer, while others wait until the fall and into the winter to ripen. Cactus with edible fruits include barrel cactus, hedgehog cactus, prickly pear, and saguaro.

Wild Grapes

Grapes were already growing in the United States when the settlers first arrived. There are at least two dozen species that occur in the United States. They are easily recognized by their woody vines that climb high into trees, often at the edges of woods. The forked tendrils and heart-shaped leaves distinguish them from other vines.

Wild grapes are the ancestors of cultivated grapes and are edible, as are the seeds. Young leaves can also be eaten. All are edible, but some are sweeter or larger than others. Most grapes are sweet to eat straight from the vine and make excellent jelly, pies, and wine. Since the fruits contain lots of natural pectin, jelly can be made without purchasing commercial pectin, and honey can be substituted successfully for sugar.

Muscadines

The most popular wild grape in areas where it grows is the muscadine grape. The fruits are larger than other wild grapes, with a thick, tart skin and sweet, juicy pulp. Scuppernong grapes that are cultivated in backyards or grown commercially are a variety of the muscadine and have light-colored skin that is thinner than the muscadine. The scuppernong also grows wild and is sometimes referred to as the blond muscadine.

▲ Muscadine grapes

Muscadines begin ripening in late summer and continue into the fall, hanging in small clusters rather than large bunches like other wild grapes. They can be gathered rather quickly by holding a bucket under the clusters and picking them by the handful, letting them drop into the bucket as they fall. Muscadines can be found from Delaware south to Florida and west to Texas and Oklahoma.

FACT

Wild grapes contain seeds that are crunchy and somewhat woody tasting. Regardless, eat them as well. Grape seeds, as well as the leaves and skin, provide a rich source of resveratrol, an anti-aging compound. Instead of buying grape seed extract, eat the wild grapes, seeds and all.

Other Grapes

There are other grape species that are more tolerant of colder temperatures and grow farther north than the muscadines. Fox grapes can be found as far north as Canada and west to Wisconsin and Michigan. The leaves are wider than other grapes with either shallow lobes or no lobes. Summer grapes have smaller fruits that are less sweet than other wild grapes. Look for the deep lobes on some of the leaves to distinguish this grape from others. Winter grapes also have small berries that get sweeter after a frost.

Oregon Grape—Not a True Grape

In the west is a fruit that looks like a grape, but it is not a grape. Its common name is Oregon grape, and it is in the barberry family. The name is referring to the fruits that grow in clusters and turn dark bluish-purple when they ripen in the fall. The leaves are dark green and shiny, somewhat resembling the leaves of American holly. The fruits are best made into jams or jellies.

Viburnums

Viburnums are in the muskroot family and are large shrubs or small trees with flat-topped clusters of red or blue-black berries that usually hang down when ripe. During the winter months they tend to shrivel up like raisins, giving them the common name "wild raisin." Some are sweet and can be eaten raw as a nibble. Others tend to be bitter. Once the plant has been identified as a viburnum, sample taste the fruit for sweetness. Some are more palatable than others.

Highbush Cranberries

As their name implies, highbush cranberries grow on bushes, not in bogs. They are also not a true cranberry. At first glance, you might think it's a small maple tree. The leaves are opposite and deeply three-lobed above the middle like a maple. But that's where the similarity ends. White flat-topped clusters of flowers appear on the highbush cranberry in late spring or early summer and are of two kinds. The outer flowers are showy with five white petals, but sterile, while in the center are almost inconspicuous fertile flowers.

These will be followed by a round fruit that turns bright red in the early fall as it ripens.

ALERT

There is a similar shrub that is also called highbush cranberry that was introduced from Europe and also has red berries, but they are very bitter. It grows in a similar habitat as the native species and looks similar except the leaves of the European species are smaller and wider. The best way to distinguish between the two is by taste.

Highbush cranberries grow in cooler climates and are common in Canada and in the northern New England states. They are found as far south as New Jersey and west to the Black Hills of South Dakota and do best along streams or along wooded borders.

Arrowwood

Arrowwood is a viburnum that is common in the eastern United States with oval, coarsely toothed leaves. It also has dark, dry fruits that are bitter and inedible, although birds do eat them.

Black Haw

The most popular group among foragers is the black haw group. There are several species of black haws that grow in wooded areas across the eastern United States. They include the northern wild raisins, nannyberries, and black haw. There is also one called possum haw that is edible and grows in the swamps but tends to have a mucky taste. The berries start out red in the late summer and then turn blue-black in the fall when they ripen. They often remain on the plants through the winter, sometimes drying on the bushes. Rehydrating them by soaking them in water may be necessary before using them.

Roots

In the fall, when the above-ground parts of a plant stop growing, the nutrients and food are stored beneath the ground in tubers, bulbs, corms, rhizomes, and roots. The time to gather these parts is while the leaves are dormant, from fall to early spring when they start showing signs of new life.

Groundnuts

Groundnuts are not nuts; rather they are members of the pea family. Their name comes from the nut-like tubers that grow underground. The plant is a bean-like vine with compound leaves that grows as a climbing vine into trees and shrubs. If there are no trees to climb, it tends to sprawl over and around the grasses and other herbaceous plants. The time to locate them is mid-summer when they develop clusters of maroon-colored blossoms. Even though it's a perennial, the leaves die back in the fall. Look for the old vines and follow them to the ground. The tubers are just beneath the surface and grow in long strings. They can be dug in the fall and into the winter, as long as the ground is not frozen. According to Dr. James Duke, groundnut tubers contain three times as much protein as potatoes.

Mallow

Mallow roots have a history of use for food. It was from the marsh mallow that the original marsh mallow cream was made. During the winter, the tops die back but underground the mucilaginous root is still alive and growing. The roots of some species have been used as cooked vegetables, made into a confection, brewed as a tea, or added to soup in the winter.

Nutgrass

Nutgrass is a sedge with many species that grow in wetlands throughout the world. It can be recognized by its umbrella-like flower head with grass-like leaves radiating out from under the flowering rays. Flower stalks have edges, a triangular stem, as is characteristic of many of the sedges. The tubers are somewhat nutty tasting and can be dug any time the ground is not frozen. They can be eaten raw, roasted, or cooked as a vegetable.

Yampa

Yampa is one of eight species and a member of the carrot family that is found throughout the west. Like other members of the carrot family, it has flat-topped clusters of small, white flowers. The narrow leaves look like stems and arise from clusters of edible roots. The time to gather them is in the fall after the plant has gone to seed. The roots should be washed and peeled before using as a cooked vegetable. They can also be dried and ground as a flour.

Seeds and Grains

Seeds are the life-lines of the plants. It is from them that new life will emerge. Even though they may be small, they are often concentrated with nutrition and sometimes flavor. These are best when harvested at midday after the dew has lifted just before they are ready to drop from the plant.

American Lotus

Also referred to as water lily, the American lotus is native to the United States as well as many other parts of the world. Its range includes most of the eastern United States, west to Texas and north to Iowa and Minnesota. The large, circular leaves, which measure up to two feet across, may rise above the surface of the water with the center somewhat depressed where the stem is attached. Water is shed from the surface, and after a rain, droplets of moisture bead up on the plant. In late summer, flowers are replaced by large, cone-shaped, flat-topped receptacles filled with edible seeds that can be harvested in early autumn.

Evening Primrose—the Night Bloomer

Evening primrose can be spotted from the car while driving down the road in mid-summer. Pale yellow flowers with four petals droop from the tops of flowering stalks that can be up to eight feet tall. In the evening after the sun has set, mature buds start swelling and within minutes burst open. The next morning as soon as the sun is up, the flowers droop and then die. The next evening new flowers open and they continue up the stalk.

FACT

Evening primrose seeds are a source of gamma linoleic acid and are grown commercially for the oil that is extracted from them. They also contain tryptophan that is removed from the oil. The oil is used to treat fibromyalgia, arthritis, and other common ailments. Gathering your own seeds and using them as food will give you the synergistic health benefits.

Following the flowers are the four-chambered seed capsules, which are green and then turn brown as they ripen. Look for the plants when they are blooming and then come back about a month later to harvest the seeds. Clip the seed heads off and turn upside down in a paper bag. The little black seeds will drop to the bottom. These can be sifted and used as a seasoning.

Grass Seeds

By the end of summer many grasses have bloomed and are developing seeds. As the leaves begin turning yellow, the seeds are reaching maturity. All grass seeds are edible but are not always easy to process. A husk that may have stiff barbs on the ends that could get stuck in your throat surrounds the seeds. Some release the seeds as they dry while others cling to the chaff. Separating the chaff from the grain is a necessary and sometimes difficult process.

Grasses whose seeds are used for food include:

- Barnyard grass is usually less than three feet tall and found in old pastures, barnyards, and other disturbed areas.
- Crabgrass is a common weed grass in lawns and gardens and grows in clumps, sometimes forming a mat.
- Foxtail barley grows in clumps up to two feet tall and can be found in old pastures, roadsides, and edges of fields.
- Foxtail grass often towers above other grasses in fields and gardens with the seeds forming tight clusters on the tips.
- Wild rice grows in wetland areas reaching up to ten feet tall and can be distinguished from other grasses by the male flowers that hang beneath the female flowers.

Grass seeds can be ground up and used as a flour substitute. In some cases they are better cooked as a gruel. Avoid using any seeds that might be moldy or wilted.

Pickerelweed

Pickerelweed is a wetland emergent plant that grows throughout the eastern United States with large, dark green heart-shaped leaves on long stalks. It blooms most of the summer with bluish-purple flowers that have two lips, each containing three lobes with two yellow spots on the upper middle lobe. Flowers grow in a cluster on a terminal spike that quickly develop into seeds following the flowers. These can be stripped off and eaten raw or added to salads or cooked vegetables.

Pine Seeds

Pine seeds are the more desirable part of the pine that is used for food. Most pine seeds are attached to wings and can be found by removing the woody scales on the pine cone. They vary in size and taste but all are edible once the outer shell has been removed.

Several species of pines in the western part of the United States have seeds that are used for food, including the pinyon pine in the southwest. Pinyon pine seeds are wingless. They are held in the cone by a membrane that is broken by the frost, releasing the seeds to the ground.

In the eastern United States, none of the pine trees produce seeds comparable to those in the west. White pine is larger than most and has been used as food.

Nut Knowledge

Using nuts as a source of food dates back to the American Indians, who taught the settlers how to gather and prepare them for food. Nuts were a mainstay of their diet, especially during the winter months when the food supply became low. To locate nuts, look for the squirrels. Since nuts are one of their most sought-after foods, locating where squirrels are most active may lead you to the nut trees.

Most nutmeats are sweet and high in protein. They are also rich in unsaturated fats which give them a high caloric value, but no cholesterol.

Beech Nuts

Beech trees are tall trees that grow in mature hardwood forests. The tree can be spotted by its smooth, light gray bark. It's the tree that people are tempted to carve their initials into. The nuts are small, only about one-half to three-fourths of an inch long. Usually two triangular nuts are enclosed in a prickly husk, and they mature in early autumn.

Black Walnuts

Black walnuts are found in most of the eastern half of the United States. They are large trees with compound leaves consisting of seven to nineteen toothed leaflets that turn yellow in autumn. The fruit is a thick-shelled nut with ridges enclosed in a green husk that does not split open at maturity.

FACT

Nuts have been referred to as "brain food" due to their serotonin content. According to Dr. James Duke, the black walnut, which looks like a brain, is one of the best sources of serotonin in this country. This is befitting of the "Doctrine of Signatures" which is based on "like cures like." In this case, the brain-shaped nut is one of the best sources of brain food.

Black walnuts begin dropping in the early fall and should be gathered soon after they fall. If they remain on the ground for more than a few days, they become infested with maggots and turn black.

The Cherished Chestnut

American chestnuts, once considered giants in eastern forests, reaching heights up to one hundred feet tall and averaging five feet in diameter, are mostly memories today for those who have lived long enough to remember them. A fungus, imported on nursery stock, spread across their range and within fifty years had almost completely wiped out the population. A few are still surviving in the higher elevations in the Appalachian mountains.

There is another native chestnut, much smaller than the American chestnut, known as the chinkapin. Chinkapins are found in the southeastern United States, from New Jersey south to central Florida, often in mature oak-hickory forests. The outer hull is a spiny bur and contains a shiny, dark brown nut.

Hazelnuts

Hazelnuts are tall shrubs in the birch family that are most easily spotted by the male catkins that form in the fall and linger through the winter until the female flower appears in early spring. These flowers are more difficult to spot. They are very small, red pistillate flowers on the ends of the branches that are pollinated by the wind. The fruits develop slowly over the summer months and are invisible to the untrained eye. The nut is enclosed in a green, leafy husk that starts turning brown as the nut matures.

▲ Hazelnuts enclosed in their leafy husk

Hickories

Hickories are tall trees, usually found in older, mature forests, where the understory is open, allowing for easy walking and visibility. In the fall the compound leaves, made up of five to nine leaflets, depending on the species, turn golden yellow, lighting up the forest floor with a warm glow as they fall to the ground. This is the time to start looking for the nuts, which are most easily found by gently kicking the leaves aside as you walk through the forest.

There are thirteen species of native hickories, which are in the walnut family and can be identified by their large, compound leaves made up of five to nine leaflets. They range through the eastern and southern part of the country. Hickory trees grow slowly, sometimes not producing nuts until they are eighty years old. When the hickory nut matures, the outer husk splits into four separate pieces and the nut drops to the ground. Even though all hickory nuts are edible, some taste better than others.

Oak Nuts

The nut of an oak tree is an acorn, and like all nuts, it has an outer hull. For the acorns, the outer hull is the scaly cap. Acorns contain tannin, which gives the acorn a bitter, drying taste. The tannin can be removed through a leaching process. Once it has been removed, acorns can be used for food.

Oaks can be divided into red oaks and white oaks. White oaks generally have less tannin than red oaks and can be distinguished from them by the leaves that lack the bristle tips on the margins. The fruits usually mature in one season rather than two, as with most red oaks.

Start gathering acorns as soon as they start falling from the tree, otherwise they will become infested with weevils. Look for the tiny hole in the shell that has been pierced by the adult laying her eggs. These can be left for the squirrels. Mature, ripe acorns should have a shiny shell. If it is dull brown or tan in color or feels light, it's probably no good.

CHAPTER 11

Winter Foraging

Wild foods are available year round, even in the winter. This is a good time to explore the outdoors, when the insect population is reduced to a minimum, and the snakes have become mostly inactive. Trees have dropped their leaves, revealing fruits that before were concealed and now partially cover the green tips of woodland herbs on the forest floor. Finding food in the winter requires knowing where to look for edible plants, how to identify them without their leaves, and which parts can be eaten.

Winter Berries

After leaves have dropped from the trees, the berries are exposed. Some of them are red and stand out against the drab grayness of the winter forest. Others are dark in color and blend in with the landscape, often going undetected. Many are edible. White berries are usually toxic and include poison ivy, poison oak, poison sumac, and mistletoe. Most provide a source of food for birds that are winter residents.

Barberries

The common barberry, not to be confused with the Japanese barberry, is a thorny shrub that grows in hedgerows and edges of fields and forests across much of the northern United States. It's most easily spotted in the spring when clusters of yellow flowers develop. The fruits of the common barberry hang in drooping clusters and ripen in mid-autumn and remain on the branches through the winter. The fruits are edible and can be used to make jelly.

Chokeberries

Chokeberries are small trees in the eastern United States. There is a red and a black chokeberry. Red chokeberry is common along waterways and in low, wet areas. The fruits turn bright red when ripe in late fall and remain through the winter. The fruits of the black chokeberry are black. The fruits are rather dry and get caught in the throat when eaten raw, giving them the name chokeberry.

Cranberries

Cranberries are in the heath family and grow in wet, boggy areas from Newfoundland all the way south to North Carolina. The large cranberry is the same species that is cultivated and sold in grocery stores for the winter holidays. It has trailing stems that can extend out two or three feet.
Other cranberries include:

- The small cranberry is similar to the large cranberry but has smaller leaves that are whiter beneath with rolled edges.
- The mountain cranberry grows more upright and has a small cluster of fruits on the stem.

Cranberries ripen in the late fall, usually after a frost and remain on the plants through the winter, needing no storage. The raw fruit is tart and astringent by itself but can be added to salads or made into desserts or juices.

Partridgeberries and Wintergreen

Partridgeberry and wintergreen, though not related, look very similar, and both grow in the shade of the forest floor in eastern and central woodlands, often together. Both plants produce red fruits that remain throughout the winter.

Partridgeberry is a trailing, evergreen vine in the bedstraw family. The woody stems have paired, roundish leaves about one-half inch long and often with white veins. White, tubular flowers with four petals appear early to mid-summer, covering the forest floor with a white carpet.

FACT

Partridgeberries are known as the two-eyed fruit. It takes two flowers to make a fruit.

The flowers are in pairs with the ovaries fusing to form a single, red, berry-like fruit that retains the two blossom scars which are referred to as the two eyes.

Partridgeberries are edible and ripen in the late fall, often remaining on the vine through the winter. Although they are lacking in taste, they make a colorful addition to fruit salads and are a pleasant nibble while hiking in the woods.

Wintergreen leaves lack the white veins, are oval shaped and slightly toothed. They also trail on the forest floor. The berries have a distinct wintergreen taste and can be nibbled or made into tea.

Prickly Pear Cactus

Prickly pear is the most widespread cactus with various species occurring throughout much of the United States. The harvest season extends into the winter in some areas. The fruits, also called tunas, vary considerably in size, color, and flavor. Usually the darker, red ones are riper and juicier.

Tongs or leather gloves are recommended for gathering cactus fruits since their surface is covered with tiny spines. These can be partially removed by rolling the fruits in sand. Use a sharp knife to remove the thin layer of skin from the fruit. The remaining spines lift off with the peel.

Once peeled, prickly pear fruits can be eaten raw. Boiled and strained, the juice can be used to make juice and jelly. Cut the fruits in half, remove the seeds, and dry the fruits to store for future use.

Toyon Berries

The toyon berry is in the rose family and is an evergreen shrub or small tree that is limited in its range to lower elevations from northern to southern California. It blooms in the summer with white flowers followed by the fruit, which looks like little apples and ripens in the winter. The berries can be eaten raw but can also be dried and ground into flour, steeped in hot water for tea, or made into pies or jellies.

Winter Greens

In the winter when the leaves have dropped and the grasses have turned brown, look for green patches. These can be in yards, meadows, edges of forests, or along waterways. They may appear at first as weeds, but once you've learned to identify some of the wild greens, you will realize this is food.

Chickweed

Chickweed is an annual that germinates in the fall and grows through the winter. Look for the patches of green in your lawn to locate it. The young plants have slender, sprawling stems with paired leaves that are small, less than one inch long. The tops can be trimmed off until the spring when it finally blooms and goes to seed. Chickweed can be eaten raw or added to salads and herb spreads.

Corn Salad

Corn salad is a low-growing annual herb in the valerian family that waits until after the weather has cooled off to germinate. It often grows in the shade of other plants along the edges of ditches, canals, or damp areas throughout the winter. The basal leaves are small with smooth margins and rounded tips. As soon as the weather starts to get warm, a flower stalk arises with small, white or pale blue flowers in flat-topped clusters surrounded by leafy bracts. The young leaves can be eaten raw and added to salads.

Crucifers

The crucifers, also known as the cross-bearers, are a worldwide group of plants belonging to the mustard family. During the winter, when most plants are dormant, the young basal leaves are growing. They appear as green patches in gardens, lawns, or forests. The young leaves can be picked throughout the winter in mild climates. In cold climates, they will die back if hit by a hard frost or snow but will re-emerge during warm interludes.

Miner's Lettuce

Miner's lettuce is an annual herb in the purslane family that comes up about mid-winter after the winter rains. Basal leaves are oval or triangular in shape, with long, succulent leaf stems. The flower stalk is distinct, with cup-like upper leaves surrounding the stem. Small, white flowers grow in clusters on stems rising above the cup. Leaves are edible raw or cooked. Miner's lettuce can be found in damp, shady areas from Alaska south to Mexico and from the Rocky Mountains west to the Pacific Ocean.

Lichens

They come in all shapes and colors—red, yellow, green, blue, brown. Some hang from branches in long strands, while others have a leaf-like shape and cling to dead trees or rocks. Others grow on the trunks of trees, while still others just sit on top of the ground. They are very abundant and can be found throughout the world.

Lichens are a combination of a fungus and an alga. Together they act as a single entity and receive minerals from rain water and from the rocks, trees, soil and other surfaces on which they grow. In a survival situation, lichens can be eaten raw, but if possible, should be soaked for several hours. Lichens contain lichenin, a starch that is water soluble and life-sustaining.

Lichens can be grouped into three general categories:

- Crustose lichens form a crust on the trunks of trees or on rocks, appearing as dabs of paint.
- Foliose lichens have a leaflike shape and are attached to rocks, branches, or logs.
- Fruticose lichens are made of thin, irregular strands woven together and hang from the trees or sit on the ground.

Rock Tripe

Rock tripe is a foliose lichen that grows on rocks in open woods from the Arctic south to the northern United States and in the mountains south to Georgia. The top surface is gray to olive-brown while the underside is black. It is attached near the center and expands outward very slowly, forming a circular shape as it grows. After a rain, while it is wet, it feels leathery and smooth. As it dries, it becomes brittle. Rock tripe can be gathered by tearing off pieces, leaving the center attached so it will continue to grow. Rock tripe is edible and can be added to soups.

Reindeer Moss

Reindeer moss is more frequently found in northern states, although it occurs in patches as far south as Virginia. It grows on the ground in large colonies with masses of round, hollow, silvery-gray stems.

Iceland Moss

Iceland moss can found in the far north and forms mats that are leaf-like and are olive-green to brown, sometimes with red blotches. It grows on the bare ground in the arctic and in the mountains and hills of the northern states and along the coast of New England. During dry conditions the stems and branches curl up and then flatten out when it is wet. Iceland moss contains bitter properties and should be parboiled before using.

Roots

Winter is when most of the plant world appears to be sleeping. Leaves drop to the ground, vines hang limply, and grasses turn brown. However, this non-living appearance is just an illusion. The plants are very much alive, and all it takes is a little digging beneath the surface to realize this is true. In colder climates this may not be possible unless there is a warm spell and the ground begins to thaw. But for those who live in mild climates, there is lots of food just beneath the surface.

Many of the edible roots in wetland areas are best when harvested in the winter, a time when the water is cold and the tops are dormant. Scouting out the area in advance and marking the area is helpful for finding the plants once the leaves have died back. Otherwise, finding and identifying the roots may be difficult.

Biennials

Biennials are herbs that form a basal rosette of leaves the first year, often in the late summer after the seeds have been dispersed from the previous year's plants. The roots of some biennials are edible and continue to grow through the winter. These can be dug at any time before the plant sends up the flower stalk the next spring.

Evening Primrose

Evening primrose is a biennial that comes up from seed in late summer or early fall and forms a basal rosette of leaves that are often speckled with red spots and remain green through the winter. A white, starchy taproot develops underground and can be dug anytime through the winter as long as the ground is not frozen. Roots can be used as a cooked vegetable or with other vegetables.

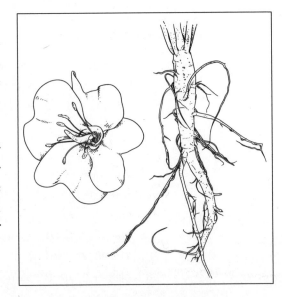

▲ Evening Primrose tap flower and root

Burdock

Burdock is a biennial herb in the sunflower family that was brought to America by Europeans, who got it from Asia, where it has always been valued as food. During its first year, it develops a basal rosette of leaves that are large and fuzzy and continues to grow through the winter. This is the time to dig up the roots.

FACT

Burdock often comes up along the edges of fields or in meadows that get mowed periodically. The plant will continue to grow until it finally gets to bloom and produce seeds. Meanwhile, the root is also growing. And even though it hasn't bloomed, it can still be tough and woody.

Thistles

Thistles are biennials in the sunflower family that develop their leaves in the fall. They are often seen in fields and pastures or along the edges of forests. Look for the large, sharply spined leaves, usually with lobes, and dig it up. The long, skinny taproot is edible and can be cooked as a vegetable.

Cattails

There is some part of the cattail that is available all year, even in the winter. Once the leaves have died back, the starch is stored in the roots. Cattails have horizontal rhizomes that spread out in all directions. The rhizome is a source of starch. Fall and winter is the time to dig for cattails. Near the base of the plant, just beneath the muck, is a small, white sprout that has already started developing for next year's growth. The size varies from one to four inches and has a taste similar to cucumber. Buried even deeper in the mud is the underground, starchy rhizome that can be used as a flour substitute. In a survival situation, you can chew on the root straight from the ground and spit out the fibers.

Chicory

When chicory is young, the basal leaves look very much like a dandelion, with deep lobes on some plants and shallow lobes on others. The difference is when it blooms. You can spot it as you're driving down the road in mid-summer. Beautiful blue flowers line the roadways and fencerows, and add color to the fields. This is chicory, whose root is used to make the commercial beverage sold as a coffee substitute. It sends up a stiff flower stalk that produces blue rays that are square at the top with fringes. By midday the flowers have closed up and will be replaced with new flowers the next day. Chicory is a perennial, so once you have located it you can return in the fall and winter to dig up the white, fleshy taproots.

Duck Potatoes

Also referred to as arrowheads or wapato, duck potatoes are distributed throughout the United States. Not all species have arrowhead-shaped leaves. Some have linear or lance-shaped leaves that emerge from the roots in shallow water. The flower stalk arises from the same root system with no apparent leaves. Flowers with three white petals grow in whorls of three on the stalk and are followed by a greenish ball also in whorls of three. Roots extend out from the base of the plant, sometimes up to two feet, with tubers that develop on the ends. The tubers look and taste very much like potatoes and can be steamed or fried as you would potatoes.

ALERT

Arrow arum also has heart-shaped leaves and is often mistaken for arrowhead. Leaves have three prominent veins arising from the base and flowers that are surrounded by a leaf-like spathe. Dark green to black seeds follow the flowers. The roots contain calcium oxalate crystals that result in intense burning of the mouth and throat if not properly prepared.

Gathering the tubers can be difficult. They mature in late fall or early winter after the leaves have started to die back, and also about the time that temperatures start to drop below freezing. Not only do the roots go deep and out, but the tubers are also embedded tightly in the muck. Breaking them free requires breaking up the muck and can best be done by using a digging fork and stomping around in the muck. Wearing waders is recommended, as they can serve as protection not only from the cold water, but also from reptiles that might be awakened from their winter sleep.

Garlic and Onions—the Smell Will Tell

Garlic and onions are in the lily family, with grass-like leaves that form clumps in the winter. The easiest way to tell the difference between garlic and onion is to dig up the roots. Field garlic has cloves, while the onion has a single bulb. The distinctive characteristic for both species is the strong smell. If it doesn't have the onion or garlic smell, don't eat it. The death camas, also in the lily family, looks similar but doesn't have the onion smell. The roots can be dug all winter as long as the ground isn't frozen.

Jerusalem Artichoke

Jerusalem artichokes are neither an artichoke nor are they from Jerusalem. They are a member of the sunflower family and native to the plains of the central United States. It is now naturalized throughout most of the United States and cultivated in England for its edible tubers that can be gathered all winter as long as the ground isn't frozen. They spread by tubers and will quickly colonize an area when introduced. It produces flower stalks that may reach six to twelve feet high with yellow sunflower-like flowers up to three inches wide in late summer. Wait until it has finished blooming and gone to seed before harvesting the tubers. A frost sometimes improves their flavor.

To harvest, pull the stalk out of the ground first and shake any tubers loose that are still attached. Use a shovel to scoop down about a foot away from the plant, being careful not to cut up the tubers. Tubers are round and knobby looking and can be several inches long. They can be scrubbed and eaten raw or cooked as a vegetable.

Toothwort—the Herb That Bites

Toothwort, pepper-root, and crinkle-root are just some of the names given to this low-lying woodland herb that belongs to the genus Dentaria.

There are several species of Dentaria that are native to North America and grow from Quebec to Florida, extending out to Louisiana and north to Minnesota.

Toothwort appears in the winter, after all the other plants have died back. Coarsely toothed leaves are in pairs and divided into three leaflets with prominent, white veins. The dense roots form a mat and appear as patches of green that stand out on the forest floor. It grows all winter until the days start getting warm, then it sends up a flower stalk and blooms. The flowers are white with four petals, characteristic of the mustard family, to which it belongs. After the plant produces seeds, it dies back and disappears until the next winter.

The root is the part that is edible and has a strong, horseradish-like flavor. It can be grated and used to add a spicy flavor to salads and salad dressings.

Tree Parts

As autumn approaches and leaves drop to the forest floor, tree branches are exposed, as are the twigs, buds, and bark. Even though the leaves are gone, it is still possible to identify trees just by looking at these skeletal features. Some trees have twigs that can be used to make tea, while the buds of others can be eaten, and in a survival situation, the bark of some trees can be used.

Inner Bark

Trees have an outer bark and an inner bark. The outer bark is the layer that protects the tree from injuries. The inner bark carries food that is made in the leaves to the branches, trunk, and roots. The sapwood, or xylem layer, carries sap from the roots to the leaves.

Harvesting the inner bark involves scoring the tree with a knife and cutting off strips, removing the hard, outer bark. The inner bark is then dried and ground into flour as an emergency food. Trees whose bark can be used for food include alder, ash, basswood, beech, birch, elm, fir, maple, pine, poplar, spruce, and willow.

Tree Sap

In late winter or early spring, certain trees are tapped to collect sap. In some places there are maple syrup festivals. Sugar maple is the one most frequently tapped. Cool, frosty nights and warm, sunny days are needed for the sap to rise. Other trees that can be tapped include birches, basswood, and hickory.

Twigs and Buds

The buds on a tree are actually made up of miniature leaves in their embryonic stage. Scales that vary in number and size according to the tree on which they are growing protect most buds. Buds that appear larger on the same tree are usually flower buds. Terminal buds appear at the end of the branch and are usually larger than the axillary buds located in the leaf axils.

The buds are arranged on the branch either in pairs or alternating. Sometimes they are in whorls, with three or more encircling the stem. Below the bud is a leaf scar where the previous year's leaf was attached. On the surface of the leaf scar is a varying number of small dots or lines, called bundle scars, where sap was channeled from the leaf to the stem. These dots and lines present a variety of patterns that can help to identify the tree. Using a hand lens is necessary in some cases when the bundle scars are very small.

Twigs and buds of some trees and shrubs can be nibbled on to relieve thirst, or in some cases, to make tea, including alder, arbor vitae, balsam fir, sassafras, spicebush, and sweet birch. Sassafras flower buds are large and can be added to salads along with the leaf buds, which are smaller.

Evergreen Leaves

Conifers have needle-like leaves and are known by most people because of their use as a Christmas tree. Most conifers are evergreen and the needles of some can be used to make a winter tea that is rich in vitamin C by steeping the needles in hot water. Other conifers that can be used to make a tea include Douglas fir, hemlock, spruce, and larch.

There are also broad-leaved evergreens that keep their leaves all year. Redbay and bay laurel are both members of the laurel family and have leaves that can be used through the winter months as a seasoning. The bay laurel grows on the west coast in California while the redbay is a native shrub on the east coast, growing from Delaware south to Florida and west to Texas.

Bayberry, also called waxmyrtle, is not related to the bays, but it has a scent that is similar to the bay leaf. It is a medium-sized shrub or small tree that grows on the east coast, with leaves that are much smaller than the other bays. It is a member of the waxmyrtle family and has leaves that are aromatic when crushed and can be used in the same way as bay leaves for seasoning. The leaves can also be steeped in hot water to make a stimulating tea.

CHAPTER 12

Growing Wild

The seeds are there. All they need is space and an opportunity to grow. If you have a yard or garden, dedicate a part of it to the wild plants. Scatter seeds of wild plants you would like to see grow there and then sit back and see what happens. Let nature take its course. Watch for the seedlings and then learn to distinguish one from another. Cultivate those that have food and nutritional value and remove those that don't. Growing wild plants is connecting with nature.

Weeds from Seeds

Thousands of tiny seeds are lying dormant in the soil, just waiting for an opportunity to germinate and grow. Sometimes all it takes is disturbing the soil by tilling the ground and removing the existing vegetation as one does when planting a garden. Soil mounds from dirt excavation or banks along ditches are other examples of disturbed areas that provide a breeding ground for young plants to grow.

Annuals

The annuals are one of the first plants to emerge in bare soil that has been disturbed. This includes amaranth, chickweed, corn salad, lambsquarters, miner's lettuce, purslane, and wild mustards. These plants bloom, produce seed, and then die, all within one season. Chickweed and members of the mustard family emerge in the early fall when it has started to cool down and will grow until it gets too cold or a heavy frost sets them back. But as soon as it starts warming up again, they come back. Not all the seeds sprout at one time. When they finally start blooming you know that spring is on the way.

Biennials

Following the annuals and sometimes mixed in with them are the biennials. Seeds of biennials, including evening primrose, thistle, and burdock may germinate from late spring to early fall. They continue to grow through the winter and in the spring of the second year send up a flower stalk, bloom, and go to seed. If mowed or cut down before they get a chance to bloom and produce seed, they may continue to come back until they finally get an opportunity to go to seed.

Perennials

Perennials are those plants that continue to come back year after year. They will come up along with the annuals and biennials, and if not controlled or eliminated, will eventually replace them. Some perennials drop their leaves in the fall and grow new ones in the spring. The tops of others die back completely but the root remains alive underground and sends up new growth the next spring. Some plants are short-lived perennials and may come back for several years and then die back.

Succession

One thing that is certain in nature is that nothing stays the same. The process of going from one plant community to the next is called succession and begins with the bare soil. It also occurs when there is a light gap created in the forest as a result of trees coming down in storms. Timbering a forest opens it up to light, and new growth emerges as well. Forest fires occur naturally as a result of lightning strikes, making it possible for seeds that need the heat from fire to germinate. Marshes or ponds that are filled in, either by nature or people, turn quickly into meadows.

Meadows

An area that has been cleared of vegetation will experience an explosion of seed sprouting that will include not only the herbaceous plants, but also grasses, vines, and tree seedlings. These are plants that like the sun and grow rapidly. Chickweed, wild mustards, oxeye daisy, plantain, wild carrot, and thistle are some of the annuals and biennials that come up in a meadow. At the same time, perennial grasses, seedlings for vines, honeysuckle, wild grapes, and tree seedlings will emerge. The brambles, including blackberries, raspberries, and wild roses will start making their appearance. If not cut back, they will eventually crowd out the low-growing annuals and some of the biennials. Mowing a meadow once or twice a year will keep it in the meadow stage and prevent the next stage of succession from happening.

Pioneer Pines

Pines are often referred to as the pioneers of the forest. While they may not always be the first tree seedlings to move into an area, they are usually the fastest growing. Pines are part of a large family that also includes larches, hemlocks, firs, spruces, and Douglas firs and can be found throughout the United States, often coming up in an area that has experienced a fire. They need a lot of sunlight, can tolerate poor soil, and are often drought resistant. They have long taproots that extend deep into the earth for water.

Pines provide shade, allowing herbaceous plants and hardwoods to grow in their understory. As the needles drop to the ground, they build up a thick layer of pine straw. Pines are not able to reproduce in their own shade, since they need a lot of sunlight to grow. The seeds however, will still germinate and may live for a couple of years before dying out.

The Growing Forest

Maples, sweetgum, and poplars are some of the fast-growing hardwood trees that come up in the understory of the forest. These arrive with the pines that eventually will tower over them. Vines of different species form tangles of dense thickets while reaching for the light, sometimes forming spirals around the trees. Sometimes a tree grows over them, leaving interesting shapes and patterns in the trunk of the tree. A diversity of understory trees and shrubs grow in these forests, including serviceberries, crabapples, hawthorns, and blueberries. These forests are usually dense and difficult to walk through. The slower-growing hardwoods in the understory will eventually replace those hardwood trees that are intolerant of shade.

A Mature Forest

When a forest reaches the stage where it is able to reproduce itself, it is a mature, or climax forest. Oaks are often the dominant trees in these forests and tower over the other plants. They form a thick canopy that prevents sunlight from reaching the forest floor and create an open understory. Fewer, if any vines grow in an older forest. A carpet of moss and ferns sometimes covers the forest floor.

ALERT

A number of the plants that grow on the forest floor are rare or endangered from overharvesting or from loss of habitat. Many of these plants, especially orchids, require the special conditions in which they are growing to live and often don't survive being transplanted. If you need to move them, include as much dirt around them as possible.

The forest floor is where you can look for early spring wildflowers that bloom before the trees have grown their leaves when they can receive the peak sunlight. Brush aside the leaf material and you will see wild ginger, partridgeberry, wintergreen, trilliums, orchids, and other regional wildflowers.

Seed Savvy

Seeds are contained in an assortment of packages in nature. Some are pretty obvious, while others are well hidden. The seeds themselves are distinct from each other. Looking for seeds forces you to look at plants in a different way and to see beyond the green leaves.

Seeds of wild plants are contained in fruits that are dispersed in nature in a number of ways. Some are attached to wings and are carried by the wind. These are the pines, maples, ash, and tulip poplar. Chestnuts and burdock have seeds that are hitchhikers with barbs that allow them to attach themselves to fur or clothing of those passing by. Most nuts simply drop to the ground, making them easy for squirrels and chipmunks to gather. They don't always eat what they gather. Instead, they store the nuts, often by burying them in the ground. However, they don't necessarily remember where they buried them and the next spring, those that were forgotten sprout and new seedlings emerge.

Many seeds are contained within edible fruits and are carried by birds to new areas where they are either dropped or passed through the digestive system. When you start seeing persimmon seeds on the trail in the fall, you know the persimmons are ripe. This is also true with other fruits. Look for the seeds in the scat of raccoons, opossums, and foxes that eat the fruits. The undigested seeds pass through the system, and the next spring, if conditions are right, they will grow into seedlings. Many seeds are dispersed this way.

Saving Seeds

Saving seeds begins in the spring, when the first wild greens bloom and go to seed. Seeds can be collected in areas where you wouldn't normally forage, such as roadsides or polluted waterways. Always be on the lookout for that wild edible that you have wanted to try and watch for it to produce seeds. Collect a few seeds to get the plant started. If you already have plants established, be sure to leave some at harvest time to reseed.

Plants that grow and reproduce in a particular region over several generations adapt to the conditions of that region, resulting in a genetically stronger plant that will maintain its health and produce more heavily under both normal and stressful situations. These plants usually have a natural resistance to insect invasion and require a minimal amount of water and fertilizers. When possible, grow native plants. They have been around for a long time and have proven they can withstand the environmental conditions of that region.

ESSENTIAL

Plastic bags are easier to carry to the field than paper for collecting seeds. However, seeds should be transferred to a paper bag as soon as you get home to dry and to prevent mold from growing. Label the bag, including the name of the plant, where you found it, and the date.

Seed Storage

If you plan to keep your seed only until the next season, or maybe for a couple of years, find the coolest, driest place in your house to store them. Avoid excess heat and humidity if possible. A filing cabinet, cardboard box, or airtight box works well. For long-term storage, seeds can be frozen. Before freezing them, put the seeds in glass jars along with silica gel packets added to reduce the moisture and seal. Wait a couple of days before removing the packets and then reseal and freeze. Even if you don't have silica gel you can still seal the seeds in jars and freeze. They will remain viable for a number of years when stored this way.

Berry seeds can also be dried and stored this way. Mash the berries first, and try to remove as much of the fleshy pulp as you can. For some berries, you will need to wash them, using a strainer with a fine enough mesh to prevent the seeds from slipping through. When the seeds have been cleaned, place them between paper towels to absorb the moisture and change as needed.

Starting Seeds

As winter settles in and most plants have gone to seed, it is time to look at seeds that have been collected through the year and start sorting and categorizing. It is also the time to decide what areas you want to dedicate to wild plants and remove any you don't want. Some plants can be started in pots and left outside through the winter, especially if they're native plants. The advantage in starting seeds in pots is that once you have planted them and labeled them you will know what they are when they come up and can get to know them as they grow through their changes.

American Lotus

The American lotus is widely planted in ponds for its aesthetic value and in some places has established itself as a weed, spreading by underground rhizomes and seeds. Lotus seeds have a hard, impermeable seed coat and can remain viable for a long period of time. Seeds may be propagated by using a file to scarify the pointed tip of the seeds and soaking them in warm water, changing the water twice a day until signs of germination appear, usually two to three weeks. Roots of established plants can also be divided in the spring. Lotus plants do best in full sun and a moist, loamy soil.

The Forager's Garden

If you want to be a successful gardener and don't have a lot of time to spend maintaining it, then grow wild plants. Many of them are disease and insect resistant and require little maintenance. If they are plants that are native to your area, then those are plants that are adapted to the environment and generally require little care or watering. Growing wild vegetables is one way of making sure you always have your favorite edibles nearby.

Plants that grow and reproduce in a particular region over several generations adapt to the conditions of that region, resulting in a genetically stronger plant that will maintain its health and produce more heavily under both normal and stressful situations. Such plants usually have a natural resistance to insect invasion and require a minimal amount of water. The only fertilizer needed is organic compost.

Sowing Wild Seeds

Having a wild vegetable garden isn't limited to those seeds that are in the soil. Prepare a garden bed as you would for any vegetable crop and include organic compost. Then scatter your seeds, including annuals and biennials that provide greens for a wild salad. If you have your own compost pile, any discarded fruits containing seeds are likely to come up also. As seedlings emerge, wait until you can identify them before you remove them.

Berries are easily started from seed. Collect them when mature or in some cases, after they have dried on the plant. If you're not going to plant them right away, they should be dried by spreading them out on a mat or tray. Scatter in disturbed soil in the fall in a partly sunny area. Cover with a layer of dirt and mulch to prevent them from drying out. Even though berry plants will come up in the forest, they will produce more fruits if they get more sunlight.

Woody Plants

Seeds from trees, shrubs, and vines that require more space to grow than the herbs, can be planted in their natural habitat. Germination rates and seed dormancy rates vary with individual seeds. They may not all germinate the first season. It may be several years before germination. Some seeds must first pass through the digestive tract of an animal, some require cold temperatures, while others need heat from a fire to break their dormancy.

Maintenance

Even a wild garden requires a certain amount of maintenance. If unattended, by the second or third year, succession becomes obvious as grasses and tree seedlings crowd out the herbaceous plants. Tend to a wild garden as you would a domesticated garden by removing unwanted grasses and undesirable weeds. Watering is generally not necessary unless it is an unusually dry season.

Creating a Wetland Community

Plants that grow in a wet area like damp soil. Many of these plants form colonies and have large, showy flowers. This includes a number of wetland plants that are also edible. These plants can usually tolerate short drying-out periods as well as occasional flooding. Creating a wetland community involves having a way to hold water. Wetland communities develop around natural and artificial ponds, along rivers and streams, marshes, and swamps.

Water Containers

Artificially created water ponds and streams or simply putting a potted plant in a container that can hold water are means of holding water for growing wetland plants. The water depth should be at least ten inches. The soil in a marsh or swamp is mucky and made up of partially decomposed plant material. If possible, use rich soil from the earth to line the container. You can build up elevation with sticks or branches for plants that like wet soil but don't like being submerged.

Containers come in all shapes and sizes. Small tubs are excellent for starters with one or two plants. Turning a children's play pool into a water pond is an excellent way to recycle the pool when the child no longer needs it. Pond liners can be used in excavated or low areas to collect water. They should be thick enough to prevent the roots of plants from breaking through. You can either put the plants in the pool or pond or you can put the potted plant directly into the pool. The plants may still need additional watering when there is a long, dry period.

Wetland Plants to Grow

Tubers and rhizomes of plants such as arrowheads, groundnuts, and cattails can fill a small pond in a short period of time. All you need to start is a few tubers and several inches of soil. Some of these tubers, such as arrowhead, are generally ready to be harvested in the winter when the water is cold and the tops are dormant, making them difficult to find in nature and even more difficult to dig. In a small pond, the roots form a mat and can be lifted by hand and the tubers removed from underneath. And there's no doubt about what it is, whereas in nature there are a multitude of other roots and tubers to distinguish it from.

Cranberries grow in wet, boggy areas, often with sphagnum moss. They can be established by building up a mound in a pool or pond so the plant is above the standing water. If you have a source for sphagnum, use that as a mulch around the plant. While they may survive in the shade, you will have a better chance of getting fruit if it gets some direct sunlight.

Forest Gardening

The word "gardening" brings to mind neat rows of vegetables with either full or partial exposure to the sun. But there is another approach one can take, and that is forest gardening. A forest garden is simply a garden modeled after a forest, complete with layers that include the canopy, understory, shrubs, herbaceous plants, and a ground cover on the forest floor. Woody vines grow up through the layers to the treetops. As a result, there is usually a diversity of plants that offer a variety of flowers for pollinating insects, food, and sometimes medicine. Forest gardening provides native plants with a habitat to grow in and requires little maintenance.

Growing Nut Trees

Nut trees often form the canopy of the forest. Fall is the time for planting nuts if you are interested in growing your own trees. It is best to choose healthy, well-formed nuts from a tree that is native to your area. Starting a tree from seed can be done quite easily. After the nuts fall and lie on the ground partially covered with moist leaves, they will start to sprout on their own in a few weeks. Nuts can sometimes be sprouted by placing them in a shallow dish of water wrapped in a moistened paper towel. Some nuts, including acorns, when gathered in a plastic bag and left in the refrigerator for too long will also sprout. They can also be started by burying them in a pot of dirt and putting them outside. Water them like you would any plant you're starting from seed. These can also be planted directly into the soil where you want them to grow. Since they naturally drop from the trees in the fall, this is a good time to plant them.

Once the nut has sprouted and the root is two to three inches long, transfer the nut to a container deep enough for the root and place outdoors in a partially shaded location and keep moist.

When the seedling is several inches tall it is ready to be transferred to its permanent home, either in the spring or fall, when conditions are favorable for growth. Water regularly until it has adjusted to its new environment.

The time it takes before nuts are produced varies with the different trees or shrubs. Oak nut production can begin in three to five years, whereas hickory trees may take up to forty years to produce nuts. Once established, they will provide you with a source of food and nutrition for many years to come.

Cultivating Woodland Shrubs

If you have a wooded area, chances are the shrubs are already there, either in a seedling stage or hidden among other plants. Find out what shrubs grow in your area and which ones provide food. Many are berry producers and can be introduced if they're not present. Native nurseries are sources for getting wild plants to cultivate.

QUESTION

Can you start trees or shrubs by digging up sprouts from the parent plant?
It depends on which plant it is. Cuttings can successfully be taken from some plants, while others, even though it may appear that you have plenty of roots, just don't survive. The survival rate is higher if you are able to get the primary root.

The Forest Floor

The forest floor is where the shade lovers live. This includes a lot of the early blooming wildflowers, mosses, and ferns. A woodland wildflower garden is fun and easy to grow. All it needs is shade, moisture, and space. It requires more maintenance than the other layers, otherwise succession will occur as taller, more aggressive plants move in.

CHAPTER 13

Into the Forager's Kitchen

The kitchen is where magic happens. It is a chemical laboratory, where you mix, measure, combine ingredients, and hopefully, come up with a dish that exceeds all expectations. A forager's kitchen doesn't look too different from a regular kitchen except for the presence of unusual or interesting looking gadgets. Plants brought in from the field often require special treatment to make them palatable, and very often that treatment requires tools that a regular kitchen wouldn't have. It's through experience that you will develop your kitchen according to your needs.

Gadgets and Utensils

Every forager has their favorite cooking gadgets and utensils. Finding tools that can help you process plants in an energy-efficient way will make it easier to include them in your diet on a regular basis. Often you will find that you already have the tools you need. Preparing wild foods often involves being creative and adapting to the situation. However, there are certain basics that everyone should have.

Strainers and Juicers

Strainers are necessary and should be included in any kitchen. They come in an assortment of sizes and have lots of uses. Extracting juice from fruits requires separating the pulp from the seeds. One way this can be done is to press the fruit through the strainer using a spoon. You can also line the strainer with a coffee filter and pour tea through it to remove plant particles. Colanders work for large items, especially when rinsing or draining liquids. Salad spinners are wonderful tools for spinning off moisture for herbs and salad greens. Reusable, cotton cloth bags can also be used as a strainer and are especially useful when making wild teas.

A foley food mill is a step above a strainer. Fruit is strained by turning a handle attached to a press. It pushes the pulp through the strainer while holding back the seeds.

ALERT

Avoid using a commercial juicer or blender when juicing fruits such as grapes, cherries, or other fruits with a hard seed. The seed will also be crushed, adding a woody taste in some instances. Cherries, apples, and plums contain cyanide in the seeds and should not be eaten.

Steam juicers are more expensive than strainers or food mills but work great to extract juice from fruit, especially if you're working with a large quantity of fruit. The juice that is extracted is concentrated, with no added liquid, retaining more vitamins and nutrients.

Grinders and Nut Pickers

Grinding tools are needed for nuts, seeds, and other dried plant parts to be turned into flour. Stones work well for this purpose. But not just any stone. It needs to fit comfortably in the palm of your hand. A larger stone is needed as a base to pound onto. If no stones are available, a hammer will do. A nut picker is handy for removing nuts from their shells. If you're not able to find one commercially, try using a nail or other object with a sharp, pointed tip. You can also buy electric coffee or seed grinders that are quicker and easier if you're going to be doing a lot of grinding. A blender or food processor will work for grinding or chopping some plants.

Pots and Pans

Every kitchen needs at least one pot to cook in and one pan for baking. More is better. They come in all sizes. Slow cookers are good for soups and stews. Skillets are handy for stir-fries and fritters. These can be either iron skillets or electric for convenience. Pots of different sizes for boiling water and steaming vegetables are also useful.

Teakettles for boiling water and teapots for steeping herbs for wild tea are a must. Any pan that can hold water and be placed on the burner can serve as a teakettle. There are also electric teakettles as well as coffee pots that can serve as a teapot. Coffee pots are good for herbs that need to simmer on a low temperature or to keep tea hot until you're ready to serve it.

Using steam to cook vegetables rather than boiling them preserves more of the flavor and nutrients. This can be done with a steam cooker that has two pots. The bottom is like a saucepan that holds the water. The other pot holds the food. It sits on the bottom pot and acts as a strainer with holes in the bottom. As the water heats, steam rises through the openings and cooks the food. The water that is used for steaming vegetables can then be used as a broth or as the liquid that is needed for a recipe.

Storage and Serving Containers

If you return from the field with a good yield you will need containers to store the excess. Before storing them, they still need some preparation. If you're going to store them in the pantry, they must be cleaned and dried first. Dried herbs can be stored in glass jars. Freezing is another way of storing plant foods. Freezer bags or plastic bowls can be used for this. An assortment of jars of different sizes and freezer bags should always be available.

Once you have prepared your dish you will need something to serve it on. Trays from natural materials such as wooden plates or bowls provide an attractive display. Otherwise, any plate or bowl works.

Trays also can be used as drying racks. Line the bottoms with newspapers or paper towels to absorb moisture and place in a well-ventilated area. Especially in humid areas, a dehydrator is handy for drying plants that otherwise would take a long time or not dry at all.

Stocking the Pantry

Just because you're cooking with wild plants doesn't mean that all the ingredients have to be wild. However, the pantry can serve as the storage area for herbs and seasonings that you have gathered and dried as well as commercial items.

Sweeteners

If you like to make desserts you will need sweeteners. It doesn't necessarily have to be white sugar. There is also raw sugar, honey, agave nectar, syrup, and molasses to choose from at the grocery store. Wild fruit preserves and syrups can also be used as a sweetener. Some fruits are sweeter than others and can be dried and ground for use as a sweetener. Persimmons are one of these fruits. When dried as fruit leather, the taste is very similar to dates. Grind it up and use as a sugar substitute.

ALERT

If you are having a problem in your kitchen or pantry with Indian meal moths, one solution that was mentioned in a local newspaper was to use the leaves of the bay tree. You can also experiment with using the leaves of bayberry or redbay if you live near the east coast, or other fragrant herbs in your area.

Flours

Flours are good to have for use as thickeners and flavors, plus they add bulk to other ingredients. Flour or meal can be obtained from a number of wild plants and either used alone or with regular flour as an extender, depending on the use. Pollen collected from cattails and pines is soft and adds fluff to pancake mix or other flour. Nuts and seeds can be ground up and used to add a nutty flavor to breads and cakes. The seeds of lambs-quarters, amaranth, wild buckwheat, dock, and most grasses can be dried, ground up, and stored in the pantry or frozen to supplement other types of flour.

Oils and Vinegars

Olive oil is good for general cooking and can be used in stir-fries, salad dressings, and other vegetable dishes. There are also a number of other oils, including peanut, sunflower seed, coconut, and sesame seed oil that add flavor. Butter can be used instead of oil in most recipes. Experiment with the different flavors in creating your recipes and see what works for you.

Nuts and Seeds

Nuts and seeds add flavor to lots of dishes. You should have a combination of wild and cultivated nuts and seeds that include evening primrose seeds, mustard seeds, sunflower seeds, pumpkin seeds, chia seeds, and hemp seeds. Nuts are good for about a year in their shell before becoming rancid. Otherwise they should be frozen until ready to use. Seeds, when dry, can be stored in glass jars in the pantry.

Wild Substitutes

Finding recipes with wild foods is usually pretty rare unless you have a wild foods cookbook on your bookshelf. However, most wild plants have a cultivated counterpart. When wondering how to use a plant, taste it first and see what it reminds you of. If the taste is unlike anything you've ever known, then look at the texture to determine what it resembles. Remember, the kitchen is a laboratory and you're experimenting. Take notes.

Milk Substitutes

Fruit beverages, juices, or teas can be used as a substitute for milk in many foods. In some cases you may need to use less than the recipe calls for. Nuts are a great source of milk, especially hickory nuts. The water that is strained from the nuts after pounding and soaking them is rich and creamy and makes a wonderful addition to any recipe calling for milk.

Pectin Sources

There are a number of fruits that are high in pectin, especially when unripe. This includes wild cherries, grapes, black gums, and especially crabapples. What crabapples lack in sweetness, they make up for in pectin, especially in the skin. Because of their high pectin content, they can be used as a source of pectin when making jams or jellies from fruits that are low or lacking in pectin. Concentrated liquid pectin can also be made and stored for later use.

Horseradish Substitutes

Toothwort, also referred to by its genus name, dentaria, is a member of the mustard family and has a root that resembles horseradish in flavor. Winter is the time to look for toothwort. This is when the low-lying herb makes its appearance on the forest floor. Three coarsely toothed leaflets with prominent, white veins help to locate it.

Other members of the mustard family that resemble horseradish in flavor include bittercress and peppergrass. Both are annuals that come up in the fall, grow through the winter, and produce small, white flowers in the early spring. The leaves, flowers, and flowerbuds can be used to add a horseradish-like flavor to salads and dressings.

Seasonings

Redbay and bay laurel are both members of the laurel family and have leaves that, when crushed, have a smell that is similar to the bay leaf and can be used as a substitute for bay leaves in cooking. Several species of bayberry in the genus Myrica have leaves with a fragrant scent similar to the bay leaf and can be used as well. Flowers and young leaves of sassafras are spicy tasting and can be added to rice, soups, and vegetable dishes.

Cultivated onions and garlic can be substituted with field garlic, wild onions, or ramps in those areas where it grows.

Spicebush—a Native Allspice

Spicebush berries turn bright red when they are ripe, turning dark in color as they dry. They can be dried by using a dehydrator or by spreading them out on a mat to air-dry. Once they are thoroughly dried, they can be ground up, using either a mortar and pestle as the Indians did, or put in a coffee grinder or blender. Some prefer to remove the hard seed in the center while others grind it up with the berry. The ground-up berries should be stored in tightly covered glass jars. Dried, ground-up berries can be used as a substitute for allspice. Because they have such a strong flavor, the amount used should be reduced to about half of the commercial brand.

Salt Plants

Without salt, some foods taste bland no matter what seasonings you add. If you live near a salt marsh on the east coast, from eastern New Brunswick and Nova Scotia south along the coast to Georgia, chances are you have plants that contain salt in their stems or leaves. Plants that live in a salty environment have to adapt by either excreting the salt or storing it in their stems.

Saltwort

Saltwort, also referred to by its genus name, Salicornia, grows on the edges of salt marshes and tidal creeks along the east coast from Eastern New Brunswick and Nova Scotia south along the coast to Georgia. There are also several species on the west coast as well as around saline and alkaline lakes on the Great Plains, in the Rockies, and the Great Basin. They are one of the first plants to colonize on bare tidal flats.

The name "Salicornia" comes from the word "sal," which means salt, and "cornus," meaning horn, from the stems on the plant that look like little horns. Common names vary from saltwort to glasswort, pickleweed, and marsh samphire. Members of the goosefoot family, they are characterized by succulent stems with leaves that are reduced to blunt scales, an adaptation to conserve water and protect themselves from dehydration. Lashed by salt winds and in some cases, immersed by incoming tides, they remain in place by spreading their roots underground to form a mat that prevents them from being uprooted by tidal waters. Minute green flowers are inconspicuous and borne in the hollows of the upper joints, followed by small seeds.

Salicornia is not the only plant from which salt can be obtained. Orach, another member of the goosefoot family, also grows in salt marshes and has a salty taste as well. The leaves are fleshy and shaped like an arrow. Small clusters of flowers grow in the leaf axils. The young leaves and tips can be used to add a salty flavor to food.

Saltmarsh cordgrass has adapted to a salty environment by excreting excess salt from its leaves. Try rubbing the leaf blade between two fingers and then lick your fingers. This process can also be used to test the saltiness of the water. If the water is mildly salty, you may not get much salt at all. At other times you may actually be able to collect salt crystals that can be used for salt. Cordgrasses often grow in the salt marsh with Salicornia.

From the Field to the Table

Bringing wild plants home for dinner involves more than just picking them. For some plants there is a process involved before they're ready to eat. Skill and patience are required, as some of the work can be tedious. The rewards come when you sit down to eat.

Making Tea

Herbs used to make teas can usually be used fresh from the field or dried for later use. Teas from flowers and leaves are usually steeped in hot water to make an infusion. To drink as a beverage, they only need to steep for a few minutes. For medicinal benefits they should steep for ten to twenty minutes. A decoction is made of roots, bark, and twigs by first bringing the water to a boil and then simmering them for ten to twenty minutes.

Plants can also be dried and used to make tea. Berries should be crushed before steeping and then strained through a filter. Generally a teaspoon of dried herbs is sufficient for a cup of tea. While steeping, they should be covered so the essence doesn't escape in the steam.

Greens and Vegetables

Many of the wild greens are good just as they are, straight from the field into the salad bowl. Those that are too bitter for your taste can be mellowed by cooking. Certain ones must be cooked before eating to remove toxins that otherwise might make you sick. Still others need additional peeling or trimming away of parts that are inedible.

Cactus Pads

Cactus pads are edible and can be made into delicious recipes, but they are armed and dangerous. They have sharp spines surrounded by tufts of bristly hairs that pierce the skin and are difficult to see. They must be removed before you can eat them. Use young cactus pads while they are tender. Tongs are recommended for removing them. Roll in the sand or grass first to remove as many spines as you can. It helps to steam or boil them to soften the remaining spines. Using a sharp knife, remove the skins and thorns. Cut off the outer edges and any rubbery tips, and then scrape or cut out any remaining spines. Rinse under running water and inspect carefully under good lighting for any additional spines. You don't want these to end up in your tongue or throat later. Otherwise, they're ready to be sliced or diced for whatever recipe you are using.

Poke

Young poke leaves and stalks are both edible but should never be eaten raw. You will throw up. The stalks are somewhat like asparagus when prepared without the leaves. Begin with the lower leaves and peel down the stalk, removing the layer of skin while you're at it. You can keep the young leaves at the top and either add to the stalks or keep separately and prepare as a cooked green. Prepare by covering the young leaves and stalks with cold water. Bring just to the point of boiling and strain. Repeat the process a second time. Poke is now ready to use in salads, cooked as vegetables, or as an asparagus substitute.

Fruits

Serviceberries, blueberries, blackberries, and raspberries are among the fruits that need no preparation to eat or use in recipes. Others, like cherries and plums have seeds in the center that must be separated before using. A simple way to do this when in the field is to put fruits like wild cherry or black gum berries in a zip-top bag, add a little water, zip the bag, and then mash the fruits between the palms of your hands. You can make your fruit juice while hiking and then strain it to remove the seeds.

A foley food mill is a must for processing certain fruits. Persimmons have large, flat seeds that are separated from the pulp by pressing the raw fruits through the food mill. Wild cherries, black gums, mayapples, and passion fruits are among those that have seeds that cling to the pulp and separate more easily when heated. Add just enough water to cover the fruits. Bring to a gentle boil for ten to fifteen minutes to get the juices flowing and then press through the food mill.

Wild grapes get special attention, depending on how you're going to use them. If you want to make a pie or jam, you will want to keep the hulls but get rid of the seeds. You can do this by squeezing the pulp out the stem end and separating it from the hulls. Heat the pulp ten or fifteen minutes until the juices are flowing and then strain through the foley food mill. Take the juice that you get and put it back in with the hulls and mix it up well. It is now ready for use.

On the higher end is the steam juicer, which can be a bit expensive. Juice is extracted from the fruits using steam. This comes in handy for small fruits like crabapples or rose hips that can be tedious to process otherwise.

Nuts

Nuts have an outer hull that contains the nut, which is a hard shell, inside which is the nutmeat. For some nuts, including the hickories and chestnuts, the outer hull splits open and the nut drops to the ground. When black walnuts mature they drop to the ground with the outer hull intact.

Once the black walnut hull has been removed, rinse the nuts in a bucket of water, removing any that float, and spread in a single layer on a mat or well-ventilated area to dry. Drying times will vary and may take from a week to a month, depending on the conditions. Once dry, black walnuts can be stored in a cool, dry place until ready to use.

Nuts have a shell that must be cracked to get to the nutmeat inside. Some are harder than others. Hickory nuts and black walnuts have a thick shell that can only be cracked with a rock or hammer. Cracking the nuts requires skill that comes with practice. Find a rock that fits in the palm of your hand. Use another flat stone to place the nut on. Then give it a sharp blow. When the right spot is hit, the shell will crack open, revealing the chambers of nutmeat inside. Nut pickers can then be used to pick out the nutmeat.

ESSENTIAL

The green hulls surrounding the black walnut should be removed right away to prevent becoming infested with maggots. Removing them without getting stained can be tricky. The easiest way is to place the walnuts in the driveway behind the wheels of your car and back out over them. Wearing gloves, break away the outer hulls and remove the nut.

Nuts can also be crushed and boiled. The nutmeat floats to the top, which can be skimmed off, and the heavier shells sink to the bottom. The strained liquid, or nut milk, can be used as a drink or added to bread, cookies, or cakes, adding a nutty flavor.

All acorns are edible. However, they also contain tannic acid that makes them taste very bitter. The tannin can be removed by soaking the acorns in water. Once acorns have been gathered, either shell them immediately or freeze them inside the shell until you're ready to use them. Otherwise they may start sprouting or get moldy.

QUESTION

Do all acorns have to be leached before you can eat them?
Live oaks that grow on the east coast from Virginia south to Florida and west to Texas produce acorns that are low in tannin and can be eaten raw. When mature they turn shiny brown and drop from the tree. Immature, green acorns sometimes drop from the trees early but taste bitter.

Once the acorns have been shelled, put them in the blender and chop them up. You can use a cloth bag to put the ground up acorn meal into and then put into a pot of water. When the water turns dark, pour it off and add more. Repeat the process until the water remains clear. You can then spread the acorn meal on a tray and dry in a dehydrator or on a baking dish in the oven on a low temperature, turning occasionally.

Roots

Most roots can be scrubbed and sliced and they're ready to use. However, some require additional preparation for specific uses, whether it's going to be for flour, beverages, or some other use.

Cattails

Cattail roots can be harvested year-round. They have underground rhizomes that contain starch and can be used as a flour substitute. The roots first have to be covered with water, then pounded and broken up to break the starch free that settles to the bottom. After the water has cleared, strain the water off, leaving the starch at the bottom. This starch can be used as is or dried and stored for later use. The best time for the rhizome is during the winter, when the above-ground parts have died back and the starch is stored in the roots.

Chicory and Dandelions

Chicory and dandelion roots are edible and can be chopped and added to soups with no additional preparation. However, if you plan to use them as a beverage or noncaffeinated coffee substitute, they have to be roasted. Scrape off as much of the tough outer skin and rootlets as possible. Place roots on a cookie sheet and dry in the oven at 200°F until brown and brittle, about two hours. Once they are completely dry, put them in the blender or coffee grinder to pulverize them.

Seeds

Seeds should be gathered in paper bags for drying. Turning the plants upside down in the bag allows the seeds to drop to the bottom. Thrashing the bag against a board helps to release the seeds. Sometimes the seeds can be stripped from the plants. Wild beans, when dry, split open and the beans pop out.

Regardless of how the seeds are gathered, there is usually plant debris mixed in with them that you don't want to include in your recipe. A strainer with holes large enough for the seeds to pass through but small enough to keep the debris out works for small seeds like evening primrose. Screens can be used as strainers and come in different mesh sizes for larger seeds like beans. Pick a windy day and go outside with your seeds and transfer them from one container to another, letting the wind carry away the chaff and outer hulls. Seeds that are round can be placed on stiff paper and held up at an angle where they will roll down, leaving the husks behind.

FACT

The seeds of the American lotus, when mature, are about the size of a small acorn and have a hard, thick shell when ripe that must be parched first to loosen the inner kernel. The seeds can then be cracked, the shell removed, and either roasted, boiled, or dried and ground into flour.

Wild Food Nutrition

Wild foods are more than just empty calories. They are concentrated with vitamins and nutrients as well as compounds that can help relieve certain ailments. If you know which plants contain certain nutrients that you need, you can harvest those plants and eat your way to good health.

Eat the Weeds

Cancer-fighting antioxidants are found in a number of wild greens. Antioxidants are a group of vitamins, minerals, and enzymes that are believed to help slow the aging process. Purslane is one that, in addition to vitamin C and beta-carotene, also is rich in omega-3 fatty acids and may help lower cholesterol.

Evening primrose seeds contain gamma linoleic acid, which has been reported to have a number of health benefits. It also contains tryptophan, which is an amino acid that is necessary for the production of niacin and is used by the brain to produce serotonin.

FACT

Eating raw is becoming popular among some people who are trying to improve their health or recover from a serious illness. Being on a raw foods diet involves eating foods that haven't been cooked, grilled, or steamed, since cooking at high temperatures may kill certain enzymes necessary to digest food. Raw foods may be dehydrated at a temperature no more than 110°F. They may also be frozen or fermented.

Following is a list of other plants and the nutrients they contain:

- Violets are a source of vitamin C and rutin, a compound that strengthens blood vessels.
- Grape seeds, leaves, and Japanese knotweed are sources of resveratrol, an anti-inflammatory compound.
- Dandelions, stinging nettles, chickweed, and other greens are good sources of calcium and iron.
- Horse balm and bee balm contain thymol, a natural antiseptic.
- Purslane, burdock, and chickweed are sources for magnesium, which is vital to enzyme activity and assists in calcium and potassium uptake.
- Red clover and groundnuts provide genistein, an isoflavone that possibly prevents the spread of breast cancer.
- Bittercress, burdock, dandelion, and lambsquarters contain phosphorous, essential for growth and maintenance of all body tissues.
- Wild greens including pokeweed, watercress, and purslane, as well as rose hips, pine needles, sumac, and false solomon's seal are sources for vitamin C.

Nuts

Hickory nuts are very nutritious. One pound of shelled hickory nuts has over three thousand calories and more than three hundred grams of fat according to the USDA *Handbook of the Nutritional Contents of Foods*. The fat includes essential fatty acids shown to prevent heart disease. They also provide protein, carbohydrates, iron, phosphorous, and trace minerals. Hickory nuts and black walnuts are a source of serotonin, a mood elevator.

CHAPTER 14

Storing Wild Plants

Wild food is seasonal. The harvest season arrives when the crop is ready. If it's a productive year, there may be more than can be eaten before it goes bad. You can stretch the season through different methods of storing the plants, making them available for use even when they're out of season. Otherwise, you won't have another opportunity until next year. There are a number of methods that you can use to store wild foods, and the one you use will depend on what you're storing and the climate where you live.

Dehydration

The easiest and oldest method of preserving and storing plants is to dry them. Drying them shrinks the volume, so they take up less space and have a shelf life of at least one year, until the next harvest season comes around. Herbs, nuts, berries, and seeds can all be dried and stored until ready to use. To reuse, depending on the part and use, you can rehydrate them by letting them steep in hot water at least ten to fifteen minutes, for some things longer.

Air Drying

Air drying is the easiest and most convenient way to dry your plant materials. All you need is space and air circulation. You can easily turn a corner of your kitchen or porch into a drying area by opening windows, getting a fan, and either hanging the plants or spreading them on a drying rack.

Hanging Herbs

Many herbs can be tied and hung in bundles in a room with good circulation to dry. Plants with long stems and small leaves work well for this. Plants collected for seeds can be dried this way as well, allowing the seeds to drop to the bottom of a paper bag. Peppergrass, evening primrose seeds, lambsquarters, amaranth, mints, and goldenrods are examples of plants to air dry. Cut them near the base, remove any yellow or insect-eaten leaves, tie at the base in small bunches with string or a rubber band, and hang them from rafters if available. Otherwise, find a corner with good circulation and use clothesline string or a decorative stick to hang them from. Make sure they are far enough apart not to touch. This will give an herbal smell to your room.

Drying Racks

Screens make good drying racks. Just make sure they're washed and sterilized and elevated enough so air can circulate underneath. These are handy to have for when you come in from the field and you don't have time to process what you have gathered. You can spread your plants on the rack and leave them. Just remember to turn them periodically. This works well for larger plant material such as roots or twigs. It also works for flowers such as oxeye daisy and mints. Large, juicy fruits should be cut in half to prevent getting moldy on the inside and to dry quicker. Placing racks on a table under a ceiling fan with open windows works really well.

Baskets

Baskets made from natural materials are convenient containers and provide storage for lots of items. Nuts stored in hanging baskets from the rafters will last at least through the winter. However, they are rich in oils and will go rancid quickly in hot, humid climates. Other plants that dry well in baskets include sumac clusters, wild beans, and the seeds of plants that are large enough not to fall through the cracks in the basket. Some roots can be stored temporarily in baskets.

Solar Drying

Using the sun to dry foods is the most natural and nutritional way to preserve them. Solar dryers are easy to build and give you an opportunity to store what you have gathered until you need it. A large, open-top cardboard box can be turned into a solar dryer with just a few modifications, or you can build one with plywood. Pizza boxes have even been used for small items. Maintaining a temperature of 110° and providing air circulation are the primary factors to consider.

Dehydrators

Dehydrators are sold commercially that can greatly speed up the drying process, especially in a humid environment. The more efficient ones have a fan and a thermostat, which is helpful for those who want to retain enzymes that otherwise would be destroyed by heat. An oven turned down to its lowest setting can be used to dry some things. A solar oven can also be used as a dehydrator.

Wild greens dry well in a dehydrator. The quick drying process enables them to retain their green color as well as nutrients. Once they are dry, you can powder them, either in a coffee grinder or between the palms of your hands, vacuum seal or put in a glass jar, label, and date.

Berries dry well but need to be turned periodically so they will dry evenly. Drying elderberries on trays in the sun helps reduce their strong flavor. You can make fruit leather by spreading puréed fruits on a drying sheet, either in a dehydrator or outdoors in partial sunlight. When drying fruits outdoors, it might be helpful to cover them with cheesecloth to prevent flies and other insects from finding them, depending on where you live.

ESSENTIAL

Vacuum sealing your food is essential if you want to store it for longer periods of time. A vacuum sealer is used for this purpose. It consists of a vacuum machine and vacuum seal bags, which usually come with the machine. It works by sucking out all the air from the bag and then using heat to seal it.

Root Storage

Harvesting and storing edible roots for winter use is a custom that has been practiced for many years. Root storage can be done using several methods, depending on where you live and how cold your winters are.

In the Ground

Some roots, like Jerusalem artichokes, evening primrose, and burdock can be stored by simply leaving them in the ground and digging them up when needed. The disadvantage with this method is that when you're ready to use them the ground may be frozen, weather may not be cooperating, or you may not want to take the time to go out and dig them. Another problem in areas with warmer temperatures is that underground rodents and beetle larvae may feed on them before you get to them. Or if there is a really warm spell, some roots, like Jerusalem artichokes, will start to sprout.

Cold Storage

Cold storage involves keeping roots alive, but dormant. In areas with cold winters where the ground remains frozen for periods of time, having roots in storage is convenient. When you dig them up, be sure to keep some soil around them. You want to keep them cool enough so they don't grow but warm enough so they don't freeze. If they dry out, they will die also. A root cellar or basement can be used for some roots. If you have an out-building or other storage facility with good ventilation, it can be turned into a drying room as well. A wooden or cardboard box can be used for small quantities or they can be layered in mounds or pits between sand or straw. Old newspapers can also be used for layering. You may want to try several methods in the beginning to see what's going to work best for you and the area where you live.

Freezing

Freezing wild foods is one way to store them and requires little time and preparation. Many plants can be brought in from the field, washed, placed in freezer containers, and frozen with no extra preparation. Freezing them stops the growth of organisms that would spoil the food. Freezer containers or packaging materials should be waterproof and easy to seal in order to protect the plants from drying out, which can result in freezer burn.

Freezing Fruits

Fruits generally do well frozen, retaining much of their nutritional value, flavor, texture, and color. This includes blueberries, blackberries, elder-berries, persimmons, and pawpaws. Cherries, grapes, and black gums are among those fruits that have seeds inside. It's a good practice to remove these seeds before freezing them to make sure they don't accidentally end up in a recipe.

Freezing Greens and Vegetables

Wild greens and vegetables can be frozen, but not all of them. Those with a high water content, like some of the salad greens, don't do as well as those with less water. Greens and vegetables should be blanched first by immersing them in hot water or steam and then cooling them. The length of time is determined by the size and texture. Cooking kills the enzymes that would cause them to lose their flavor, color, and texture.

Vegetables that have been cooked and are left over can be frozen for future uses. This includes soups, stir-fries, and casseroles. Put in freezer containers or jars to freeze. Always leave room at the top for expansion from the moisture in the food.

FACT

Grape leaves can be frozen in advance to use through the year for stuffing. To prepare for freezing, rinse each leaf and lay it in a large pot, stacking the leaves on top of each other. Cover with water and sprinkle with salt. Cook on low heat for 20 to 30 minutes, until the leaves turn dark green. Drain and put in a freezer bag or container, keeping flat. Let cool before freezing.

Freezing Nuts and Seeds

Freezing nuts and seeds extends their shelf life longer than drying. Put the entire nut in its shell in a freezer bag, label and date it, and it's ready. No thawing is necessary when you're ready to use them. They can be used straight from the freezer. If space is a factor, you will want to shell them first.

Canning

Canning is the process whereby sterilized food is stored in sterilized jars that are sealed. The processing times and method used will depend on the types of foods and their acidity level. Always use good-quality canning jars, regardless of the process used, as well as new canning lids and tongs for lifting hot jars. Sterilize the lids by pouring boiling water over them and letting them soak for at least ten minutes before using.

Open Kettle Method

The easiest method is the open kettle method. Hot, fully cooked food is poured into hot, sterilized jars, topped with hot, sterilized canning lids, and sealed. A vacuum is formed that seals the lid in place. After the jars have cooled test the seal by pressing down on the lid in its center. If it doesn't spring back and is somewhat concave, it has sealed. Otherwise, store it in the refrigerator and use it right away. This method is usually only used for jams, jellies, and syrups.

Boiling Water Bath

The boiling water bath is used to increase the shelf life of your canned foods and is used for strong-acid foods including jams, jellies, and syrups as well as some acidic vegetables. It's a good practice to use the boiling water bath for any foods that you're preserving, just to be on the safe side. A large canner is used for this purpose. It has a rack inside the canner to set the jars into and is filled with boiling water, covering the tops of the jars by one or two inches. The water is then boiled for a period of time, depending on what's being canned.

QUESTION

Can you increase the acidity of low-acid foods that you want to can using the boiling water bath?
Vinegar, lemon juice, and citric acid are used to increase the acidity for specific foods being canned to prevent the growth of microorganisms that cause food to spoil. The one used and the amount is determined by what you're canning. If it's a wild food not on the canning charts, follow the guidelines for one that is similar in texture and size.

Pressure Canning

Pressure canning is the method used for low-acid foods that need higher temperatures than the boiling water bath to kill off the bacteria that cause spoilage. The temperature must reach 240°F and is done by creating steam under pressure. A pressure canner is necessary for this.

ALERT

Always check your pressure canner in advance to make sure it is operating correctly. Gauges used to indicate the pressure must be accurate. Gaskets should be intact without nicks or breaks that will allow steam to leak out. Follow the directions that come with the pressure canner for safe usage.

Preserves

Fruits are preserved in a number of ways in different forms. Making jelly or jam out of wild fruits is one way of preserving the fruit and enjoying it year round. These foods can provide you with sweeteners for desserts and additions to other dishes. The process is simple and can be done with little effort or expense.

Some wild fruits have more pectin than others and can be made into jelly without adding extra pectin. Wild grapes, for instance, contain natural pectin, especially in the unripe state and will jell without commercial pectin. Other fruits high in pectin include barberry, blackberry, cranberry, currants, and plums.

Pawpaw, persimmon, sumac, blueberry, and elderberry are among those that are low in pectin. Combine fruits that are high in pectin with those that aren't to ensure that they will jell. Liquid pectin can be made from some fruits such as crabapples or hawthorns.

Jelly

Jelly is made from fruit juice that is generally extracted from the fruit through a cooking process and strained through a sieve or foley food mill to remove the seeds. Jelly is clear and firm, holding its shape when removed from the jar. Wild cherry, wild plum, black gum, blackberry, passionfruit, and mayapple are among those fruits used to make jelly.

Jam

Jam is made by crushing or grinding the fruit and mixing it with sugar. Cooking it will cause the mixture to thicken and gel, depending on the fruits and the amount of natural pectin in them. Blueberries, elderberries, and strawberries are examples of fruits used to make jams.

Preserves

Preserves are made with large chunks of fruit immersed in a syrup. Sometimes they are cooked, but the process can also be done with raw fruits and requires no cooking. The syrup can be made with honey, sugar, maple syrup, or agave nectar sprinkled or dribbled over the fruit and letting it stand for a period of time. It can also be made with hot water and sugar or honey poured over the fruit.

Syrup

Honey or maple syrup is sometimes used as a sweetener when making preserves. This will often result in a syrup that can be poured rather than a jelly, which is firm, especially if no pectin is used. The syrup can be used as a topping on pancakes or as a sauce for fruit dishes.

Fruit Butter

Fruit butters are made by blending or puréeing fruits, either in a blender or a food processor and then cooking with sugar until it is thick with a smooth consistency. The pulp left over when steam-juicing fruits like black cherry or black gum is good for making fruit butters.

Other types of preserves include these:

- Marmalade has citrus and other fruits added.
- Conserve has raisins, nuts, and spices.
- Chutney has spices, vinegar, and a sweetener mixed with chopped fruits or vegetables.

Fermentation

Fermentation is the process that occurs when sugar and yeast come together and alcohol is the result. Many wild fruits, including persimmons, have naturally occurring yeast in them as well as sugar. When the fruits drop to the ground and lie there for a couple of days, the sugar and yeast start interacting and getting bubbly. If it feels soft when you pick it up, sniff it. Chances are fermentation is happening.

Wild Wines

Making wild wines is an activity that has been happening for a long time. It's one way of preserving your harvest of not only fruits, but flowers and herbs as well. Making wine can be a scientific process that requires the measuring and adding of chemicals to ensure a superior product, or it can be a simple process with nothing added but sugar. However, the scientific process usually isn't necessary. Most wild fruits are already covered with wild yeasts that start the fermentation process. Wine yeast can be added to assure that fermentation occurs.

There are a few items that will be needed for winemaking. They include:

- A large crock (2–5 gallons), bucket, or one-gallon glass jars
- Cheesecloth or muslin to cover the container
- An airlock for the secondary fermentation
- A small hose or plastic tubing for siphoning wine
- Wine bottles with corks to siphon the wine into

Vinegars

Sometimes the winemaking process doesn't stop when it reaches wine. If fruit flies have managed to get into your winemaking container, they may have contaminated it with bacteria that turns wine to vinegar. Or if the process is allowed to continue naturally without being interrupted with a secondary fermentation or bottling process, it will turn into vinegar.

You can start the process by using the leftovers from winemaking after siphoning off the wine for its secondary fermentation. Put the leftovers in a container and let it stand for two or three days, uncovered. When you begin to smell vinegar, you'll know it's ready. Pour warm water over the mixture and strain. Vinegar that comes from wine is aptly known as wine vinegar.

There are also other types of vinegars. Apple cider vinegar comes from apple cider and rice vinegar comes from rice wine. Distilled white vinegar is made from grains and is the cheapest and most commonly used for making herb vinegars. Steeping herbs in vinegar is one way to preserve them. You can use your imagination to make some interesting vinegars to use in salad dressings.

Tinctures, Cordials, and Elixirs

Tinctures, cordials, and elixirs are made with herbs preserved in alcohol. Tinctures are highly concentrated extracts of herbs and are usually preserved in a solution of alcohol and water. Vinegar or glycerin can also be used as a substitute for alcohol. They can be used as a form of medication or as a food supplement.

Cordials and elixirs are similar to tinctures except that they have a sweetener added. Cordials are stimulating beverages that are meant to be shared with friends and are both warming and heart-warming. Elixirs are made with herbs that are tonics and can be taken daily for a specific period of time.

CHAPTER 15

Beverages

Bee Balm and Black Tea

*A refreshing drink to have in the summer when the bee balm is in bloom.
Combine with black tea for a taste similar to Earl Grey.*

INGREDIENTS | SERVES 8

1 quart of water

1 cup fresh bee balm leaves

2 bags of black tea

1 tablespoon honey (optional)

1. Bring water to a boil.

2. Put leaves and tea bags in a teapot. Pour hot water into the teapot.

3. Cover and let steep 5–10 minutes.

4. Strain and add honey. Chill before serving.

Berry Leaf Tea

*For a caffeine-free tea, use the leaves of wild strawberry, blackberry,
and raspberry to make a pleasant-tasting beverage.*

INGREDIENTS | SERVES 4

1 quart boiling water

½ cup dried strawberry, blackberry, or raspberry leaves

1 tablespoon fresh or dried berries

1 tablespoon maple syrup or agave nectar

1. Pour water over leaves and berries.

2. Cover and let steep 10–15 minutes.

3. Sweeten to taste with maple syrup.

Infusions and Decoctions

When leaves, flowers, or tender tips of plants are steeped in hot water, it is called an infusion. Tougher plant parts such as stems, inner bark, thick leaves, or roots need to be simmered for at least 10–20 minutes to extract their properties and are called decoctions.

Black Cherry Juice

Served over ice, this is a flavorful drink that energizes and rejuvenates on a hot summer day.

INGREDIENTS | SERVES 4

2 cups wild black cherries

1 quart of water

2 tablespoons maple syrup

Surviving the Heat

When hiking in the summer months, look for the cherry trees. Sometimes water just isn't enough in the heat. If you find a cherry tree, pick some ripe cherries and put them in a zip-top bag to nibble on as you hike.

1. Place washed cherries in a pan and add just enough water to cover them.

2. Bring to a boil and continue boiling for 15 minutes, mashing the cherries as they cook to release the juice.

3. Pour through a strainer or foley food mill to separate the juice from the seeds.

4. Sweeten with maple syrup and add water to equal 1 quart. Chill and serve.

Blackberry Cordial

A tasty drink to share with friends after dinner.

INGREDIENTS | MAKES 1 QUART

2 cups crushed blackberries

½ cup honey

3 cups blackberry brandy

Berry Topping

Save the berries from the Blackberry Cordial and use as a topping on ice cream, cakes, and other desserts. This is one way to preserve your surplus of berries in the summer.

1. Add honey to crushed blackberries in quart jar.

2. Cover with brandy and shake well.

3. Let stand for at least 1 week.

4. Pour mixture through strainer and bottle.

Blackberry Wine

A smooth-tasting wine that is good to drink as a dessert wine.

INGREDIENTS | 10–12 WINE BOTTLES

1½ gallons blackberries

1½ gallons water

5 pounds sugar

Crock versus Crock Pots

Crocks are large, earthenware containers that were frequently used by country people for pickling, fermenting, or winemaking. Crock pots are electric cookers and are also earthenware containers but they sit inside another container and are used for slow cooking.

1. Wash berries carefully and remove any that are moldy. Crush them and put into a 5-gallon crock or large sterilized bucket, adding enough water to cover them. Put a lid, muslin, or cheesecloth over the top and let stand for 24 hours.

2. Strain the berries through the cloth and return the juice to the crock. Add the sugar. Cover and let stand for 4–5 days.

3. Stir each day and skim the foam off the top.

4. Strain the juice. Add enough water to make 2 gallons. Put in gallon jars with airlocks and rubber stoppers in place. Let stand 2 weeks.

5. When the fermentation is complete, use the plastic tubing to siphon the wine into sterilized bottles. Cork and wait at least 3 months before opening your first bottle.

Black Gum Juice

Use the juice to make jelly, syrup, or glaze for cakes, pies, and ice cream.

INGREDIENTS | MAKES APPROXIMATELY 1 CUP JUICE

2 cups black gum berries

Water, to cover berries

Raw sugar, to taste

1. Remove fruits from stems, place in a saucepan, and add just enough water to cover the fruits.

2. Bring to a gentle boil for about 10 minutes, until the juice is flowing.

3. Press through a sieve or foley food mill to extract the juice.

4. Dilute the juice to desired strength and add sugar to taste.

Clover-Mint Tea

Poured over ice, this is a refreshing tea to drink on a hot summer day.

INGREDIENTS | SERVES 2

2 cups boiling water

1 tablespoon fresh red clover flowers

2 tablespoons fresh mint leaves

1. Pour boiling water over the flowers and mint leaves.

2. Cover and let steep for 10–15 minutes. Chill and serve.

Tea Aroma

Herbs contain essential oils that are extracted by hot water when steeped for a period of time. Covering the teapot with a lid prevents the oils from escaping with steam. Mints often have a strong fragrance and add flavor to teas that otherwise would taste bland.

Chrysanthemum Tea

*A sweet, fragrant beverage that is relaxing to have
in the evening to help you sleep at night.*

INGREDIENTS | SERVES 4

1 quart boiling water

1 tablespoon dried oxeye daisy flowers

1 tablespoon dried life everlasting leaves

2 tablespoons fresh lemon balm leaves

1. Pour boiling water over herbs.

2. Cover and let steep 10–15 minutes.

3. Strain and serve.

Dandy Fizz

This is the teetotaler's version of dandelion wine.

INGREDIENTS | MAKES ½ GALLON

1 cup dandelion flower petals, pulled apart from stem

2 cups boiling water

2 lemons, cut in thin slices

2 oranges, cut in thin slices

½ cup maple syrup

1. Cover flowers with boiling water. Cover and let steep until cool.

2. Add remaining ingredients and let stand 1–2 days.

3. Strain and serve.

Elderflower Punch

Enjoy the flowery flavor of this refreshing punch.
Float elder flower petals on the surface for an added decorative touch.

INGREDIENTS | SERVES 8

6 large heads elder flowers

2 quarts boiling water

2 lemons, squeezed and cut in wedges

3 tablespoons maple syrup

1. Use scissors to remove flowers from stems.

2. Cover with boiling water.

3. Add lemons and maple syrup. Chill and serve.

Elder Wisdom

Elder is a diaphoretic herb that eliminates toxins through perspiration. It has gentle cleansing properties that stimulate blood flow. Drinking elder flower tea on a regular basis will help to detoxify the body.

Elder-Lemon Elixir

Serve with lemonade over ice for a refreshing drink on a hot summer day.

INGREDIENTS | MAKES 1 QUART

10–15 heads elder flowers

20–25 lemon verbena leaves

3–6 sprigs of fresh lemon balm

3–6 sprigs of sweet goldenrod leaves

2 cups boiling water

2 cups lemon liqueur

Honey or maple syrup, to taste

1. Steep the elder flowers, lemon verbena leaves, lemon balm, and sweet goldenrod leaves in boiling water for 15–20 minutes and strain.

2. Add lemon liqueur and sweeten to taste with honey or maple syrup.

3. Serve over ice.

Iced Drinks

If you like your beverages iced, make the same drink ahead of time and freeze it in ice cube trays. This will prevent the ice cube from diluting the strength of your drink.

Grape Wine

This is a robust wine that only gets better with age.
Drink to your good health, as it is rich in resveratrol, a heart-healthy compound.

INGREDIENTS | MAKES 1 GALLON

6 pounds wild grapes (muscadine, fox, or summer)

3 quarts water

2 pounds sugar

1½ cups orange juice

1 package wine yeast

Airlocks

Airlocks are made of plastic or glass that fit into a cork or rubber stopper and are placed on the jug or container for the secondary fermentation, which is anaerobic. They are filled initially halfway with water. As fermentation occurs, it allows the gases to escape and at the same time prevents unwanted materials from getting in.

1. Mash grapes with your hands in 5-gallon crock or bucket.

2. Add water and sugar to the crock or bucket. Cover with cheesecloth or muslin and let stand 24 hours.

3. Let orange juice reach room temperature by setting it out for 2 hours. Add room-temperature orange juice to wine yeast in closeable container. Cover and shake vigorously. Let stand until bubbly before adding to the grape mixture.

4. Stir daily, pressing pulp at the same time to extract more juice.

5. After about a week, siphon wine into gallon jugs and attach airlock.

6. When the fermentation is complete, after about 3 weeks, siphon into clean jugs and reattach airlock.

7. After 2 months, siphon into bottles.

Green Drink

Drink your way to health with this vibrant, energizing drink.

INGREDIENTS | SERVES 2

2 cups fresh, wild greens (dandelion, stinging nettle, violets, chickweed, etc.)

1 carrot, cut in chunks

2 cups pineapple juice

1 frozen banana

Put all the ingredients in a blender and mix until creamy.

Smoothies

The arrival of blenders brought with it a new way of blending foods. Smoothies were created, using fruits or vegetables and a liquid base, such as juice, milk, yogurt, or tea. They can be hot or cold, with or without ice, or even frozen. A cold smoothie is a great way to cool off on a hot summer day.

Nut Milk

Use this milk as a substitute for regular milk to add a nutty flavor to your recipe. Nut milks can be stored in the refrigerator for up to one week. Freeze it for longer storage. Shake well before using.

INGREDIENTS | MAKES 1 QUART

1 cup shelled, pre-soaked nuts (hickory, beech, hazelnut, pecan)

3 cups water

1. Put nuts and half the water into a blender and mix until smooth.

2. Add remaining water and blend again.

3. Store in the refrigerator until ready to use.

Persimmon Smoothie

A smooth, creamy texture with all the sweetness of ice cream.

INGREDIENTS | SERVES 2

½ cup persimmon pulp

1 cup vanilla or maple yogurt

¼ cup orange juice

Crushed ice

Place all ingredients in a blender and blend until smooth.

Persimmon Wine

You will be amazed at the taste and appearance of this fine-tasting wine. Not for the teetotaler.

INGREDIENTS | MAKES 1 GALLON

1 package wine yeast

Juice from 4 oranges, room temperature

3 pounds persimmon pulp

2¼ pounds sugar

7 pints water

Juice of 3 lemons

1. Add yeast to orange juice and let stand until bubbly.

2. In a wide-mouth gallon jug, combine persimmon pulp, half of the sugar, 2 pints water, lemon juice, and orange juice with yeast added.

3. Let stand for 1 week, stirring daily.

4. Strain mixture through cheesecloth and return to wide-mouth jug.

5. Add remaining sugar and let stand 2 days.

6. Siphon into a gallon jug for secondary fermentation and attach an airlock.

7. Fill the airlock with water to the halfway line.

8. Fermentation is complete when the brew stops bubbling, about 10–12 days. Siphon into bottles and insert a cork in the top.

Pine Needle Tea

A drink high in vitamin C that is available year-round.
Spruce needles can be used as well.

INGREDIENTS | SERVES 4

3–5 clusters of pine needles

1 quart boiling water

Juice of 1 lemon

Maple syrup, to taste

1. Using kitchen scissors, snip needles into 1 to 2-inch-long pieces.

2. Pour boiling water over needles. Add lemon juice.

3. Cover and let steep 5 minutes.

4. Sweeten to taste with maple syrup and serve.

Make It Medicinal

The longer you steep pine needle tea, the stronger it becomes, making it more of a medicine than a tea. Drink the tea as a cold or flu remedy or to boost the immune system.

Rose Hip Cider

A rich blend of winter fruits in a hot tea that is rich in vitamins C and E.
A good tea to drink during the flu and cold season.

INGREDIENTS | SERVES 8–10

½ cup rose hips, cut in half

¼ cup hawthorn berries

½ cup cranberries, chopped

4 cups boiling water

2 cinnamon sticks

2 cups crabapple juice

2 cups apple juice

2 cups cranberry juice

1. Chop rose hips, hawthorn berries, and cranberries in blender.

2. Put in saucepan and cover with boiling water. Let simmer for 20–30 minutes.

3. Add remaining ingredients and simmer on low for 1 hour.

4. Ladle into cups and serve.

Rose Petal Tea

A flowery flavor that is both thirst-quenching and refreshing.

INGREDIENTS | SERVES 4

12 wild roses, or any roses that haven't been sprayed with pesticides

16 ounces water

Remove petals and place in a glass or jar filled with water. Let stand 2–3 hours, preferably in the sun, before serving.

Flower Essences

The essence of a flower can be captured by placing fresh flowers in a glass bowl of spring water on a sunny day after the dew has lifted. Fill the bowl three-quarters full of water. Snip the flower heads off near the top and let them float in the water in full sunlight for at least three hours. Preserve the essence by adding one teaspoon brandy, vodka, or other spirits per cup of water.

Sassafras Tea

This is the root that was originally used to flavor root beer and the tea has a distinctive root beer flavor.

INGREDIENTS | SERVES 4

12 sassafras roots about the size of a pencil

1 quart water

Sweetener to taste (optional)

1. Wash roots and place in water. Bring to a boil. Reduce heat and cook until water turns a dark red. The longer you cook the roots the more concentrated the tea.

2. Strain through a filter to remove sediments, add sweetener if desired, and serve hot or cold.

Safrole

Safrole is a compound found in sassafras roots that was used in experimental research. It was discovered to possibly be a carcinogen, so the FDA banned it. Sassafras is used as a tonic that is generally only drunk in the spring to thin and purify the blood. Practice moderation when making and drinking sassafras tea.

Sleepy Time Herb Tea

A calming and relaxing tea to drink before retiring for the evening.

INGREDIENTS | SERVES 4

2 tablespoons fresh skullcap leaves

2 tablespoons fresh passionvine leaves and stems

2 tablespoons fresh mint leaves

2 tablespoons fresh lemon balm leaves

2 tablespoons life everlasting leaves

1 quart boiling water

Sweetener, to taste (optional)

1. Wash herbs and place in teapot. Pour boiling water over herbs.

2. Cover and let steep for 10–15 minutes. Sweeten if desired and serve.

Combining Herbs for Tea

When combining herbs to make a tea, know what the effects of individual herbs are first. Combine no more than three to five herbs at one time when making tea.

Sumac Ade

Enjoy this citrus-tasting beverage that is good hot or cold.

INGREDIENTS | SERVES 6–8

4–6 large clusters of ripe sumac fruits

2 quarts cold water

Sweetener, to taste (optional)

1. Over a large bowl, rub the stems between your fingers, loosening the fruits and letting them drop into the bowl.

2. Put the fruits in a quart-size bottle or pitcher and cover with cold water. The water should start turning pink right away. The longer it sits, the pinker it will become.

3. Pour through a strainer lined with a coffee filter and sweeten to taste.

Sumac Elixir

A tonic to take through the winter to help fight against colds and viruses.

INGREDIENTS | SERVES 4–6

1 cup sumac berries

2 cups cold water

Honey, to taste

Splash of pineapple juice

1 shot vanilla vodka

1 shot lemon liqueur

1 shot pomegranate liqueur

1. Steep the sumac berries in cold water for 8–10 hours, until the water turns red.

2. Strain and add remaining ingredients.

3. Serve over ice.

Sweet Summer Tea

A tea that is both cooling and refreshing. Be sure to chill the serving pitcher ahead of time.

INGREDIENTS | SERVES 4

1 quart boiling water

½ cup fresh sweet goldenrod leaves

½ cup fresh lemon balm leaves

½ cup lemon verbena leaves

1. Pour boiling water over leaves in teapot. Cover and let steep for 10–15 minutes.

2. Chill and serve.

Wild Grape Juice

A sparkling, alcohol-free drink that can be served with any meal.

INGREDIENTS | SERVES 6–8

4 cups wild grapes

½ cup water

1 liter ginger ale

1. Add water to grapes and bring to a gentle boil.

2. Continue to cook for about 15 minutes or until the grapes are soft.

3. Strain through a food mill or sieve to extract the juice.

4. Add ginger ale and chill.

Twig Tea

Making this tea fills your kitchen with a wonderful aroma of wintergreen mixed with a spicy smell. Make this tea concentrated and then dilute to desired strength.

INGREDIENTS | SERVES 4

1 cup sweet birch twigs, cut into 2-inch pieces

1 cup spicebush twigs, cut into 2-inch pieces

1 quart boiling water

Sweetener, to taste (optional)

Cover twigs with boiling water and let simmer 10–20 minutes. Sweeten if desired and serve hot or chilled.

Wintergreen Toothpicks

The twigs from sweet birch were at one time used to make toothpicks that were naturally flavored with a wintergreen taste. Twigs can also be frayed on the ends and used as a toothbrush.

Wintergreen Tea

Add sweet birch twigs to the pot for a more intense wintergreen flavor.

INGREDIENTS | SERVES 4

1 cup wintergreen leaves

1 quart boiling water

Sweetener, to taste (optional)

1. Crush the leaves and cover with boiling water.

2. Cover and let simmer for 15–20 minutes. Sweeten if desired and serve.

Basic Yaupon Tea

A caffeinated tea that has a taste and appearance similar to green tea.

INGREDIENTS | SERVES 4

1 cup yaupon leaves, removed from the twigs or branches

1 quart boiling water

Sweetener, to taste (optional)

1. Roast leaves in 200°F oven until dry and crumbly (about 30 minutes).

2. Cover with boiling water and simmer about 20 minutes.

3. Strain through a coffee filter and sweeten to taste.

Yaupon Chai Tea

The extra spices and seasonings turn this into a gourmet wild tea. You can preserve this tasty beverage by adding vanilla rum to the drink.

INGREDIENTS | SERVES 4

4 teaspoons roasted yaupon leaves

4 cups boiling water

3–4 ginger slices

Pinch of cardamom seeds

¼ vanilla bean, cut into small pieces

Maple syrup, to taste

1. Cover roasted leaves with boiling water.

2. Add ginger slices, cardamom seeds, and vanilla bean.

3. Steep about 20 minutes. Strain through a coffee filter and sweeten to taste with maple syrup.

CHAPTER 16

Appetizers, Salads, Sauces, and Spreads

Blackberry Preserves

This is an excellent preserve that requires no cooking and is easy to make.

INGREDIENTS | MAKES 1 CUP

1 cup fresh blackberries (or raspberries)

¼ cup raw honey

1. Add honey to blackberries and mash.

2. Chill for 1 hour before serving.

Crabapple Sauce

Use this sauce as a topping on cakes, hot biscuits, or as a pie filling.

INGREDIENTS | SERVES 8–10

2 cups crabapples

1 quart water

¼ cup honey

¼ teaspoon cinnamon

1. Wash crabapples and remove blossom ends and brown parts. Place in a large saucepan, cover with water, and bring to a boil.

2. Cover and simmer until soft, about 15 minutes.

3. Remove crabapples from pot and set water aside.

4. Cut crabapples into quarters and remove seeds.

5. Put in blender with enough water from cooking the crabapples to puree.

6. Return to saucepan and add honey and cinnamon. Continue to cook on low heat 10–15 minutes.

7. Serve hot or store in the refrigerator in glass jars until ready to use.

Cranapple Salad

A fruity, nutty salad that will tease your taste buds with its sweet and sour flavors. To keep it raw, put the cranberries into a blender and chop into fine pieces.

INGREDIENTS | SERVES 8

2 cups wild cranberries (if available)

1 cup maple syrup, or to taste

1 stalk celery, chopped

2 medium apples, chopped

¼ cup nuts, chopped

1. Put cranberries and maple syrup in small saucepan.

2. Bring to a gentle boil and continue to cook about 15–20 minutes, until berries have popped and start to thicken.

3. Remove from heat and add remaining ingredients. Chill 1 hour before serving.

Cranberries for Cystitis

Research studies show that cranberries and blueberries both contain compounds that prevent bacteria from adhering to the bladder walls, thus preventing a bladder infection, also called cystitis. They also contain arbutin, which is both an antibiotic and a diuretic.

Cranberry Sauce

This is a basic cranberry sauce recipe that can be used alone or with other salads.

INGREDIENTS | SERVES 8–10

2 cups wild cranberries (if available)

1 cup maple syrup

1 cup water

1. Combine cranberries, maple syrup, and water in a saucepan.

2. Bring to a boil. Reduce heat and continue to cook about 10–15 minutes, until berries burst and sauce has thickened.

3. Cool in refrigerator for 1–2 hours before serving.

Cactus Salad

A tasty topping for salads, beans, and other vegetable dishes.

INGREDIENTS | SERVES 4

4–5 cactus pads, steamed until tender and spines removed

1 green bell pepper, thinly sliced

1 hot pepper, chopped

3 wild onions (or green onions), chopped finely

¼ cup vinegar and olive oil dressing

1. Cut cactus pads into strips.

2. Toss with peppers and onions in a large bowl.

3. Pour dressing over mixed vegetables and marinate at least 30 minutes.

Dipping Sauce

Great to use with spring rolls or as a sauce on cooked vegetables.

INGREDIENTS | MAKES ½ CUP SAUCE

¼ cup tamari

¼ cup water

1 tablespoon cornstarch

1 tablespoon sesame seeds, browned

1 tablespoon ground garlic mustard seeds (or other mustard seeds)

½ cup finely chopped garlic mustard or peppergrass leaves

2 tablespoons sesame oil

2 cloves garlic, grated

¼ teaspoon ginger, grated

2 tablespoons lime juice

1 tablespoon maple syrup

1. Combine tamari, water, and cornstarch in a small sauce pan. Cook on medium-high heat until mixture comes to a boil.

2. Reduce heat and continue to cook about 10 minutes until the sauce has thickened and become clear.

3. Add remaining ingredients and mix well.

4. Cool and serve.

Elderberry Syrup

Use alone or with other fruit juices to boost the immune system against flu viruses.

INGREDIENTS | MAKES 2 CUPS

1 cup dried elderberries

1 quart water

½ cup honey

Stabilizers

Stabilizers are preservatives and are used to extend the shelf life of a particular herb or fruit. The most common stabilizer is alcohol, whether it is vodka, brandy, or grain alcohol. If you want to prepare enough elderberry syrup to have through the flu season, add ½ cup brandy to the recipe.

1. Cover elderberries with water in a medium pot and bring to a boil.

2. Reduce heat and continue to simmer until water is reduced by half, about 30–45 minutes.

3. Strain through a sieve or foley food mill to remove the seeds.

4. Mix in the honey and store in the refrigerator until ready to use.

Fruit Nut Spread

Spread on nut breads or crackers or as a filling in wonton wrappers.

INGREDIENTS | SERVES 8–10

1 cup wild berries, mashed

¾ cup nuts, finely chopped

8 ounces cream cheese, softened

¼ cup maple yogurt

Stir wild berries and nuts into cream cheese and yogurt until creamy and smooth. Use as a spread on bread or crackers.

Ground Cherry Salsa

*This salsa has a rich flavor that makes it a favorite as a dipping sauce
or served over stir-fried vegetables.*

INGREDIENTS | MAKES 2 CUPS

1½ cups ground cherries

1 hot pepper

1 clove garlic

½ small onion

1. Remove cherries from their papery husks and rinse in cold water.

2. Cover with water and simmer until they are soft but not bursting open (about 10–15 minutes).

3. Chop peppers, garlic, and onion into large pieces.

4. Put all ingredients into the blender with ¼ cup water from the cooking liquid and blend for a few seconds until mixed.

Herb Vinegar

Use to mix with oil for salad dressings or as a marinade for vegetables.

INGREDIENTS | MAKES 12 OUNCES

3–5 sprigs of peppergrass

¼ cup dentaria root, chopped

1 tablespoon mustard seeds

1 tablespoon field garlic cloves or wild onion

12 ounces apple cider vinegar (or white wine vinegar)

1. Put the herbs in a sterilized jar and cover with vinegar, filling to within ½ inch of the top.

2. Cover the top with plastic wrap first if using a metal lid to prevent rust.

3. Put in a cool, dark place for 2–3 weeks.

4. Strain and bottle.

Jerusalem Artichoke Salad

An earthy tasting salad that can be enjoyed all winter.

INGREDIENTS | SERVES 6–8

10 medium-sized Jerusalem artichokes, scrubbed and grated

3 wild onions or field garlic, chopped finely with tops included

½ cup cranberries or blueberries

1 teaspoon Wild Herb Seasoning (Chapter 18) or Seed Seasoning (Chapter 16)

¼ cup Sweet and Sour Dressing (Chapter 16)

2 cups wild salad greens

1. Place Jerusalem artichokes and wild onions in a large bowl. Mix well.

2. Add cranberries and seasoning.

3. Pour dressing over mixture and let marinate for 1 hour.

4. Serve on a bed of wild salad greens.

Persimmon Jam

Makes a delicious spread for hot, buttered biscuits.
Add cream cheese to make a frosting to put on cakes.

INGREDIENTS | MAKES APPROXIMATELY 3 CUPS

2 cups persimmon pulp

1 cup sugar

2 ounces liquid pectin

1. Combine persimmon pulp and sugar and bring the mixture to a boil.

2. Add the liquid pectin and boil for 1 minute longer.

3. Pour into hot, sterilized jars and seal.

Petal Petits

Use the flower petals as a base for your favorite jelly or spread to make an attractive, edible display.

INGREDIENTS | SERVES 8–10

10 yucca flowers

8 ounces cream cheese, softened

1 tablespoon wild syrup or preserves (black gum, cherry, blackberry)

¼ teaspoon vanilla flavoring

1 cup edible flowers (violet, wild pansy, redbud)

1. Remove petals from yucca flowers, discarding the center parts.

2. In a medium bowl, mix cream cheese with preserves and vanilla flavoring.

3. Spoon a dollop of cream cheese mixture in the center of each petal.

4. Top each one with an edible flower. Chill and serve.

Be Creative

There are a number of edible flowers that can be used a base for preserves or other filling. Hibiscus flowers work well for this purpose. Look for flowers that are large enough and stiff enough to contain the filling. Use small berries as a topping instead of flowers for a variation.

Prickly Pear Jelly

A delightfully colorful jelly to use as a spread on crackers, breads, and cakes.

INGREDIENTS | MAKES APPROXIMATELY 2 CUPS

2½ cups prickly pear juice

6 ounces fruit pectin

Juice of 1 lemon

2 cups sugar

1. Combine juice and fruit pectin in a saucepan. Bring to a boil, stirring constantly.

2. Add the lemon juice and sugar.

3. Bring to a hard boil and boil for 3 minutes.

4. Remove from the burner, pour into sterilized jars, and seal.

Roasted Chestnuts

Try roasting these over an open fire to capture the wood flavor from the smoke.

INGREDIENTS | SERVES 6

2 dozen chestnuts

1. Preheat oven to 400°F.

2. Cut an X into each chestnut on the flat side.

3. Place on a baking sheet and bake for 30–35 minutes, turning frequently.

4. Peel while still warm.

Roasted Live Oak Acorns

Live oak acorns, when ripe, are low in tannin and can be roasted straight out of the shell with no leaching process necessary.

INGREDIENTS | SERVES 6

2 cups unbroken live oak acorns, shells removed

1 tablespoon peanut oil

1. Preheat oven to 350°F.

2. Coat acorns with peanut oil and spread on a cookie sheet. Bake for 10–15 minutes.

3. Cool and serve.

Seed Seasoning

A healthy seasoning that is rich in omega-3s and omega-6s.
Sprinkle on wild salads or vegetable dishes. Make a spread by adding
2 tablespoons sunflower seed oil, finely minced garlic, and grated ginger.

INGREDIENTS | MAKES APPROXIMATELY 1 CUP

2 tablespoons sunflower seeds

2 tablespoons chia seeds

2 tablespoons pumpkin seeds

2 tablespoons flax seeds

1 tablespoon evening primrose seeds

2 tablespoons hemp seeds

Pinch of ground cardamom seeds

Pinch of ground turmeric

Pinch of cinnamon

1. Grind sunflower seeds, chia seeds, pumpkin seeds, flax seeds, and evening primrose seeds in a coffee grinder. Place in bowl.

2. Add remaining ingredients and mix well.

Sugar Cookie Pizza Crust

The perfect crust to bring out the sweetness of spring wildflowers.

INGREDIENTS | SERVES 6–8

⅓ cup butter, softened

½ cup raw sugar

⅓ cup honey

1 egg

1 teaspoon vanilla

1 cup whole wheat flour

¼ cup ground nuts

2 teaspoons baking powder

1. Preheat oven to 350°F.

2. In a large mixing bowl, cream together butter, sugar, honey, and egg. Add vanilla.

3. Stir together flour and baking powder and add to creamed mixture.

4. Drop by spoonfuls onto greased cookie sheet about ½ inch apart. Use the back of a spoon to flatten until dough is touching to create one large cookie.

5. Bake about 12 minutes. Cool. Use as the crust to make a wildflower pizza.

Sweet and Sour Dressing

Great to use on wild salads, stir-fries, or other vegetable dishes.

INGREDIENTS | SERVES 10

1 tablespoon maple syrup

Juice from ½ lemon

¼ cup rice vinegar

1 cup sunflower seed oil

1 tablespoon finely chopped hickory nuts

½ teaspoon ground garlic mustard seeds

1 tablespoon peppergrass leaves, finely chopped

1 teaspoon evening primrose seeds, ground

Combine all ingredients in a closed jar and shake until blended.

Toasted Maple Nuts

A tasty way to boost your serotonin levels on a wintry day when you have to be inside.

INGREDIENTS | SERVES 4

1 cup nuts (black walnuts, hickory, pecans)

1 tablespoon coconut oil or butter

2 tablespoons maple syrup

1. Preheat oven to 350°F.

2. Heat oil or butter in saucepan. Add maple syrup and mix well.

3. Coat nuts in oil mixture. Spread evenly on a baking dish.

4. Roast nuts in oven 10–12 minutes, turning after 5 minutes.

Wild Muscadine Preserves

*The texture and flavor make this a favorite. Use as a spread on hot biscuits,
as a filling for fruit roll-ups, or to make a pie.*

**INGREDIENTS | MAKES APPROXIMATELY
4 CUPS**

3 cups muscadine grapes, hulled and
seeded

½ cup honey

¼ cup water

1. Combine grapes, honey, and water in a saucepan and
   bring to a boil.

2. Continue to boil gently for 10–15 minutes, stirring
   occasionally, until it is thickened.

3. Pour into sterilized jars and seal.

Grape Seeds

If you miss removing all the seeds from the grapes when
processing them, that's okay. Grape seeds, like the skin
and young leaves, contain resveratrol, an antioxidant that
helps reduce inflammation as well as other health benefits. Instead of buying seedless grapes at the grocery
store, and then grape seed extract at the health food
store, try nibbling on wild grapes, seeds and all.

Wild Plum Butter

*Use any of the wild plums to make this butter.
Serve on hot biscuits or scones.*

INGREDIENTS | MAKES 2 CUPS

2 cups wild plum pulp

1 cup raw sugar

1. Combine the pulp and sugar. Bring to a boil.

2. Reduce heat and simmer 15–20 minutes, until it has
   thickened.

3. Pour into sterilized glass jars and seal.

Wildflower Pitas

*This is a wonderful way to use the edible spring wildflowers.
Reduce the calories by eliminating the pita and add as a topping to your salad.*

INGREDIENTS | SERVES 6

2 cups assorted edible flowers (henbit, dead nettle, wood sorrel, violets, wild pansies, redbud, wild mustard)

1 cup mixed salad greens

1 tablespoon lemon juice

1 tablespoon maple syrup

6 pita breads

1. Combine flowers and greens in a large bowl.

2. In a small bowl, mix lemon juice and maple syrup and pour over salad mixture.

3. Stuff in pita breads and serve.

Wildflower Pizza Topping

All the colors of spring arranged on a tasty cookie crust.

INGREDIENTS | SERVES 6

8 ounces cream cheese, softened

2 tablespoons honey

1 teaspoon vanilla

1 tablespoon wild berry syrup

1 Sugar Cookie Pizza Crust (Chapter 16)

2 cups assorted wild edible flowers (redbud, violet, pansy, oxalis, black locust)

1 tablespoon raw sugar

1. In a large mixing bowl, cream together cream cheese and honey.

2. Add vanilla and berry syrup.

3. Spread on cooled Sugar Cookie Pizza Crust.

4. Arrange wildflowers on top of pizza. Sprinkle with raw sugar.

5. Chill and serve.

Yucca Flower Cakes

Serve as a base for cheese spreads, spreads, or sauces.

INGREDIENTS | SERVES 6

1 cup yucca flower petals

2 eggs

½ cup sour cream

¼ cup flour

1 tablespoon Wild Herb Seasoning (see Chapter 18)

Vegetable oil or butter, for frying

1. Remove the petals of the flowers and discard the centers.

2. Blend yucca flowers, eggs, and sour cream in the blender.

3. Add flour and herb seasoning.

4. Drop by spoonfuls on hot, oiled griddle and cook until brown on each side.

5. Serve with pesto or Ground Cherry Salsa (Chapter 16).

CHAPTER 17

Soups and Vegetable Dishes

Artichokes and Groundnuts Casserole

This hearty casserole with its earthy flavors makes a tasty side dish for any meal.

INGREDIENTS | SERVES 8

1 tablespoon butter or oil

2 cups Jerusalem artichokes scrubbed and sliced

1 cup groundnuts, scrubbed and sliced

1 small onion, chopped

½ cup flour

1 tablespoon Wild Herb Seasoning (Chapter 18)

Salt and pepper, to taste

½ cup sour cream or milk

1 cup grated cheese

1. Preheat oven to 350°F.

2. Grease the bottom of a baking dish with butter or oil.

3. Spread artichokes, groundnuts, and onions on bottom of baking dish.

4. In a small bowl, mix flour, herb seasoning, salt, and pepper. Sprinkle over the roots.

5. Spoon sour cream or pour milk over mixture.

6. Top with a layer of cheese.

7. Bake for 40–45 minutes.

Broiled Japanese Knotweed

Easy-to-prepare side dish that can be served alone or with other vegetables.

INGREDIENTS | SERVES 6–8

10–12 Japanese knotweed spears, about 6 inches in length

1 tablespoon butter for greasing baking dish

1 teaspoon Wild Herb Seasoning (Chapter 18)

2 tablespoons butter, melted

1. Preheat oven to 350°F.

2. Arrange knotweed spears on bottom of buttered baking dish.

3. Mix herb seasoning with melted butter. Dribble over knotweed spears.

4. Bake for 10 minutes.

Cattail and Cheese Casserole

Serve as a side dish along with a wild salad to make your meal complete.

INGREDIENTS | SERVES 4

1 egg, beaten

½ cup sour cream

3 cups steamed cattail buds, scraped from the stalks

1 teaspoon Wild Herb Seasoning (Chapter 18)

1 cup soft bread crumbs

Hot water as needed for mixing

1 cup grated cheese

1. Preheat oven to 350°F.

2. In a large bowl, combine egg and sour cream.

3. Add cattail buds, herb seasoning, and bread crumbs. Mix well.

4. Pour into greased baking dish and sprinkle cheese on top.

5. Bake approximately 30 minutes, or until done.

Creamed Arrowhead Tubers

If you didn't know better, you would think you're eating seasoned, buttered potatoes.

INGREDIENTS | SERVES 4

2 cups arrowhead tubers, washed and scrubbed

1 tablespoon butter

1 small onion, chopped

2 celery stalks, chopped

2 carrots, chopped

¼ cup sour cream

1 teaspoon Wild Herb Seasoning (Chapter 18)

1. Slice arrowhead tubers. Place into a large saucepan and cover with water. Boil gently about 20–30 minutes, until tender.

2. Drain tubers, reserving liquid.

3. In a saucepan over medium heat, melt the butter. Add the onion, celery, and carrots and sauté until tender, about 10 minutes.

4. Add sautéed vegetables, sour cream, and seasonings to cooked tubers. Mix well to combine and serve.

Fried Nopales

Chop and sprinkle over beans and other cooked vegetables.
This is good served with Ground Cherry Salsa (Chapter 16).

INGREDIENTS | SERVES 4–6

2 tablespoons olive oil

1 medium onion, chopped

1 medium green bell pepper, chopped

1 cayenne or chili pepper, chopped

6–8 cactus pads, spines removed, cut into strips

1 tablespoon Wild Herb Seasoning (Chapter 18)

1. In a skillet over medium-high heat add the olive oil. Once it is hot add the onions, peppers, and cactus strips and sauté about 10–15 minutes, until tender.

2. Reduce heat, add Wild Herb Seasoning, and let simmer 10–20 minutes.

Herb Tofu

A blend of tofu with wild greens that is good served
with rice or pasta, on the side or as a topping.

INGREDIENTS | SERVES 6–8

16 ounces extra-firm tofu, cut into cubes

2 tablespoons olive oil

4 garlic cloves, chopped

1 medium onion, chopped

2 cups wild greens, chopped (dandelion, nettles, heal-all, lambsquarters, wild mustard)

1 cup Ground Cherry Salsa (Chapter 16) (or diced tomatoes)

1. In a medium-size sauce pan sauté tofu in olive oil about 10 minutes, until brown and crispy, and set aside.

2. In a separate medium-size pan, sauté garlic and onions in olive oil about 10 minutes, until golden.

3. Reduce heat and add greens. Cook about 5–10 minutes, until wilted.

4. Combine sautéed tofu with cooked vegetables.

5. Add salsa or tomatoes and let simmer about 10 minutes and serve.

Kitten-on-the-Cob

A taste that is amazingly similar to corn. It even has a spike going through the center to hold on either end. Eat like you would corn-on-the-cob.

INGREDIENTS | SERVES 4–6

10–12 male cattail buds

2 tablespoons melted butter

1 teaspoon Wild Herb Seasoning (Chapter 18)

1. Remove the green sheath around the cattail buds and place in the top of a steamer.

2. Steam cook about 10–15 minutes. Place in shallow dish.

3. In a small bowl combine herb seasoning and melted butter. Dribble over kittens and serve.

Milkweed Buds

Once properly prepared, these tasty buds can be added to salads, soups, or other vegetable dishes.

INGREDIENTS | MAKES 2 CUPS

2 cups milkweed buds, large stems removed

Water to cover milkweed buds

1. Bring pot of water to a boil. Add milkweed buds and flowers. Boil for 1 minute. Strain water.

2. Bring a second pot of water to a boil. Again, add buds and flowers and boil for 1 minute. Drain and serve as a side dish or added to other vegetables.

Pink Mashed Potatoes with Evening Primrose Roots

*Evening primrose roots, when cooked, take on a pinkish hue,
tinting regular potatoes with their color.*

INGREDIENTS | SERVES 4–6

3 medium-sized potatoes, chopped

4 evening primrose roots, scraped and chopped

1 tablespoon dried Wild Herb Seasoning (Chapter 18)

½ teaspoon evening primrose seeds

½ teaspoon celery seeds

Salt and pepper, to taste

½ cup sour cream

2 tablespoons butter

1. Steam cook the potatoes, evening primrose roots, herb seasoning, primrose seeds, and celery seeds for about 20 minutes.

2. Put in a large bowl and add remaining ingredients. Mash with a fork or potato masher, adding broth from cooking to desired thickness.

Poke and Pasta

Turn this into a salad by adding wild salad greens and edible flowers.

INGREDIENTS | SERVES 6

2 tablespoons butter or vegetable oil

2 tablespoons flour

1 cup milk (or milk substitute)

2 cups prepared (cooked twice) poke shoots, cut in 1-inch lengths

1 cup cheese, grated

1 tablespoon Wild Herb Seasoning (Chapter 18)

2 cups cooked pasta

1. Heat butter in skillet. Stir in flour until smooth and cook 5–10 minutes until light brown.

2. Add milk and cook on medium heat, stirring constantly, about 10 minutes, until sauce starts to bubble.

3. Remove from heat and add cooked poke, cheese, and seasonings. Serve over cooked pasta.

Purslane-Potato Soup

This is a delicious soup that can also be made with watercress, poke leaves, nettles, or other wild greens that are available.

INGREDIENTS | SERVES 6–8

2 tablespoons oil

1 medium onion, chopped

2 stalks celery, finely chopped

1 quart water

1 cup purslane leaves or other wild greens; use ½ cup if dried

3 medium potatoes, scrubbed and diced

2 medium evening primrose roots, scrubbed and chopped

1 cup sour cream

2 tablespoons butter

½ teaspoon evening primrose seeds

Salt and pepper, to taste

Optional seasonings: basil, dill, chives, parsley, wild onion tops

1. Heat oil in saucepan and sauté onions and celery about 10 minutes, until the onions are transparent.

2. Bring water to a boil in medium-sized soup pot.

3. Add sautéed vegetables, greens, potatoes, and evening primrose roots. Cook on medium heat about 20–30 minutes, until roots are tender.

4. Stir in sour cream, butter, evening primrose seeds, and seasonings.

5. Let flavors blend at least 5 minutes before serving.

Purslane—More Than Just a Weed

The weedy purslane that shows up in most people's gardens who don't spray herbicides need be a weed no longer. In addition to several cancer-fighting antioxidants, it's also loaded with ascorbic acid, beta carotene, vitamin E, and omega-3 fatty acids that have been shown to help lower cholesterol levels as well as other health benefits.

Redbud Stir Fries

These are like snow peas but with a tart flavor.
Serve with rice, potatoes, or other vegetables.

INGREDIENTS | SERVES 4

2 tablespoons butter

1 cup redbud pods, ends removed

1 small onion, chopped

2 carrots, chopped

1 teaspoon Seed Seasoning (Chapter 18)

1. Melt butter in a skillet over medium heat. Add the redbud pods, onion, and carrots and sauté 10–15 minutes.

2. Turn off heat, add seed seasoning, mix well, and cover. Let stand for 5 minutes before serving.

Roasted Roots

You can use whatever roots are available for this recipe as well as other vegetables.

INGREDIENTS | SERVES 8–10

6 evening primrose roots, scraped and cut in small pieces

3 burdock roots, peeled and chopped

1 pound Jerusalem artichokes, scrubbed and sliced

½ cup coconut milk

¼ cup butter, melted

¼ cup maple syrup

2 tablespoons grated ginger

2 tablespoons Wild Herb Seasoning (Chapter 18)

1. Steam evening primrose roots and burdock roots 20 minutes, until tender.

2. Combine with Jerusalem artichoke roots in a 12-inch iron skillet.

3. Add the coconut milk, butter, syrup, Wild Herb Seasoning, and ginger. Coat vegetables with mixture.

4. Place the vegetables in the iron skillet and place in the oven. Roast about 20 minutes.

5. Remove from oven, toss and turn roots and then roast about 20 minutes more, until the roots are tender and nicely glazed.

6. Serve as a side dish or over rice.

Rock Tripe Soup

This is a strengthening and warming soup to have during the cold winter months.
Serve with quinoa, rice, or other grain.

INGREDIENTS | SERVES 4

2 quarts water

½ cup rock tripe, broken up into small pieces

1 medium onion, chopped

2 stalks celery, chopped

2 carrots, chopped

2 tablespoons butter or vegetable oil

2 tablespoons Wild Herb Seasoning (Chapter 18)

½ teaspoon evening primrose seeds

Salt, to taste

1 cayenne or chili pepper, cut in half and seeds removed

1 teaspoon filé powder

1. In a medium soup pot, bring water to a boil and add the rock tripe. Reduce heat to medium.

2. In a skillet over medium heat, sauté the onion, celery, and carrots in butter or vegetable oil for 10–15 minutes. Add Wild Herb Seasoning and evening primrose seeds and mix well.

3. Add to soup pot along with salt and cayenne pepper. Simmer for 1 hour.

4. Remove from heat and add filé powder.

Filé Powder

Filé powder is used in gumbo recipes as a thickener and is sold in specialty stores and gourmet shops. If you look at the ingredients, the only thing listed is sassafras leaves. You can make your own filé powder by gathering the young leaves and either dehydrating them in a dehydrator or spreading them on a screen until dry and then powdering them. Add to the cooked dish after you have removed it from the heat. Cooking with filé will result in a stringy, unappealing texture.

Root Soup

A robust soup to have on a cold, winter day, packed with vitamins and nutrients.

INGREDIENTS | SERVES 8–10

1 quart water

2 cups stinging nettle greens, chopped

4–6 evening primrose roots, peeled and chopped

4–6 Jerusalem artichoke tubers, chopped

1 cup chopped roots, combination of dandelion roots, burdock roots, yellow dock roots, or other roots, depending on what's available

½ cup rock tripe broken up into small pieces

2 tablespoons vegetable oil or butter

1 medium onion, chopped

2 celery stalks, chopped

3 carrots, chopped

Field garlic or wild onion tops, chopped

1 dried cayenne or chili pepper

½ teaspoon evening primrose seeds

Salt and pepper, to taste

1. Heat water to boiling in a medium-sized soup pot.

2. Add nettles and let cook for 2 minutes.

3. Add chopped roots.

4. Heat oil or butter in saucepan and sauté onions, celery, and carrots.

5. Add to soup pot, along with field garlic or onion tops, pepper, and evening primrose seeds. Cook on medium low heat for at least 30 minutes. Season with salt and pepper to taste.

Liver Cleansers

Herbs that are used to cleanse the liver are called hepatic herbs. They help by triggering the flow of bile and include dandelion root, burdock root, and yellow dock root. Their roots grow deep into the ground, making them rich in minerals and useful as a liver tonic.

Saltwort Balls

Add your own special blend of wild herbs and seasonings. Serve with soups or salads.

INGREDIENTS | SERVES 4

1 cup saltwort, chopped fine

½ cup wild greens (dandelions, mustards, lambsquarters, etc.), chopped

1 egg

1 cup prepared stuffing mix, corn meal, or other flour

¾ cup grated cheese

½ cup minced onion

Vegetable oil or butter for frying

1. In a medium bowl, combine saltwort and wild greens and mix well. Add the remaining ingredients and mix.

2. Form into balls and fry in heated oil or butter 5–10 minutes, rolling with a spoon on all sides until brown.

Sassaf-Rice

A wonderful blend of flavor and color.
Serve with stir-fries or other cooked vegetables.

INGREDIENTS | SERVES 6–8

2 cups cooked wild rice

2 tablespoons butter, melted

1 cup sassafras flowers

1 teaspoon filé powder

Sprinkle of ground turmeric

Sprinkle of ground cardamom seed

1 teaspoon Wild Herb Seasoning (Chapter 18)

3 green onions, chopped

½ cup greenbrier tips

1. In a large bowl, add butter to wild rice and mix well. Stir in sassafras flowers.

2. Combine filé powder, ground turmeric, ground cardamon seed, and Wild Herb Seasoning and mix in with rice.

3. Garnish with green onions and greenbrier tips.

Spring Fries

*This is a great dish to serve over wild rice with
Ground Cherry Salsa (Chapter 16) or cactus salad on top.*

INGREDIENTS | SERVES 4

3–4 wild onions or field garlic (or 1 medium onion), chopped

2 tablespoons butter or olive oil

4 thistle stalks, peeled

2 cups wild mustard flower buds and flowers

4–5 cattail hearts or flower buds, steamed and stripped

1 cup yucca flowers, petals removed

In a skillet over medium heat, sauté onions or garlic 5–10 minutes in butter or olive oil. Add remaining ingredients and simmer for 10–15 minutes.

Spring Rolls

These can be served raw, retaining the fresh and crisp flavor of spring vegetables.

INGREDIENTS | MAKES 2 DOZEN ROLLS

2 cups wild greens, chopped (peppergrass, heal-all, oxeye daisy, chickweed, dandelion)

6 wild onions (marinated overnight in sugar water)

½ teaspoon ginger, grated

1 carrot, grated

¼ teaspoon finely minced mint leaves

1 tablespoon lime juice

1 tablespoon soy sauce

Spring roll wrappers

Hot water for dipping wrappers

1. In a large bowl, combine greens, vegetables, ginger, and mint leaves. Add lime juice and soy sauce, mixing well.

2. Dip wrappers into hot water and hold until soft and pliable, about 10 seconds.

3. Spoon 1 tablespoon mixture onto wrappers and roll.

Marinated Wild Onions and Garlic

The strong smell and taste of wild onions and wild garlic can be mellowed by marinating them in sugar water. Layer them in a jar with onions or garlic on the bottom layer. Sprinkle sugar over the bulbs and continue to layer. Add enough water to cover the bulbs and let sit overnight.

Stir-Fried Milkweed Buds, Flowers, and Pods

*These flower buds look just like little green peas when cooked
and make a nice addition to potato dishes.*

INGREDIENTS | SERVES 6–8

2 tablespoons butter (or vegetable oil)

1 medium onion, chopped

2–3 carrots, chopped

2 cups precooked milkweed buds, flowers, and pods

1. Melt butter in saucepan over medium heat.

2. Sauté onions and carrots in melted butter about 5 minutes.

3. Add precooked milkweed buds and flowers to onions and carrots. Reduce heat and simmer for 5–10 minutes.

4. Serve as a side dish or with rice.

Stuffed Wild Grape Leaves

*When gathering grape leaves, look for the tender, lighter green leaves
rather than the darker, older ones for better taste and texture.*

INGREDIENTS | SERVES 12

3 dozen grape leaves

Sea salt, as needed

2 cups Wild Rice and Groundnuts (Chapter 17) as a stuffing mix

2 tablespoons olive oil

Grape Casserole

Grape leaves come in different sizes, depending on the species. If the leaves are too small for rolling, layer them in the bottom of an oiled or buttered casserole dish and put the wild rice stuffing mix on top of the leaves. End with a layer of grape leaves on top. Sprinkle with olive oil and bake at 325°F for about 20 minutes.

1. Rinse each leaf and lay it in a large pot, stacking the leaves on top of each other.

2. Cover with water and sprinkle with salt. Cook on low heat for 20–30 minutes, until the leaves turn dark green.

3. Put a tablespoon of the stuffing mix near the stem end of the leaf.

4. Fold in the sides and roll tightly.

5. Place on an oiled baking dish and brush the tops with olive oil.

6. Bake at 325°F for about 20 minutes. Serve warm or cold.

Sourwood Potatoes

Using the leaves from the sourwood tree in cooking imparts a mild, lemony flavor.

INGREDIENTS | SERVES 4

3 tablespoons butter

15–20 sourwood leaves

3 medium potatoes, sliced thinly

1 tablespoon Wild Herb Seasoning
(Chapter 18)

1. Preheat oven to 400°F.

2. Use 1 tablespoon of butter to grease the bottom of baking dish.

3. Line the bottom of the dish with half the sourwood leaves.

4. Layer the potatoes on top of the sourwood leaves.

5. Sprinkle herb seasoning on top of the potatoes.

6. Thinly slice the remaining butter and lay the slices of butter on top of seasoning.

7. Layer remaining sourwood leaves on top. Sprinkle a little water over the leaves.

8. Cover and bake 40–45 minutes.

Thistle Stalks with Hazelnut Butter Dip

Sweeter than celery once you get past the spines.

INGREDIENTS | SERVES 6

½ cup hazelnut butter (or other nut butter)

¼ cup plain yogurt

3 tablespoons honey

2 teaspoons sesame oil

½ teaspoon lemon juice

12 thistle stalks, peeled and cut in half lengthwise

1. In a large bowl combine the hazelnut butter, yogurt, honey, sesame oil, and lemon juice. Mix until smooth.

2. Fill thistle stalks with dip and serve.

Vegetable Pizza

*Adding a few wild toppings to your pizza can transform it into
a gourmet pizza with flavors found only in the wild.*

INGREDIENTS | SERVES 4

4 cloves garlic, chopped

1 tablespoon olive oil

2 cups chopped wild greens

1 cup Ground Cherry Salsa (Chapter 16) (or other pizza sauce)

1 pizza crust

1 small red onion, thinly sliced

1 cup grated cheese

1. Preheat oven to 425°F.

2. In a skillet over medium heat, sauté garlic for 2–5 minutes in olive oil.

3. Reduce heat and add greens. Cook 5–10 minutes, until wilted.

4. Spread ground cherry salsa (or sauce) on bottom of pizza crust.

5. Add greens with a layer of sliced onions on top of the greens.

6. Sprinkle with cheese and bake 15–20 minutes, until cheese has melted.

Watercress Soup

Upland cress, bittercress, or winter cress can also be used to make this nutritional soup.

INGREDIENTS | SERVES 4

4 tablespoons butter

1 onion, chopped

4 cloves garlic, finely chopped

1 cup watercress leaves, chopped

2 cups vegetable broth

1 bay leaf

1 cup sour cream

Several sprigs of oxeye daisy leaves, for garnish

1. Melt butter in saucepan and sauté onions and garlic for 5–10 minutes.

2. Reduce heat and add chopped greens. Cover and let simmer 5–10 minutes.

3. Put vegetable broth in a soup pot and bring to a boil.

4. Add vegetables and bay leaf to the soup pot, cover and simmer for 20 minutes.

5. Stir in sour cream, garnish with oxeye daisy leaves, and serve.

Vegetable Broth

Water that has been used for steaming vegetables is good to use as a vegetable broth. You can also make a broth by adding 1 tablespoon Wild Herb Seasoning (Chapter 18) to 2 cups of hot water and let it steep.

Wild Bean Tacos

A high-protein dish full of flavor that is satisfying and filling.

INGREDIENTS | SERVES 6

½ cup wild onion or field garlic, minced

1 tablespoon olive oil

2 cups cooked, shelled wild beans, mashed

1 cup cooked wild rice

12 taco shells

1 cup Ground Cherry Salsa (Chapter 16)

1 cup Cheddar cheese, grated

1. Sauté wild onions or field garlic in olive oil 5–10 minutes, until tender.

2. Add the wild beans and cooked rice to the onions or garlic and mix well.

3. Spoon 2 tablespoons mixture into taco shells.

4. Add 1 teaspoon Ground Cherry Salsa to each shell.

5. Sprinkle with grated cheese. Melt in oven on low broil.

Wild Beans and Greens

Serve as a topping on wild rice, pasta, or other cooked grain.

INGREDIENTS | SERVES 4

4 cloves garlic, chopped

1 medium onion, chopped

2 tablespoons olive oil

2 cups wild greens, washed and chopped (lambsquarters, dandelion, heal-all, wild mustard)

2 cups wild beans, cooked

½ cup Ground Cherry Salsa (Chapter 16) (or 1 cup diced tomatoes)

1 tablespoon rice vinegar

1. In a skillet over medium heat, sauté garlic and onion in olive oil 5–10 minutes, until soft.

2. Lower heat and add greens. Cover and let simmer about 10 minutes.

3. Add cooked beans and salsa (or tomatoes) and cook another 10 minutes.

4. Turn off heat and add vinegar. Cover and let stand for 2–3 minutes before serving.

Wild Rice and Groundnuts

Use as a stuffing with grape leaves to make dolmas or as a main dish.

INGREDIENTS | SERVES 4–6

1 medium onion, minced

1 stalk celery, chopped

2 tablespoons olive oil

1 cup wild rice

½ cup groundnuts, scrubbed and thinly sliced

2½ cups hickory nut milk (or water)

½ cup shelled hickory nuts

½ cup dried cranberries or blueberries

1. In a skillet over medium heat, sauté onions and celery in olive oil. Add rice and groundnuts and stir until rice is coated with oil.

2. Add rice mixture to nut milk (or water) in medium pan and bring to a boil. Cover and simmer about 30 minutes, or until water is absorbed.

3. Add nuts and berries. Cover and let steep for 5–10 minutes.

Yucca Flower Stalks au Gratin

Gather these before the flower buds have started to develop. Some stalks are bitter, so sample each one before cooking with them.

INGREDIENTS | SERVES 4

2 cups yucca stalks, peeled and cut into 2-inch pieces

3 tablespoons butter

½ cup grated cheese

2 tablespoons sour cream

1. Steam-cook yucca stalks for 25–30 minutes, until tender.

2. Arrange in bottom of serving dish.

3. Melt butter in saucepan. Add cheese and sour cream. Stir until blended.

4. Pour over yucca stalks and serve.

Wild Stuffed Squash

Use this stuffing mix for any winter squash or as a side dish for your holiday dinner.

INGREDIENTS | SERVES 4

2 acorn squashes (or butternut squash)

1 clove garlic, crushed

½ cup onion, chopped

2 stalks celery, chopped

¼ cup nuts, chopped (hickory, walnut, hazelnut, pecan)

¼ cup sunflower seeds

½ teaspoon garlic mustard seeds, ground

½ teaspoon evening primrose seeds, ground

3–4 tablespoons butter

½ teaspoon sage

1 cup whole wheat bread crumbs

¼ cup dried wild cranberries or blueberries

½ cup cheese, grated

1. Preheat oven to 350°F.

2. Cut squash in half, remove seeds, and bake for 30 minutes.

3. In a skillet over medium heat, sauté garlic, onions, celery, nuts, and seeds for about 10 minutes in butter or until soft.

4. Add remaining ingredients except cheese. Cook 5 minutes.

5. Remove from heat. Mix in cheese.

6. Pack stuffing into squash and bake for 25 minutes.

Green Cuisine

Baked Purslane

*This dish is good for all occasions and can be served
for breakfast as well as lunch or dinner.*

INGREDIENTS | SERVES 4–6

1 tablespoon butter

2 cups purslane greens, fresh tips

1 cup dried bread crumbs

3 eggs, well beaten

¼ cup sour cream

1 cup cheese, grated

1. Preheat oven to 350°F. Butter a casserole dish.

2. In a large bowl, toss together purslane and bread crumbs

3. Add sour cream to beaten eggs and combine with purslane and bread crumbs.

4. Pour into buttered casserole dish. Top with grated cheese. Bake 30–35 minutes, until firm.

Dandelion Quiche

*The quiche that's full of vitamins. This is one way to use the dandelions growing
in your yard and get your vitamins at the same time.*

INGREDIENTS | SERVES 6

1 tablespoon olive oil

2 cloves garlic, minced

2 cups dandelion greens, chopped

3 eggs

½ cup sour cream

1 teaspoon Wild Herb Seasoning (Chapter 18)

1 unbaked pie shell

1 cup cheese, grated

1. Preheat oven to 325°F.

2. In a skillet over medium heat, heat the olive oil. Add garlic and sauté for 2–5 minutes. Reduce heat and add dandelion greens. Cover and let simmer 5–10 minutes.

3. In a separate bowl, mix eggs and sour cream. Add dandelion mixture and herb seasoning.

4. Pour into the pie shell and sprinkle cheese on top.

5. Bake 45 minutes or until firm.

Dandelion as a Diuretic

Dandelion has diuretic properties that cleanse the kidneys and urinary tract by flushing out toxins through increased urination. Use the leaves as greens or the roasted roots to make a tea to help detoxify the body.

Green Cakes

*Top these cakes with a wild herb cheese spread and
edible wildflowers and serve with soup or salad.*

INGREDIENTS | SERVES 6–8

¾ cup sour cream or milk

2 eggs, beaten

1½ cups cornmeal or flour

1 teaspoon baking powder

1¼ cups wild greens, chopped

3 green onions or wild onions,
chopped

1 chili or cayenne pepper, chopped

1 cup Cheddar cheese, grated

1. Combine sour cream or milk with eggs in large mixing
   bowl.

2. Add cornmeal and baking powder.

3. Fold in greens, onions, peppers, and cheese.

4. Drop by spoonfuls onto hot, oiled griddle or frying
   pan.

5. Fry 5–10 minutes on each side or until golden brown.

Herb Dip

Use this as a dip for vegetables or as a spread on crackers or bread.

**INGREDIENTS | MAKES APPROXIMATELY
2 CUPS**

2 tablespoons vegetable oil

1 medium onion, chopped

3 cloves garlic, chopped

3 cups chopped wild greens (or ½
cup dried greens)

1 cup sour cream

1 cup grated cheese

1 cup wild mustard flowers/flower
buds

1. In a skillet over medium high heat, add the vegetable
   oil. Once the oil is hot, sauté onions and garlic.

2. Add wild greens and cook on low heat 10–15 minutes.

3. Remove from heat and fold in sour cream, grated
   cheese, flowers, and flower buds.

Kudzu Chips

Use the youngest, most tender leaves for cooking.
Eat while still warm to enjoy the crispness of this exotic dish.

INGREDIENTS | SERVES 6

1 cup flour

1 tablespoon cornstarch

Dash of cayenne pepper

1 cup cold water

30 young kudzu leaves

2 tablespoons coconut oil or butter for frying

1. In a medium bowl, combine flour, cornstarch, and cayenne pepper.

2. Add water and stir until smooth.

3. Dip leaves in batter and fry in hot oil 2–5 minutes on both sides until brown.

Kudzu for Hangovers

Research has shown that kudzu contains a compound known as daidzen that may help those suffering from hangovers. Even better, it may reduce the craving for alcohol, preventing the hangover before it ever happens.

Lambsquarters Pie

Like a quiche but without a crust.
Use the Ground Cherry Salsa (Chapter 16) as a spread on top.

INGREDIENTS | SERVES 4

2 tablespoons butter

1 onion, diced

3 eggs, beaten

1 cup sour cream

2 cups lambsquarters, chopped

1 teaspoon Wild Herb Seasoning (Chapter 18)

1 cup whole wheat flour

2 teaspoons baking powder

1 cup Cheddar cheese, grated

1. Preheat oven to 350°F.

2. Melt butter in a saucepan. Sauté onions about 5 minutes until translucent.

3. Add eggs and sour cream to a blender and mix well. Add lambsquarters and herb seasoning and blend until greens are coarsely chopped.

4. In medium bowl, combine egg mixture with flour and baking powder. Mix well.

5. Stir in sautéed onions and grated cheese. Pour into buttered pie pan and bake for 35 minutes, or until firm.

Mallow Lasagna

The mucilaginous quality of the mallow leaves acts as a natural thickener for the lasagna.

INGREDIENTS | SERVES 8–10

6 wild onions, marinated overnight in sugar water (or 1 medium onion, chopped)

4 cloves garlic, chopped

2 tablespoons olive oil

¼ cup Wild Herb Seasoning (Chapter 18)

½ cup grated Parmesan cheese

1 teaspoon dried basil

1 cup ricotta cheese

8 ounces lasagna noodles, cooked

2 cups tomato sauce

2 cups common mallow leaves, chopped fine

1 cup mozzarella cheese

1. Preheat oven to 375°F.

2. In a skillet over medium heat, sauté garlic and onions in olive oil 5–10 minutes or until tender.

3. In a large bowl, mix Wild Herb Seasoning, half the Parmesan cheese, and dried basil with ricotta cheese.

4. Butter or oil a baking dish and put a layer of noodles on the bottom.

5. Add layers of sauce, mallow leaves, ricotta cheese, and mozzarella cheese.

6. Repeat the process, ending with a layer of mozzarella cheese.

7. Cover and bake about 40–45 minutes.

8. Uncover and sprinkle with the remaining Parmesan cheese and bake another 10 minutes.

9. Remove from oven and let cool about 5–10 minutes before serving.

Nettle Pesto

Nettle is one of the best sources of protein in the plant world.
It is also rich in iron, calcium, magnesium, zinc, and other vitamins and minerals.

INGREDIENTS | SERVES 6–8

2 cups fresh stinging nettle (can also use chickweed, cress, or garlic mustard)

¼ cup fresh parsley

2 cloves garlic

1 cup toasted pecans

½ teaspoon salt

¼ cup olive oil

½ cup grated Parmesan cheese

1. Process all ingredients in food processor until a smooth paste is formed.

2. Serve on crackers, bread, or with pasta.

Poke Roll-Ups

These can be eaten alone or dipped into Ground Cherry Salsa (Chapter 16) for added flavor.

INGREDIENTS | SERVES 10

10–12 poke shoots, peeled and parboiled in 2 changes of water

1 cup Herb Dip (Chapter 18)

Wonton wrappers

Coconut oil or butter for frying

1. Cut poke into 1-inch sections (or the length of wonton wrappers being used).

2. Spread 1 tablespoon Herb Dip on wonton wrapper and place a poke shoot in the center.

3. Moisten the edges and roll the wrapper like a cigar, pinching the ends together.

4. Fry in oil or butter about 5 minutes until brown on both sides.

Poke and Pesto

Serve this as a side dish or with other vegetables.
It has the taste and texture of asparagus.

INGREDIENTS | SERVES 8–10

1 large onion, thinly sliced

2 cloves garlic, minced

2 tablespoons coconut oil or butter

2 dozen pokeweed shoots, peeled and parboiled in 2 changes of water

Juice of 1 lemon

⅓ cup Nettle Pesto (Chapter 18)

Poke—Edible, Poisonous, and Medicinal

Poke, when eaten raw, will make you throw up. However, when cooked through two changes of water, it becomes a nutritional green. Poke-weed contains vitamin A, large quantities of vitamin C and minerals. According to Dr. James Duke, the leaves also contain antiviral proteins that might help to fight cancers and viruses.

1. Preheat oven to 350°F.

2. In a skillet over medium heat, sauté onions and garlic in oil or butter until golden.

3. Spread pokeweed shoots in bottom of shallow baking dish.

4. Squeeze lemon juice over the poke.

5. Layer onions and garlic on top of pokeweed shoots.

6. Top with Nettle Pesto, evenly distributed.

7. Bake for 20 minutes.

Rice with Wild Greens

Add cooked redbud pods, cattail shoots, thistle stalks,
or other wild vegetables that are in season for added flavor.

INGREDIENTS | SERVES 6–8

1½ cups wild onions, leeks, or garlic, thinly sliced

1 tablespoon vegetable oil or butter

1 cup fresh greens, chopped

1 cup cooked rice

Parmesan cheese, optional

Splash of lemon juice or balsamic vinegar

Oxeye daisy leaves, for garnish

1. Sauté leeks in oil or butter for 2–3 minutes. Reduce heat and add wild greens and cook 5–10 minutes, until wilted. Add a splash of lemon juice or balsamic vinegar. Stir in cooked rice and let stand 5 minutes.

2. Sprinkle Parmesan cheese on top and garnish with oxeye daisy leaves and serve.

Sow Thistle Tempura

Serve dipped in tamari and sprinkled with Parmesan or with your favorite dipping sauce.

INGREDIENTS | SERVES 8

1 cup pancake mix

¼ cup pine or cattail pollen (if available)

½ teaspoon cayenne pepper

1½ cups beer

2 dozen young sow thistle leaf rosettes

2 tablespoons coconut oil or olive oil for frying

1. In a medium bowl combine pancake mix, pollen, and pepper.

2. Add beer to dry ingredients and stir until well blended.

3. Dip leaf rosettes into batter and fry in hot, coconut oil about 5 minutes, until brown on each side.

Spring Salad

Salad making is at its best in the early spring. Take advantage of this time to gather the wild greens and edible wildflowers for a beautiful and tasty salad. Stuff into a pita or use as a filling for a salad wrap.

INGREDIENTS | SERVES 8–10

1 cup chickweed flowers and tips

1 cup field pansy and violet flowers

1 cup dandelion leaves

1 cup sheep sorrel leaves

1 cup heal-all leaves

1 cup greenbrier tips

1 cup upland cress leaves, flower buds, and flowers

1 cup redbud flowers

½ cup young sassafras leaves

Plantain seeds from 1 flower stalk (optional)

Juice of 1 lemon

1 tablespoon maple syrup

1. In a large mixing bowl, toss all greens together.

2. In a small bowl, combine lemon juice and maple syrup. Pour over salad mixture and serve.

Plantago Seeds

Seeds of Plantago species, commonly known as plantain, contain psyllium, which is a fiber laxative that helps prevent constipation by cleansing the bowels. Seeds can be stripped and added to the seed seasoning or to salads as needed.

Stuffed Violets

These make an attractive display and are good for edible arrangements.

INGREDIENTS | MAKES 2 DOZEN

8 ounces cream cheese, softened

1 tablespoon fruit preserves or jam

2 dozen violet leaves

4 dozen violet and wild pansy flowers

1 tablespoon maple or raw sugar

1. In a medium bowl, mix cream cheese and fruit preserves.

2. Put a dab in the center of each violet leaf.

3. Top with a couple of flowers. Sprinkle sugar over flowers.

4. Chill 30 minutes and serve.

Wild Frittatas

This is like a lazy cook's omelet. It requires no flipping.
Put it in the pan, cover it, and set the timer so you don't forget it.

INGREDIENTS | SERVES 8

1 medium onion, chopped

3 cloves minced garlic

3 tablespoons butter

2 cups wild greens, chopped

3 eggs, beaten

1 cup milk or sour cream

1 cup grated cheese

Dash of cayenne pepper

1. In a skillet over medium heat, sauté garlic and onions 5–10 minutes in butter. Reduce heat to a low temperature.

2. Add wild greens and mix well. Spread evenly in pan.

3. In a separate bowl, beat eggs and add sour cream.

4. Pour over sautéed garlic and onions and greens.

5. Sprinkle with cayenne pepper and grated cheese. Cover pan and cook on low heat 30–45 minutes, until firm.

What Is a Frittata?

A frittata is similar to an omelet except that the ingredients are mixed in with the egg mixture, covered, and cooked on low heat or baked without having to flip it.

Wild Green Burritos

Use whatever greens are in season to make these wild burritos.
Substitute cooked pokeweed shoots for the greens for a little variation.

2 tablespoons olive oil

1 medium onion, chopped

3 cloves garlic, chopped

2 cups wild greens, chopped

½ cup sour cream

6 flour tortillas

2 cups grated Cheddar cheese

1. In a skillet over high heat, sauté onions and garlic in hot olive oil for 5–10 minutes, until soft.

2. Lower heat and add greens. Cook on low heat 10–15 minutes, until leaves are wilted.

3. Stir in sour cream.

4. Fill each tortilla with a large spoonful of cooked greens. Sprinkle with grated cheese. Fold in one end of tortilla and roll.

Bitter Herbs

Bitter herbs taste bitter. There are taste zones on the tongue for sweet, salty, sour, and bitter. The bitter zone reacts to the taste of bitter herbs by stimulating saliva flow, enhancing digestion and assimilation of food. Bitter herbs are both adaptogens and tonics, helping the body absorb nutrients and flush out toxins.

Wild Green Quesadillas

Use wild greens as the filling and serve with Ground Cherry Salsa (Chapter 16).

INGREDIENTS | SERVES 4–6

1 medium onion, chopped

2 cloves garlic, chopped

1 chili pepper, chopped

2 tablespoons olive oil

3–4 cups wild greens, chopped

¼ cup sour cream

10 flour tortillas

1 cup grated cheese

2 tablespoons butter or coconut oil for frying

1. In a skillet over medium heat, sauté garlic, onions, and pepper in hot olive oil 5–10 minutes, until soft.

2. Lower heat and add chopped greens. Cook for 15–20 minutes, until tender.

3. Stir in sour cream.

4. Spread 2 tablespoons of greens mixture onto half of flour tortilla. Top with grated cheese and fold in half.

5. Brown each side in hot buttered or oiled skillet 5–10 minutes until brown on each side.

Wild Herb Seasoning

A blend of dried greens and just enough spice to add flavor and nutrition to any vegetable dish.

INGREDIENTS | MAKES 1 CUP

1 cup dried greens (cress, purslane, stinging nettle, kudzu)

¼ cup dried saltwort (if available)

1 tablespoon dried wild chives (wild onion and garlic tops)

¼ teaspoon garlic mustard seeds (or other mustard seeds)

¼ teaspoon evening primrose seeds

1. Blend ingredients in blender or coffee grinder.

2. Use as a sprinkle on your favorite vegetable dishes, salads, or soups.

Salt Substitute

Using saltwort or any of the other plants with a high salt content eliminates the need for using commercial table salt in a recipe. When available, use these plants as a substitute for salt.

CHAPTER 19

Breads

Acorn Griddle Cakes

*A fulfilling way to start the day with griddle cakes
served with real maple syrup.*

INGREDIENTS | SERVES 12

2 cups acorn meal

2 cups flour or pancake mix

1 cup maple-flavored yogurt

½ cup water or enough for pancake
consistency

¼ cup butter or vegetable oil for
frying

1. Combine ingredients and mix until well blended.

2. Drop by spoonfuls onto hot, oiled griddle pan.

3. Brown 5–10 minutes on each side or until brown and serve.

Bean Bread

*This can also be baked in a baking dish at 350°F.
Serve with Ground Cherry Salsa (Chapter 16).*

INGREDIENTS | SERVES 8

2 eggs, beaten

¾ cup sour cream

1¼ cups wild beans, cooked

2 cups cornmeal

1 teaspoon baking powder

¼ cup hot water

3 green onions, chopped

1 chili pepper, chopped

1 tablespoon molasses

1 cup Cheddar cheese, grated

1. Combine sour cream with eggs.

2. Add beans, cornmeal, and baking powder. Add enough hot water for pancake consistency. Stir in the molasses.

3. Fold in onions, peppers, and cheese.

4. Drop by spoonfuls onto hot, oiled griddle or frying pan.

5. Fry 5–10 minutes on each side or until golden brown.

Cattail Pollen Cakes

Amazingly delicious blend of cattail pollen and corn meal.

INGREDIENTS | SERVES 12

3 eggs

2 cups corn meal

2 cups cattail pollen

2 tablespoons molasses

2 tablespoons butter, melted

1 cup hot water or enough for mixture to be consistency of pancake batter

¼ cup coconut oil for frying (can also use regular vegetable oil)

1. In a large mixing bowl, combine ingredients in order listed.

2. Drop by spoonfuls on hot, oiled griddle pan.

3. Brown 5–10 minutes on each side and serve.

Blueberry Pancakes

Use a wild berry syrup with butter as a tasty topping.

INGREDIENTS | SERVES 4

1 cup pancake mix

1 tablespoon butter, melted

1 cup maple yogurt

Enough water for pancake consistency

1 cup wild blueberries

Oil or butter for frying

1. In a large mixing bowl, combine pancake mix, butter, and yogurt.

2. Add enough water for desired pancake consistency.

3. Stir in blueberries.

4. Drop by spoonfuls on hot, oiled griddle and brown 5–10 minutes on each side.

Cranberry Nut Bread

Just the bread to serve with cheese spreads for the holidays.

INGREDIENTS | SERVES 8–10

2 tablespoons vegetable oil or butter, softened

¾ cup honey

2 eggs, slightly beaten

1½ teaspoon baking powder

½ teaspoon baking soda

2 cups flour

1 cup wild cranberries, chopped (if available)

1 cup hickory nuts, chopped

1. Preheat oven to 350°F.

2. Cream butter or vegetable oil with honey. Add eggs.

3. Combine dry ingredients and add to creamed mixture.

4. Stir in wild cranberries and nuts.

5. Spoon into greased loaf pan.

6. Bake 40–45 minutes, until done.

Dandelion Fritters

Enjoy the flowery taste of these fritters while gaining the health benefits of this nutritional herb.

INGREDIENTS | SERVES 6–8

2 cups dandelion flowers

2 eggs, beaten

¾ cup sour cream

3–4 field garlic bulbs or green onions, chopped

2 cups cornmeal muffin mix

1 cup Cheddar cheese, grated

1 tablespoon molasses (optional)

½ cup hot water

Butter or coconut oil for frying

1. Remove sepals from base of dandelion flowers using kitchen scissors or sharp knife and break up petals.

2. Stir into beaten eggs and add sour cream. Add remaining ingredients and enough hot water for the consistency of pancake batter.

3. Drop by spoonfuls onto hot, oiled griddle or frying pan. Fry 5–10 minutes on each side until golden brown.

The Dandelion Harvest

The secret to getting good-tasting dandelions is to watch for that first burst of yellow color in the early spring. These are the best tasting and make the best fritters, wine, and cordials. They tend to get more bitter as the days get warmer.

Elder Flower Fritters

A nutritious, flowery-tasting fritter that is good served with wild preserves or syrup.

INGREDIENTS | SERVES 10–12

2 eggs, beaten

1 cup sour cream

2 cups elder flowers, large stems removed

2 cups pancake mix

2 tablespoons butter or coconut oil for frying

1. In a large bowl, combine beaten eggs and sour cream, and add flowers.

2. Add pancake mix and mix well.

3. Drop by spoonfuls on hot, oiled skillet or griddle and cook 5–10 minutes until brown on each side.

Green Bars

Easy to make and full of flavor. Add Ground Cherry Salsa (Chapter 16) on top for added flavor.

INGREDIENTS | SERVES 10–12

2 tablespoons butter or shortening

3 eggs, beaten

1 cup sour cream

1 cup flour

1 teaspoon baking powder

2 cups wild greens, chopped fine

1 cup cheese, grated

1. Preheat oven to 350°F.

2. In a saucepan over medium heat, melt butter in pan.

3. Mix sour cream with beaten eggs and combine with remaining ingredients.

4. Pour into medium-size baking pan.

5. Bake for 35 minutes, until firm.

6. Cool 10 minutes, cut into squares, and serve.

Green Fritters

These are good with soups or salads and can be eaten hot or cold.

INGREDIENTS | SERVES 4–6

¾ cup sour cream (or milk)

2 eggs, beaten

1½ cups pancake mix

1¼ cups wild greens

3 wild onions (or green onions)

1 cup Cheddar cheese, grated

Oil or butter for frying

1. In a large bowl, combine sour cream with eggs.

2. Add pancake mix, wild greens, onions, and cheese.

3. Drop by spoonfuls onto hot, oiled griddle or frying pan and cook on each side 5–10 minutes, until brown.

Nut Bread

A mildly sweet bread that goes well with any wild berry preserve or jam.

INGREDIENTS | MAKES 1 LOAF

2 tablespoons butter, melted

¾ cup honey

2 eggs, beaten

2 teaspoons baking powder

2 cups flour

1 cup hickory nuts, chopped (or other available wild nuts)

1. Preheat oven to 350°F.

2. Cream melted butter with honey and add beaten eggs in medium-size mixing bowl.

3. Add baking powder and flour to creamed mixture.

4. Stir in nuts. Spoon into greased loaf pan.

5. Bake for 40–45 minutes.

6. Cool 10–15 minutes before removing from pan.

Pawpaw Nut Bread

This bread is similar in taste to banana bread.

INGREDIENTS | MAKES 1 LOAF

⅓ cup butter, softened

⅔ cup honey

2 eggs

3 tablespoons plain yogurt

½ cup pawpaw pulp

2 cups whole wheat flour

1 teaspoon baking powder

½ cup chopped pecans

1. Preheat oven to 350°F.

2. Cream butter and honey in large bowl. Add eggs and beat.

3. Stir in yogurt and pawpaw pulp.

4. Combine flour and baking powder with yogurt mixture.

5. Stir in pecans. Pour into a greased loaf pan. Bake for 40–45 minutes or until done.

6. Cool 10 minutes before removing from pan.

Persimmon Biscuits

These are delicious served hot with butter and honey.

INGREDIENTS | SERVES 12

2 cups biscuit mix

½ cup butter, melted

½ cup persimmon pulp

¼ cup maple yogurt

1. Preheat oven to 350°F.

2. Put the biscuit mix in a round bowl. Make a well in the center.

3. Pour melted butter, persimmon pulp, and yogurt into the well.

4. Work from the inside out, stirring the flour into the mixture gradually. When the dough starts to thicken, use your fingers to form a ball, dusting it with flour to keep it from sticking to your fingers.

5. Roll into small, flattened balls.

6. Bake 10–12 minutes, until golden brown.

Queen Anne's Lace Cornbread

A dainty-looking bread with a hint of carrot taste.

INGREDIENTS | SERVES 12–16

2 tablespoons butter

3 eggs, beaten

2 cups sour cream

1½ cups corn meal muffin mix

1½ cups flour

1 cup grated cheese

½ cup hot water

2 cups Queen Anne's lace flowers, large stems removed

1. Preheat oven to 350°F.

2. Melt butter in large cast iron skillet.

3. In a large bowl, combine eggs and sour cream.

4. Add corn meal, flour, cheese, and water, and mix well.

5. Add melted butter to corn meal mixture. Fold in Queen Anne's lace flowers and pour into hot, buttered, cast iron skillet. Bake for 35 minutes, or until firm.

Positive Identification

One way to positively identify Queen Anne's lace when in bloom is to look for the red dot, which is actually a floret located near the center.

Persimmon Bread

This is a sweet bread that is good with a fruit and nut cheese spread and served with hot cider.

INGREDIENTS | SERVES 6

2 eggs, beaten

¼ cup vegetable oil or butter, softened

⅔ cup honey

2 tablespoons plain yogurt

2 cups flour

1 teaspoon baking powder

1 cup persimmon pulp

½ cup chopped nuts (optional)

1. Preheat oven to 350°F.

2. Combine ingredients in the order listed. Mix well.

3. Pour into a greased loaf pan.

4. Bake 45–50 minutes.

5. Cool 10–15 minutes before removing from pan.

Raspberry Scones

Serve with butter or wild preserves while still warm.
Leftovers can be frozen and heated up as needed.

INGREDIENTS | MAKES 12

2 cups flour

2 tablespoons baking powder

1 egg, beaten

½ cup maple yogurt

1 tablespoon maple syrup

1 cup raspberries

⅓ cup butter, melted

Scones

Scones are like biscuits but they are sweeter and are often made with different fruits, including blueberries, blackberries, and raspberries. Sometimes they are cooked on a griddle and are usually served with butter and jam.

1. Preheat oven to 400°F.

2. Mix the flour and baking powder in a large bowl and create a well in the center.

3. Add the egg, yogurt, maple syrup, raspberries, and butter into the well.

4. Gradually stir the flour into the middle, working from the inside out.

5. Use a large tablespoon to drop the dough onto the baking sheet and bake for 15–20 minutes.

6. Serve warm.

Rock Tripe Crackers

Try these with friends for a dinner party served with a wild fruit jam or preserves.

INGREDIENTS | SERVES 10–12

¾ cup whole wheat flour

1 cup all-purpose flour

¼ cup nut flour

2 tablespoons sunflower seeds, ground

1 teaspoon salt

1½ teaspoons baking powder

¼ cup rock tripe, ground

¼ cup sour cream

1 tablespoon butter, melted

½ cup ice water

1. Preheat oven to 350°F.

2. In a large bowl, mix together the dry ingredients.

3. Stir in sour cream and melted butter.

4. Add the ice water and knead lightly.

5. Roll to one-eighth-inch thickness on a floured surface. Add more flour as needed to prevent the dough from sticking. Cut to desired shape and size.

6. Place on a lightly greased cookie sheet and prick tops with a fork.

7. Bake 10 minutes or until lightly browned.

Strawberry Bread

A wonderful springtime treat spread with cream cheese and strawberry preserves across the top.

INGREDIENTS | MAKES 1 LOAF

¼ cup honey

¼ cup butter, melted

1 egg, beaten

1½ cups whole wheat flour

3 teaspoons baking powder

1 cup wild strawberries

1. Preheat oven to 325°F.

2. Add honey and butter to beaten egg and blend.

3. Put flour and baking powder in a large bowl and make a well in the center.

4. Pour in egg mixture and add strawberries. Blend well.

5. Pour into a greased loaf pan and bake about 1 hour.

6. Cool 10–15 minutes before removing from pan.

CHAPTER 20

Desserts

Acorn Chip Cookie Bars

A high-protein cookie to serve with hot, mulled apple cider with rose hips.

INGREDIENTS | MAKES 16 SQUARES

¼ cup butter, softened

¼ cup molasses

2 tablespoons honey

¼ cup plain yogurt

¼ cup cream cheese

½ teaspoon vanilla

1 cup acorns, finely chopped

1 cup whole wheat flour

1 teaspoon baking powder

1. Preheat oven to 350°F.

2. Cream together butter, molasses, and honey.

3. Blend yogurt, cream cheese, and vanilla and add to butter mixture.

4. Stir in remaining ingredients.

5. Spread in 8-inch square baking dish.

6. Bake for 25–30 minutes.

7. Cool 10–15 minutes, cut into squares and serve.

Berry Cheesecake

So yummy you will want to go out and gather lots of berries.

INGREDIENTS | SERVES 8

8 ounces cream cheese, softened

½ cup plain yogurt

¼ cup honey

1 granola or graham cracker crust

1 cup blueberries, blackberries, or raspberries, sweetened with honey

1 tablespoon corn starch

¼ cup water

1. Mix cream cheese, yogurt, and honey and spread onto crust.

2. Drain liquids from berries. Spread berries on top of cream cheese mixture.

3. Add water and corn starch to drained liquid and cook on medium heat until mixture begins to boil, stirring constantly, for 1 minute, or until clear.

4. Spoon glaze over berries. Chill at least 30 minutes and serve.

Berry Cheesecake Pie

Use black gum syrup or black cherry syrup to swirl a decorative touch on this pie.

INGREDIENTS | SERVES 8

8 ounces cream cheese, softened

¼ cup sugar

1 egg, beaten

2 tablespoons milk

½ teaspoon vanilla

¼ cup berry syrup

1 pie crust

1. Preheat oven to 350°F.

2. Combine sugar and cream cheese and beat until smooth.

3. Add egg, milk, and vanilla. Spread over pie crust.

4. Swirl berry syrup into cream cheese mixture.

5. Bake 25–30 minutes.

Beech Nut Pie

Even though they're small, beech nuts are sweet and tasty and, when available, make delicious pies.

INGREDIENTS | SERVES 8

½ cup butter

¾ cup raw sugar

3 eggs

1 cup maple syrup

1 cup beech nuts (or pecans)

1 teaspoon vanilla

1 unbaked pie shell

1. Preheat oven to 350°F.

2. Cream butter and raw sugar.

3. Beat in eggs, one at a time.

4. Stir in maple syrup, nuts, and vanilla.

5. Pour into pie shell and bake 45 minutes.

Finding Beech Nuts

Beech nuts are not always easy to find. Beech trees bloom early in the spring and are often followed by a late, heavy frost. This prevents the nutmeat from developing, even though the outer hull and the shell have developed. Very often the shell is empty of nutmeat. You will know it's a good year when you see the crows arriving in flocks and landing in the beech trees, knocking the nuts out in the process.

Berry Cream Puffs

So yummy! They melt in your mouth.

INGREDIENTS | MAKES 24

1 cup berries (blueberries, serviceberries, blackberries, mulberries)

¼ cup sugar

8 ounces cream cheese, softened

24 wonton wrappers

Oil or butter for frying

1. Place berries in a saucepan with just enough water to get the juices flowing. Add sugar and cook on medium heat for 10–15 minutes, mashing the berries while cooking.

2. Remove from heat and mix wild berry mixture with cream cheese in a medium-size bowl.

3. Place 1 tablespoon berry mixture in the center of each wonton wrapper and fold edges around the mixture, moistening the edges of the wrapper with water so they will stick.

4. Fry in oil or butter 5–10 minutes, or until brown on each side.

5. Cool 5–10 minutes before serving.

Black Cherry Ice Cream

Incredibly delicious! And strengthening as well, with all the blood-building benefits of black cherries.

INGREDIENTS | MAKES 1 GALLON

4 cups milk

2¾ cups sugar

3 cups black cherry juice

5 cups whipping cream

2 tablespoons vanilla

1. Combine all ingredients in large bowl.

2. Pour into the ice cream canister and freeze according to directions.

Blackberry Cobbler

Capture the tastes of summer berries in this easy-to-make recipe.
Use strawberries, raspberries, mulberries, or whatever juicy fruit is available.

INGREDIENTS | SERVES 8–10

4 cups blackberries

¼ cup honey

1½ tablespoons cornstarch

¼ cup brown sugar (or raw sugar)

1 tablespoon butter

1 tablespoon lemon juice

½ cup flour

½ cup raw sugar

2 tablespoons butter, softened

1 egg, slightly beaten

Berries for Better Vision

Scientific research has shown that blueberries, huckleberries, blackberries, wild cherries, elderberries, and other dark-colored fruits contain anthocyanosides, an antioxidant that helps prevent macular degeneration and improve vision.

1. Preheat oven to 350°F.

2. Add honey to blackberries and mix well. Let stand for 30 minutes.

3. Drain liquid from blackberries into a saucepan.

4. Spread blackberries in bottom of baking dish.

5. Mix cornstarch, sugar, and drained fruit juice. Cook until mixture is thickened, about 15 minutes.

6. Add butter and lemon juice and mix well. Pour mixture over fruit.

7. In a separate bowl, combine flour, raw sugar, butter, and egg. Beat with spoon until batter is smooth.

8. Drop by spoonfuls over fruit mixture, spreading evenly. Bake 30–35 minutes, until done.

Blackberry Crumb Cake

Can also be used with raspberries and mulberries.

INGREDIENTS | SERVES 8

¼ cup butter, softened

¼ cup honey

1 egg, beaten

1 cup flour

1½ teaspoons baking powder

⅓ cup plain yogurt

1 teaspoon vanilla

2 cups blackberries, sweetened

½ cup raw sugar

¼ cup butter, softened

⅓ cup flour

1. Preheat oven to 350°F.

2. In a large mixing bowl, cream butter and honey.

3. Add beaten egg.

4. In a separate bowl, combine dry ingredients. Add to creamed mixture.

5. Fold in yogurt and vanilla.

6. Pour batter into greased and floured cake pan.

7. Cover with blackberries.

8. To make the topping, cream the sugar and butter. Stir in flour until mixture is crumbly. Sprinkle crumb topping over blackberries.

9. Bake for 45 minutes.

Black Gum Syrup

*It's amazing to taste the flavor transformation that occurs
when you add a little sugar to black gum juice.*

INGREDIENTS | MAKES 1 CUP SYRUP

1 cup black gum juice

½ cup raw sugar

1. Combine juice and sugar in a saucepan and bring to a rapid boil for 30 minutes.

2. Pour into sterilized glass jar and seal.

Healthy Desserts

When supplementing recipes with commercial products, it is best to avoid white flour, white sugar, margarine, and other saturated, polyunsaturated, and hydrogenated fats. Choose organic fruits and vegetables that are grown locally when possible.

Blueberry Pound Cake

*A creamy, moist cake that needs no topping.
It's delicious as it is.*

INGREDIENTS | SERVES 12–16

1 standard-size package vanilla-flavored cake mix

½ cup butter, softened

8 ounces cream cheese, softened

3 eggs

2 cups wild blueberries (or serviceberries)

1. Preheat oven to 350°F.

2. Combine cake mix, butter, cream cheese, and eggs and mix until smooth.

3. Fold in blueberries. Pour into buttered, 9" × 13" baking pan.

4. Bake for 45 minutes, or until done.

Blueberry Oatmeal Bars

Contains the rich, full flavor of blueberries.
Can also use wild strawberries, elderberries, or blackberries.

INGREDIENTS | SERVES 12

1¾ cup quick-cooking oats

1 cup flour

1 cup ground nuts (hickory or pecans)

¾ cup raw sugar

¾ cup butter, melted

2 cups wild blueberries

2 tablespoons honey

¼ cup water

2 tablespoons cornstarch

Quick-Cooking Oats Versus Old-Fashioned Oats

The difference is the way the oats are processed. Oat groats are steamed, rolled, and flaked to produce rolled oats. Quick-cooking oats have thinner flakes and cook more quickly. They are less chewy than old-fashioned oats. To turn old-fashioned oats into quick-cooking oats, put in the blender and grind to desired texture.

1. Preheat oven to 350°F.

2. In a large bowl, combine oats, flour, nuts, and sugar.

3. Add butter and mix until crumbly.

4. Press half the mixture into bottom of medium-size, buttered baking dish. Set remaining mixture aside.

5. Combine blueberries, honey, water, and cornstarch in a saucepan and bring to a boil. Reduce heat and cook 10–15 minutes, until mixture thickens and becomes clear.

6. Pour over mixture in baking dish.

7. Sprinkle remaining oats mixture over the berries.

8. Bake 20 minutes, until golden brown.

Chocolate Cherry Bars

Serve with black cherry ice cream to get the full black cherry flavor.

INGREDIENTS | SERVES 10–12

½ cup butter, melted

1 cup honey

3 eggs

⅓ cup black cherry syrup

1 teaspoon vanilla

1½ cups whole wheat flour

½ cup cocoa

2 teaspoons baking powder

1. Preheat oven to 350°F.

2. In a large bowl, mix butter and honey.

3. Beat in eggs, black cherry syrup, and vanilla.

4. Stir in flour, cocoa, and baking powder.

5. Pour into greased 9" × 13" baking dish.

6. Bake for 35–40 minutes.

7. Cool. Cut into squares.

Elder Coffeecake

This can also be made with blueberries. Serve with ice cream or yogurt.

INGREDIENTS | SERVES 8–10

½ cup butter, softened

¾ cup honey

2 eggs, beaten

1¾ cup flour

2 teaspoons baking powder

1¼ cup plain yogurt

1 teaspoon vanilla

1 cup elderberries, sweetened to taste

½ cup chopped nuts

¼ cup raw sugar

1. Preheat oven to 350°F.

2. Cream butter, honey, and eggs until fluffy.

3. Add flour and baking powder to butter mixture and blend.

4. Fold in yogurt and vanilla.

5. Pour into greased and floured cake pan.

6. Spoon elderberries over surface, pressing lightly into batter.

7. Combine nuts and sugar and sprinkle over berries.

8. Bake for 40–45 minutes.

Fruit-Nut Crunch

A healthy dessert that you can enjoy during the holidays.

INGREDIENTS | SERVES 6–8

½ cup butter, softened

½ cup oats

½ cup nuts, chopped

½ cup whole wheat flour

1 cup raw sugar

2 cups berries (blueberries, cranberries, blackberries, raspberries)

¼ cup honey

1. Preheat oven to 350°F.

2. Mix butter with oats, nuts, flour, and sugar until crumbly.

3. Press half the mixture evenly on bottom of buttered baking dish. Reserve remaining crumbs for topping.

4. Place the berries in a saucepan and cook gently for 10–15 minutes.

5. Add honey and mix.

6. Pour the berries over the oat mixture in the baking dish. Top with remaining oat mixture.

7. Bake for 30–35 minutes.

Great Grape Pie

So incredibly full of taste and texture that you want to keep coming back for more.

INGREDIENTS | SERVES 8

3 cups muscadine grapes, hulled and seeded

½ cup honey

3 tablespoons flour

1 unbaked pie shell

1. Preheat oven to 350°F.

2. Place grapes in saucepan and add honey and flour. Cook on medium heat for about 15–20 minutes, until mixture is thickened and clear.

3. Pour into unbaked pie shell.

4. Bake for 30–35 minutes.

Hazelnut Tart

A delicious way to enjoy the bounty of your harvest.

INGREDIENTS | SERVES 8

6 tablespoons butter, melted

1 cup raw sugar

2 eggs, beaten

¼ cup maple yogurt

1 cup hazelnuts, chopped

1 prepared crumb crust

1. Preheat oven to 350°F.

2. In a large bowl, mix butter and sugar.

3. Add beaten eggs, yogurt, and hazelnuts.

4. Pour into pie crust and bake for 30–35 minutes.

Hickory Bites

These high-protein bites are good to take with you when hiking or doing outside activities for quick bursts of energy.

INGREDIENTS | MAKES 7 DOZEN

⅔ cup butter, softened

⅔ cup raw sugar

¼ cup honey

2 eggs

⅔ cup chopped hickory nuts

2 cups oats

2 cups flour

1 teaspoon baking soda

⅔ cup wild blueberries

⅔ cup hickory nut milk

1. Preheat oven to 350°F.

2. In a large mixing bowl, cream butter, sugar, and honey.

3. Add remaining ingredients and mix thoroughly.

4. Drop by teaspoonfuls onto baking dish.

5. Bake for 12 minutes.

Freezing Tips

When making a large quantity of cookies, freeze what you don't need now by arranging the cooled cookies in a plastic container lined with plastic wrap, placing the wrap between the layers. When ready to use, thaw and heat in oven to desired temperature.

Hickory Crepes

Use wild strawberries, blueberries, blackberries, raspberries,
or whatever berries are in season as a filling.

INGREDIENTS | 6-8 CREPES

1 cup hickory nut milk

¾ cup pancake mix

2 eggs

2 tablespoons butter or coconut oil

1. Mix nut milk, pancake mix, and eggs.

2. Heat butter or oil in small, nonstick skillet. Pour ¼ cup batter across the bottom. Cook about 2 minutes on each side until lightly brown. Use warm crepes when adding filling.

Nut Topping

A tasty addition to most cakes or pies.
Sprinkle this topping over the top before baking.

INGREDIENTS | COVERS 1 CAKE OR PIE FOR 6-8 PEOPLE

2 cups nuts

¼ cup raw sugar

¼ cup softened butter

1. Put nuts in blender or coffee grinder and grind. Place in a bowl and mix with sugar.

2. Add softened butter and mix thoroughly until crumbly.

3. Sprinkle mixture over cakes or pies.

Soaking Nuts Before You Eat Them

According to nutrition experts, nuts contain enzyme inhibitors that prevent them from sprouting. Soaking them releases this enzyme, making the nut easier to digest.

Nutty Crumb Crust

Use as a crust or topping on baked fruit pies, cakes, or other desserts.

INGREDIENTS | MAKES 1 PIE CRUST

⅓ cup butter, softened

⅓ cup sugar

1 cup flour

½ cup ground nuts (hickory, beech, hazelnut, pecan)

1. Preheat oven to 400°F.

2. Cream butter and sugar.

3. Combine butter mixture with flour and nuts until mixture is crumbly. Set aside half of the mixture for topping.

4. Press lightly in buttered pie pan.

5. Bake for 10–12 minutes.

6. Cool.

Passionfruit Bars

A dessert with the tartness of lemons. Use a berry sauce as a topping.

INGREDIENTS | SERVES 12

⅓ cup butter

¾ cup honey

2 eggs

1½ cups flour

1 teaspoon baking powder

2 cups passionfruit juice

1. Preheat oven to 350°F.

2. In a large mixing bowl, blend butter and honey.

3. Beat in eggs one at a time.

4. Add flour and baking powder. Stir in passionfruit juice.

5. Pour into a medium-size baking dish and bake for 35–40 minutes.

Passionfruit Cream Pie

A smooth, creamy texture with all the flavors of passionfruit.

INGREDIENTS | SERVES 8

1 cup passionfruit juice

1 can sweetened condensed milk

1 cup whipping cream

Prepared pie crust

1. Whip passionfruit juice, condensed milk, and whipped cream together. Place into prepared pie crust.

2. Chill for 30 minutes and serve.

Passionfruit Pie

Serve with whipping cream or homemade ice cream.

INGREDIENTS | SERVES 8

1 cup flour

½ teaspoon baking powder

1 cup sugar

3 eggs, separated

2 cups passionfruit juice

1 crumb pie crust

1. Preheat oven to 350°F.

2. Sift flour, baking powder, and ½ cup sugar together.

3. In a separate bowl, beat egg whites until soft peaks form.

4. Add remaining ½ cup sugar gradually and beat until stiff peaks form. Set aside.

5. In a separate bowl beat egg yolks. Stir in passionfruit juice.

6. Add flour mixture gradually.

7. Fold in beaten egg whites.

8. Spoon mixture into crumb pie crust.

9. Bake for 35–40 minutes. Cool. Chill for 1 hour.

Passionfruit Tarts

This pie is similar in texture to lemon or key lime pie but with the wild flavor of passionfruit. Serve with whipped cream or cool whip.

INGREDIENTS | MAKES 1 PIE

1 cup raw sugar

2 tablespoons butter, softened

4 eggs, beaten

1 cup passionfruit pulp, seeds removed

1 crumb or nut pie crust

1. Preheat oven to 350°F.

2. Cream butter and sugar together. Add sugar and butter mixture to beaten eggs and mix well.

3. Stir in passionfruit pulp.

4. Pour into pie shell and bake 20 minutes, until firm.

Pawpaw Pudding

This can also be made with persimmon pulp, which also has a pudding-like texture.

INGREDIENTS | SERVES 8–10

¼ cup pawpaw pulp

2 cups maple yogurt

1 vanilla bean, sliced in half and the inside pulp scraped out (or 1 teaspoon vanilla flavoring)

1. In a large bowl, add pawpaw pulp to yogurt.

2. Stir in vanilla and serve.

Persimmon Ice Cream

Creamy and delicious! Serve with persimmon pudding, cake, or pie.

INGREDIENTS | SERVES 8–10

3 cups persimmon pulp

1 cup sugar

½ cup honey

¼ teaspoon cinnamon

1 cup plain yogurt

¼ cup orange juice

1 teaspoon vanilla flavoring

2 cups whipping cream

1. In a large bowl, combine all ingredients, mixing well.

2. Pour into ice cream canister.

3. Freeze in ice cream maker according to manufacturer's directions.

Persimmon Cake

You can't beat this for a holiday dessert, with richness and texture not found elsewhere.

INGREDIENTS | SERVES 12

½ cup vegetable oil or butter

2 cups raw sugar

3 eggs, slightly beaten

½ cup plain yogurt

2 cups persimmon pulp

3 cups flour

4 teaspoons baking powder

1 teaspoon cinnamon

1 cup nuts

1 (9" × 13") baking pan or 2 8" cake pans

1. Preheat oven to 350°F.

2. Cream vegetable oil (or butter) and sugar.

3. Add beaten eggs, yogurt, and persimmon pulp.

4. Combine dry ingredients and stir into mixture.

5. Pour into greased and floured cake pan(s).

6. Bake until firm, about 35 minutes.

Persimmon Frosting

A rich and creamy frosting that melts in your mouth.

INGREDIENTS | COVERS 1 CAKE

1 cup confectioner's sugar

2 tablespoons persimmon pulp

½ teaspoon vanilla flavoring

1. Combine confectioner's sugar and persimmon pulp.

2. Add vanilla flavoring and mix until smooth.

3. Spread thinly across cooled persimmon cake.

Persimmon Pie

Serve with whipped cream or your favorite homemade ice cream.
Great for the holidays!

INGREDIENTS | SERVES 6–8

1 cup flour

¾ cup raw sugar

½ teaspoon baking powder

¼ teaspoon cinnamon

1 cup persimmon pulp

⅓ cup plain yogurt

1 egg, beaten

1 teaspoon vanilla extract

1 (9-inch) unbaked pie shell

1. Preheat oven to 350°F.

2. Combine dry ingredients.

3. Stir in persimmon pulp, yogurt, egg, and vanilla.

4. Pour into pie shell and bake for 30–35 minutes, until firm.

Persimmon Pudding

Serve with whipping cream or homemade ice cream.

INGREDIENTS | SERVES 8

1 egg, slightly beaten

½ cup maple yogurt

½ cup butter, softened

2 cups persimmon pulp

2 cups biscuit mix

1 cup raw sugar

1 teaspoon vanilla flavoring

1. Preheat oven to 350°F.

2. Mix ingredients until smooth.

3. Pour into a greased baking dish and bake for 30 minutes, or until firm.

4. Cut into squares and serve.

Rose Hip Cookies

A cookie that is rich in vitamin C and full of flavor.

INGREDIENTS | MAKES 4 DOZEN

¾ cup butter, softened

1 cup raw sugar

2 eggs, beaten

¾ cup plain yogurt

2 cups flour

2 cups oatmeal

1 teaspoon cinnamon

1 cup large rose hips, deseeded and chopped

½ cup nuts, chopped

1. Preheat oven to 400°F.

2. Cream butter and sugar. Add eggs and yogurt.

3. In a separate bowl, combine dry ingredients. Add to yogurt mixture.

4. Stir in remaining ingredients. Drop by spoonfuls on baking sheet.

5. Bake for 15 minutes.

Serviceberry Coffee Cake

A berry cake with the flavor of almonds.

INGREDIENTS | SERVES 8

½ cup butter, softened

1¼ cups raw sugar or ¾ cup honey

2 eggs, beaten

1¾ cups flour

1¾ teaspoons baking powder

1¼ cups plain yogurt

1 cup serviceberries (or blueberries)

1 cup chopped nuts (hickory, hazelnut, black walnut, pecan)

2 tablespoons coconut oil, melted

1 tablespoon raw sugar

1. Preheat oven to 350°F.

2. Cream together butter, sugar, and eggs until fluffy.

3. Add flour and baking powder. Stir in yogurt.

4. Pour into greased baking pan.

5. Add chopped nuts to melted coconut oil, coating well.

6. Spread berries and nuts evenly over the top. Sprinkle with raw sugar. Bake for about 30–35 minutes, or until firm.

Wild Berry Crepes

Use whatever berry is in season and top with yogurt or your favorite wild syrup.

INGREDIENTS | MAKES 6–8 CREPES

1 cup ricotta cheese

8 ounces cream cheese

½ cup wild berries

1 tablespoon maple syrup

6–8 hickory crepes (or regular)

Butter or coconut oil for frying

1. In a large bowl, blend ricotta and cream cheese with berries and maple syrup.

2. Place a spoonful of berry mixture in the center of each crepe.

3. Fold the sides in and roll to enclose the filling.

4. Heat butter or oil in skillet and brown crepes for about 5–10 minutes on each side.

Wild Strawberry Pie

You will know it's wild by the intense flavor and sweetness.
You can also use other berries, depending on what's in season and available.

INGREDIENTS | SERVES 8

2 cups wild strawberries

3 tablespoons honey

1 granola or graham cracker pie crust

1 tablespoon corn starch

¼ cup water

1. Add honey to wild strawberries and allow to stand at least 1 hour.

2. Drain liquid from strawberries into saucepan.

3. Arrange strawberries on crust.

4. Add water and corn starch to drained liquid and cook on medium heat until mixture begins to boil, stirring constantly, for 1 minute, or until clear.

5. Spoon glaze over strawberries. Chill at least 30 minutes and serve.

Wildflower Cheesecake

An enticing dessert that reflects all the colors and fragrances of spring.

INGREDIENTS | SERVES 8

1⅓ cups graham cracker crumbs

¼ cup butter, softened

8 ounces cream cheese, softened

½ cup plain yogurt

¼ cup honey

1 teaspoon vanilla

2 cups edible wildflowers

1 teaspoon sugar

1. In a medium bowl, combine graham cracker crumbs and butter.

2. Press the mixture evenly on bottom of buttered 8" pie pan.

3. In a large bowl, combine cream cheese, yogurt, honey, and vanilla until well blended.

4. Spoon mixture over crumbs, spreading gently with spatula.

5. Arrange wildflowers on top. Sprinkle sugar over wildflowers.

6. Chill for at least 2 hours before serving.

APPENDIX A

Common Names to Latin Names

Alder *Alnus* spp.

Amanita *Amanita* spp.

Amaranth *Amaranthus* spp.

American chestnut *Castanea dentata*

American lotus *Nelumbo lutea*

American plum *Prunus americana*

Arborvitae, Northern white cedar *Thuja occidentalis*

Arrow arum *Peltandra virginica*

Arrowhead *Sagittaria* spp.

Arrowwood *Viburnum dentatum*

Ash *Fraxinus* spp.

Asiatic dayflower *Commelina communis*

Atlantic white cedar *Chamaecyparis thyoides*

Autumn olive *Elaeagnus umbellate*

Azalea *Rhododendron* spp.

Bacopa *Bacopa monnieri*

Balsam fir *Abies balsamea*

Barnyard grass *Echinochloa crus-galli*

Barrel cactus *Ferocactus cylindraceus*

Basket bush sumac *Rhus trilobata*

Basswood *Tilia americana*

Bay laurel *Laurus nobilis*

Bayberry *Myrica pennsylvanica*

Beach plum *Prunus maritima*

Bearberry *Arctostaphylos alpina*

Bedstraw *Galium* spp.

Bee balm *Monarda didyma*

Beech *Fagus grandifolia*

Big-toothed aspen *Populus grandidentata*

Birch *Betula* spp.

Bittersweet nightshade *Solanum dulcamara*

Black chokeberry *Aronia melanocarpa*

Black gum *Nyssa sylvatica*

Black haw *Viburnum prunifolium*

Black locust *Robinia pseudo-acacia*

Black needlerush *Juncus roemerianus*

Black nightshade *Solanum nigrum*

Black walnut *Juglans nigra*

Black willow *Salix nigra*

Blackberry *Rubus* spp.

Blueberry *Vaccinium* spp.

Buckeye *Aesculus* spp.

Buckwheat *Eriogonum fasciculatum*

Bunchberry *Cornus canadensis*

Burdock *Arctium* spp.

Buttercup *Ranunculus* spp.

Cactus *Opuntia* spp.

Cattail *Typha* spp.

Chaparral *Croton corymbulosus*

Cherry *Prunus* spp.

Chestnut *Castanea dentata*

Chickasaw plum *Prunus angustifolia*

Chickweed *Stellaria media*

Chicory *Cichorium intybus*

Chinkapin *Castanea pumila*

Chokeberry *Aronia* spp.

Coffeeberry *Rhamnus crocea, R. californica, R. purshiana*

Common barberry *Berberis vulgaris*

Common milkweed *Asclepias syriaca*

Corn salad *Valerianella* spp.

Crabapple *Malus* spp.

Crabgrass *Digitaria sanguinali*

Cranberry *Vaccinium macrocarpon*

Cress *Barbarea* spp.

Crotalaria *Crotolaria* spp.

Dandelion *Taraxacum officinale*

Dangleberry *Gaylussacia frondosa*

Dead nettle *Lamium purpureum*

Death camas *Zigadenus* spp.

Deerberry *Vaccinium stamineum*

Dewberry *Rubus* spp.

Dogbane *Apocynum cannabinum*

Douglas fir *Pseudotsuga mensiesii*

Eastern red cedar *Juniperus virginiana*

Elder *Sambucus canadensis*

Elm *Ulmus* spp.

Epazote *Chenopodium ambrosioides*

Ephedra *Ephedra* spp.

Evening primrose *Oenothera biennis*

False dandelion *Pyrrhopappus carolinianus*

False hellebore *Veratrum viride*

False morel *Gyromitra* spp.

Farkleberry *Vaccinium arboreum*

Field garlic *Allium oleraceum*

Fir *Abies* spp.

Fox grape *Vitis labrusca*

Foxtail grass *Setaria* spp.

Garlic mustard *Alliaria petiolata*

Goldenrod *Solidago* spp.

Gooseberry *Ribes* spp.

Ground cherry *Physallis* spp.

Groundnut *Apios americana*

Groundsel *Senecio vulgaris*

Hawthorn *Crataegus* spp.

Hazelnut *Corylus* spp.

Heal-all *Prunella vulgaris*

Hedgehog cactus *Echinocereus* spp.

Hemlock *Tsuga* spp.

Henbit *Lamium amplexicaule*

Hickory *Carya* spp.

Highbush cranberry *Viburnum opulus*

Hobblebush *Viburnum* spp.

Honey locust *Gleditsia triacanthos*

Honeysuckle *Lonicera* spp.

Horse balm *Monarda punctata*

Horse nettle *Solanum carolinense*

Huckleberries *Gaylussacia* spp.

Iceland moss *Cetraria islandica*

Indian cucumber root *Medeola virginica*

Inkberry *Ilex glabra*

Jack-in-the-pulpit *Arisaema triphyllum*

Japanese barberry *Berberis thunbergii*

Japanese honeysuckle *Lonicera japonica*

Japanese knotweed *Polygonum cuspidatum*

Jerusalem artichoke *Helianthus tuberosus*

Jewelweed *Impatiens* spp.

Jimsonweed *Datura stramonium*

Johnson grass *Sorghum halepense*

Kinnikinnick *Arctostaphylos uva-ursi*

Kudzu *Pueraria montana*

Lambsquarters *Chenopodium album*

Larch *Larix* spp.

Lemonade berry sumac *Rhus integrifolia*

Life everlasting *Pseudognaphalium obtusifolium*

Live oak *Quercus virginiana*

Locoweed *Astragalus* spp.

Longleaf pine *Pinus palustris*

Lupine *Lupinus* spp.

Mad-dog skullcap *Scutellaria lateriflora*

Mallow *Malva* spp.

Manzanita *Arctostaphylos* spp.

Maple *Acer* spp.

Mayapple *Podophyllum peltatum*

Mesquite *Prosopis* spp.

Miner's lettuce *Claytonia perfoliata*

Moonseed *Menispermum canadense*

Mormon tea *Ephedra* spp.

Morning glory *Ipomoea* spp.

Mountain cranberry *Vaccinium vitis-idaea*

Mountain laurel *Kalmia latifolia*

Mulberry *Morus* spp.

Multiflora rose *Rosa multiflora*

Mustard *Brassica* spp.

Nannyberry *Viburnum lentago*

Nutgrass *Cyperus* spp.

Oak *Quercus* spp.

Ocotillo *Fouquieria splendens*

Ogeechee gum *Nyssa ogeche*

Orache *Atriplex* spp.

Orchard grass *Dactylis* spp.

Oregon crabapple *Malus fusca*

Oregon grape *Berberis* spp.

Oxeye daisy *Leucanthemum vulgare*

Paper birch *Betula papyrifera*

Partridgeberry *Mitchella repens*

Passionflower *Passiflora incarnata*

Pawpaw *Asimina triloba*

Peppergrass *Lepidium virginicum*

Persimmon *Diospyros virginiana*

Peyote *Lophophora williamsii*

Phragmites *Phragmites australis, P. communis*

Pickerelweed *Pontederia cordata*

Pine *Pinus* spp.

Pinyon pine *Pinus edulis, P. mono-phylla, P. quadrifolia*

Pitch pine *Pinus rigida*

Plantain *Plantago* spp.

Plum *Prunus* spp.

Poison hemlock *Conium maculatum*

Poison ivy *Toxicodendron radicans*

Poison oak *Toxicodendron pubes-cens, T. diversilobum*

Poison sumac *Toxicodendron vernix*

Pokeweed *Phytolacca americana*

Poplar *Populus* spp.

Possum haw *Viburnum nudum*

Prairie crabapple *Malus ioensis*

Precatory bean, rosary pea *Abrus precatorius*

Prickly pear cactus *Opuntia* spp.

Purslane *Portulaca oleracea*

Quaking aspen *Populus tremuloides*

Queen Anne's lace *Daucus carota*

Ragweed *Ambrosia* spp.

Ramps *Allium tricoccum*

Raspberry *Rubus* spp.

Red chokeberry *Aronia arbutifolia*

Red clover *Trifolium pratense*

Red mulberry *Morus rubra*

Red oak *Quercus falcata, Q. gravesii, Q. rubra, Q texana*

Redbay *Persea borbonia, P. palustris*

Redbud *Cercis canadensis*

Reindeer moss *Cladonia rangiferina*

River birch *Betula nigra*

Rock tripe *Umbilicaria* spp. and *Gyrophora* spp.

Rose mallow *Hibiscus moscheutos*

Russian olive *Eleagnus angustifolia*

Sagebrush *Artemisia* spp.

Saguaro cactus *Carnegiea gigantea*

Saltwort *Salicornia* spp.

Sassafras *Sassafras albidum*

Sea rocket *Cakila edentula*

Seaside evening primrose *Oenothera humifusa*

Sedge *Carex* spp.

Serviceberry *Amelanchier* spp.

Sheep sorrel *Rumex acetosella*

Skullcap *Scutellaria* spp.

Small cranberry *Vaccinium oxycoccos*

Smooth sumac *Rhus glabra, R. pulvinata*

Sourwood *Oxydendrum arboreum*

Southern crabapple *Malus angustifolia*

Sow thistle *Sonchus oleraceus*

Sparkleberry *Vaccinium arboreum*

Spicebush *Lindera benzoin*

Spring beauty *Claytonia* spp.

Spruce *Picea* spp.

St. Johnswort *Hypericum* spp.

Staghorn sumac *Rhus typhina*

Stinging nettle *Urtica dioica*

Sugar bush sumac *Rhus ovata*

Summer grape *Vitis aestivalis*

Swamp azalea *Rhododendron viscosum*

Swamp black gum *Nyssa biflora*

Sweet birch *Betula lenta*

Sweet crabapple *Malus coronaria*

Sweet goldenrod *Solidago odora*

Sweetgum *Liquidambar styraciflua*

Tepary bean *Phaseolus acutifolius*

Texas mulberry *Morus microphylla*

Thistle *Cirsium* spp.

Toothwort *Dentaria* spp.

Toyon *Heteromeles arbutifolia*

Trillium *Trillium* spp.

Viburnum *Viburnum* spp.

Violet *Viola* spp.

Virginia creeper *Parthenocissus quinquefolia*

Water hemlock *Cicuta maculata*

Water lily *Nymphaea* spp.

Water parsnip *Sium suave*

Watercress *Nasturtium officinale*

Waxmyrtle *Myrica cerifera*

White oak *Quercus alba*

Wild bean *Strophostyles helvola*

Wild black cherry *Prunus serotina*

Wild carrot *Daucus carota*

Wild garlic *Allium* spp.

Wild ginger *Asarum canadense*

Wild grape *Vitis* spp.

Wild lettuce *Lactuca canadensis*

Wild mustard *Brassica* spp.

Wild onion *Allium* spp.

Wild rice *Zizania aquatica, Z. latifolia, Z. palustris, Z. texana*

Wild rose *Rosa* spp.

Wild strawberry *Fragaria* spp.

Willow *Salix* spp.

Winter grape *Vitis cinerea*

Wintergreen *Gaultheria procumbens*

Wood sorrel *Oxalis* spp.

Yampa *Perideridia* spp.

Yaupon holly *Ilex vomitoria*

Yellow dock *Rumex crispus*

Yellow jessamine *Gelsemium sempervirens*

Yucca *Yucca* spp.

Helpful Reading

Arora, David. *Mushrooms Demystified.* Berkeley, CA: Ten Speed Press, 1979.

Benyus, Janine M. *The Field Guide to Wildlife Habitats of the Eastern United States.* New York: Simon & Schuster Inc., 1989.

Brill, "Wildman" Steve, and Evelyn Dean. *Identifying and Harvesting Edible and Medicinal Plants.* New York: Hearst Books, 1994.

Cohen, Russ. *Wild Plants I Have Known and Eaten.* Essex, MA: Essex County Greenbelt Association, Inc., 2004.

Derby, Blanche Cybele. *My Wild Friends—Free Food from Field and Forest.* Northampton, MA: White Star Press, 1997.

Derig, Betty B., and Margaret C. Fuller. *Wild Berries of the West.* Missoula, MT: Mountain Press Publishing Co., 2001.

Duke, James A. *Amazing Secret Healers in Your Backyard.* Emmaus, PA: Rodale Press, Inc., 1998.

Duke, James A. *The Green Pharmacy.* Emmaus, PA: Rodale Press, 1997.

Duke, James A. *Handbook of Edible Weeds.* Boca Raton, FL: CRC Press, 1992.

Elpel, Thomas J. *Botany in a Day—The Patterns Method of Plant Identification.* Pony, MT: HOPS Press, LLC. 1996.

Fernald, Merritt Lyndon, and Alfred Charles Kinsey. Revised by Reed C. Rollins. *Edible Wild Plants of North America.* New York, Hagerstown, San Francisco, London: Harper & Row, Publishers, 1943.

Freitus, Joe. *Wild Preserves.* Washington, DC: Stone Wall Press, Inc. 1977.

Gibbons, Euell, and Gordon Tucker. *Handbook of Edible Wild Plants.* Virginia Beach/Norfolk, VA: Donning, 1979.

Greenspan, Sharon. *Wildly Successful Eating™: Raw and Living Food Basics.* Unpublished duplicated paper, 2009.

Hertzberg, Ruth, Beatrice Vaughan, and Janet Greene. *Putting Food By.* Brattleboro, VT and Lexington, MA: The Stephen Greene Press, 1973.

Johnson, Cathy. *The Wild Foods Cookbook.* New York: Penguin Books USA, Inc. 1989.

Kallas, John. *Edible Wild Plants.* Layton, UT: Gibbs Smith, 2010.

Kavasch, Barrie. *Native Harvests—Recipes and Botanicals of the American Indians.* New York: Random House, Inc. 1977.

Kingsbury, John M. *Deadly Harvest—A Guide to Common Poisonous Plants.* New York: Holt, Rinehart and Winston, 1965.

Kirk, Donald R. *Wild Edible Plants of the Western United States.* Healdsburg, CA: Naturegraph Publishers, 1970.

Knopf, Alfred A. *The Audubon Society Field Guide to North American Wildflowers: Eastern Region.* New York, NY: Chanticleer Press, 1979.

Krochmal, Connie, and Arnold Krochmal. *A Naturalist's Guide to Cooking with Wild Plants.* New York: Quadrangle/The New York Times Book Co., 1974.

Moerman, Daniel E. *Native American Ethnobotany.* Portland, OR: Timber Press, 1998.

Mogelon, Ronna. *Wild in the Kitchen: Recipes for Wild Fruits, Weeds and Seeds.* New York: M. Evans and Company, Inc., 2001.

Muenscher, Walter Conrad. *Poisonous Plants of the United States.* New York: Collier Books, 1975.

Niethammer, Carolyn. *American Indian Cooking.* Lincoln and London: University of Nebraska Press, 1999.

Nyerges, Christopher. *Guide to Wild Foods and Useful Plants.* Chicago, IL: Chicago Review Press, 1999.

Radford, Albert E., Harry E. Ahles, C. Ritchie Bell, C. Ritchie. *Manual of the Vascular Flora of the Carolinas.* Chapel Hill: The University of North Carolina Press. 1964.

Shababy, Doreen. *The Wild & Weedy Apothecary.* Woodbury, MN: Llewellynm Publications, 2010.

Shurtleff, William, and Akiko Ayoagi. *The Book of Kudzu.* Brookline, MA: Autumn Press, 1977.

Stadelmann, Peter. *Water Gardens.* Hauppauge, NY: Barron's Educational Series, Inc., 1990.

Sutton, Ann, and Myron Sutton. *Eastern Forests.* New York: Alfred A. Knopf, 1985.

Tatum, Billy Joe. *Wild Foods Field Guide and Cookbook.* New York: Workman Publishing Co., 1976.

Thayer, Sam. *Nature's Garden.* Birchwood, WI: Forager's Harvest, 2010.

Thayer, Sam. *The Forager's Harvest.* Ogema, WI: Forager's Harvest, 2006.

Vargas, Pattie, and Rich Gulling. *Country Wines—Making & Using Wines from Herbs, Fruits, Flowers & More.* Pownal, VT: Storey Communications, Inc., 1992.

Website Resources

Forestry Outreach Site
This site contains information on forest communities.
www.fw.vt.edu/dendro/Forsite/contents.htm

National Park Service
This site contains information on ecosystems in the national parks.
www.nps.gov/index.htm

Plants Poisonous to Livestock
This site contains information on plants that have caused livestock poisoning.
http://extension.missouri.edu/publications

Poisonous Plants of North Carolina
This is a site for poisonous plants.
www.ces.ncsu.edu/depts./hort/consumer/poison/poison.htm

Invasive Plant Atlas
This site contains information on invasive plants of the United States.
www.invasiveplantatlas.org/index.html

National Invasive Species Information Center
This site contains information on invasive species.
www.invasivespeciesinfo.gov/plants/main.shtml

USDA Natural Resources Conservation Service
This site contains information on invasive and noxious weeds.
http://plants.usda.gov/java/noxiousDriver

Weeds Gone Wild
This site has information on alien plant invaders of natural areas.
www.nps.gov/plants/alien

Dr. Duke's Phytochemical and Ethnobotanical Databases
This website contains information on phytochemicals.
www.ars-grin.gov/duke

Green Pharmacy Botanical Desk Reference
This is Dr. Jim Duke's site for green pharmacy botanicals.
www.greenpharmacy.com

Harvard Gazette
This site contains the study on kudzu being used to cut alcohol consumption.
http://news.harvard.edu/gazette/story/2005/05/kudzu-cuts-alcohol-consumption

Wetlands
This is the United States Environmental Protection Agency site on wetlands.
http://water.epa.gov/type/wetlands

USDA Plants Database
This site contains plant profiles for the United States.
http://plants.usda.gov/index.html

Storing Seeds
This site contains information on seed storage times and viability.
http://growingtaste.com/storage.shtml - DIR

NW Farms & Food
A website with news, local food, and farms in the Pacific Northwest.
http://nwfarmsandfood.com/index.php

National Center for Home Food Preservation
This site contains information on preserving food using pressure canners.
www.uga.edu/nchfp/publications/uga/using_press_canners.html

Canning Pantry
A site with information on pressure canners and pressure canning.
www.canningpantry.com/using-pressure-canners.html

Home Appliances and Kitchen Machines
This is a site with a listing of home appliances and kitchen tools.
www.galttech.com/research/household-DIY-tools

Index

Photo Credits

We Have
EVERYTHING®
on Anything!

With more than 19 million copies sold, the Everything® series has become one of America's favorite resources for solving problems, learning new skills, and organizing lives. Our brand is not only recognizable—it's also welcomed.

The series is a hand-in-hand partner for people who are ready to tackle new subjects—like you!

For more information on the Everything® series, please visit *www.adamsmedia.com*

The Everything® list spans a wide range of subjects, with more than 500 titles covering 25 different categories:

Business	History	Reference
Careers	Home Improvement	Religion
Children's Storybooks	Everything Kids	Self-Help
Computers	Languages	Sports & Fitness
Cooking	Music	Travel
Crafts and Hobbies	New Age	Wedding
Education/Schools	Parenting	Writing
Games and Puzzles	Personal Finance	
Health	Pets	

Heal-all flowers in late spring

Wild thistle blooms in spring

Chickweed flowers, with leaves in the background

A cluster of violets in bloom

Red clover with distinctive petal arrangement

A grouping of stinging nettles leaves

Recognizable mayapple leaves on the forest floor

A ripe serviceberry cluster

Oxeye daisies in a summer field

Wild garlic with distinctive white flowers

Cattails (bulrushes) near a marsh

A grouping of elderberries in late summer

Dewberries, relatives of the blackberry

Crabapple tree in autumn

A ground cherry exposed in its husk

A grouping of red Hawthorn berries

Black walnuts on the tree

Chestnut with open husk

Ripe persimmons ready to be picked

Chicory flowers in late bloom

Reindeer lichen on a rock

Wintergreen berries and leaves

The fruit of the prickly pear cactus

A cluster of barberries in winter